IMAGES
of America

Hockessin Colored School #107C

I0806374

On September 6, 1920, the students of Hockessin Colored School #107C transitioned from their wooden frame schoolhouse to a new brick school building. Dr. Joseph H. Odell presided over the ceremony. The children walked through the doors of their new school shouting: "Chica laca, chica laca/Siss! Boom! Rah!/duPont! duPont!/Rah! Rah! Rah!" The following list of names is a special recognition of the former students of Hockessin Colored School #107C: June Bantum, Laura Bantum, Maryann Bantum, Melvin Bantum, Arlene Battin, Dorothy Battin, Ethel Battin, James Battin, Mary Battin, Oliver Battin Jr., Oliver Battin Sr., Rosetta Battin, Ruth Battin, Shirley Battin, Robert Berry, Charles Bolden, Jean Bolden, Reba Bolden, William Bolden, Beverly Brock, Shirley Brock, Addie Bulah, Ardella Bulah, Emily Bulah, Fred Bulah Jr., Hilda Bulah, Shirley Bulah, Thomas Bulah, Carl Cannon, Richard Cannon, Virginia Cannon, Edna Carter, Ethel Carter, Herbert Carter, Joseph Carter (a), Joseph Carter (b), Mary Carter, Orville Carter, Norman Casson, Hilda Chapman, Arlene Coleman, Charles Coleman (a), Charles Coleman (b), Janet Coleman, John Coleman, Lottie Coleman, Marshall Coleman, Mary Coleman, Ronald Coleman, Sandra Coleman, Sara Conrad, Darryl Copper, Richard Copper, Irvin Cornish, Orpha Cornish, Gertalene Davis, James Davis, Lola Davis, Mitchell Davis, Robert Davis, Harriet Denby, Joseph Denby, Charles Dodson, John Dorsey, William Ferrell, Charles Folks, Edward Folks, Grace Folks, Herbert Folks, James Folks, Leroy Folks, Percy Folks Jr., Robert Folks, Bertha Frisby, Harold Frisby, Les Frisby, Charles Gasby, Dorothy Gasby, Ella Mae Gasby, Jacqueline Gasby, John Gasby, Linda Gasby, Mabel Gasby, Robert Gasby, Shirley Gasby, Sylvia Gasby, Thomas Gasby, Velma Gasby, Walter Gasby, Reginald Gray, Stanley Gray, Wilmer Gray, Andrew Harris, Barbara Harris, Dorothy Harris, Orville Harris, Romaine Harris, William Hickman, Arthur Hodges, Arthur Hunter, Barbara Hunter, Ernest Hunter, Ethel Hunter, Florence Hunter, George Hunter, James Hunter, Leon Hunter Jr., Leon Hunter Sr., Mable Hunter, Margaret Hunter, William Hunter, Abe Jackson, Carol Ann Jackson, Charles Jackson Jr., Charles Jackson Sr., Charles Lee Jackson, Edna Jackson, James Jackson, Jerome Jackson, Lottie Jackson, Mary Jackson, Nancy Jackson, Patricia Jackson, Clarence Jamison, Ernest Jamison, Margaret Jamison, Berna Johnson, Bernice Johnson, Charles Johnson, Charles Johnson Sr., Charles H. Johnson Jr., Earl Johnson, Edna Johnson, Katherine Johnson, Margaret Johnson (a), Margaret Johnson (b), Marie Johnson, Nancy Johnson, Rachel Johnson, Ralph Johnson Jr., Reba Johnson, Rosetta Johnson, Samuel Johnson, Velma Johnson, Vienna Johnson, William Johnson, Alice Jones, Donald Jones, Dorothy Jones, Etta Jones, Robert Jones, Ruby Jones, Blanche Knott, Charlotte Knott, James Henry Knott, James Sonny Knott, Edna Lewis, Lawrence Lewis, Phillip Lewis, Ruth Lewis, Thelma Lewis, Willard Lewis, Walter Macklin, Charles Miller, Edward Miller, Richard Miller, James Nickens, Alan Peterson, Bettye Peterson, Gregory Peterson, Gwendolyn Peterson, Lawrence Peterson, LeRoy Peterson, Lester Peterson, Linwood Peterson, Louis Peterson, Luther Peterson, Pia Peterson, Walter Plater, Beatrice Poe, Bertwell Poindexter, Clifford Poindexter, Edwina Poindexter, George Poindexter, Jean Poindexter, Jorita Poindexter, Dorothy Purdy, Clara Raisin, Horace Raisin, Ella Mae Rawleigh, Richard Reid, William Skinner, Alma Smith, Beatrice Smith, Bertha Smith, Chandler Smith Jr., Lester Smith, James Sutton, Earl Taylor, Ethel Taylor, Garfield Taylor, Henry Taylor, Isa Taylor, Pauline Taylor, Spencer Taylor, Victoria Taylor, Joseph Thomas, Charles Tillman, Ava Tinnin, Gladys Tinnin, Luther Tinnin, John Tinnin, George Washington, Hestine Washington, Lula Washington, John Washington, William Washington, Beatrice Watters, Isaiah Watters, Ruth Watters, Alice Williams, Cornelius Williams, Delores Williams, Emanuel Williams, George Williams, Irvin Williams, Lillian Williams, Lois Williams, Lorraine Williams, Prince Williams, Ronald Williams, Sarah Williams, Theodore Williams, and Thomas Williams.

On the Cover: This 1957 photograph features the annual holiday banquet sponsored by the Stitch in Time Sewing Club. The event was held at the Hockessin Colored Grand Union Hall, located on the grounds of Chippey Church and Hockessin Colored School #107C. See page 48 for additional information about this image. (Hilda Bulah Morris.)

IMAGES
of America

Hockessin Colored School #107C

Lanette R. Edwards, EdD

ARCADIA
PUBLISHING

ISBN 978-1-4671-6013-1

Published by Arcadia Publishing
Charleston, South Carolina

Printed in the United States of America

Library of Congress Control Number: 2023935532

For all general information, please contact Arcadia Publishing:
Telephone 843-853-2070
Fax 843-853-0044
E-mail sales@arcadiapublishing.com
For customer service and orders:
Toll-Free 1-888-313-2665

Visit us on the Internet at www.arcadiapublishing.com

I dedicate this book to the former students of Hockessin Colored School #107C and my husband, Tony, and our children Calann, Trevor, Tyler, and Tony Jr.

CONTENTS

Acknowledgments

Thanks go to my husband, Tony, my knight in shining armor, and to our wonderful children Calann, Trevor, Tyler, and Tony Jr., you are simply the best, truly the wind beneath my wings.

To my dear former students of Hockessin Colored School #107C (especially those of you who are among the last standing soldiers of patrimony), Hilda Bulah, Gwendolyn Peterson, James Sonny Knott, Ike Watters, Robert Berry, LeRoy Peterson, Lois Williams, Blanche Knott, Charlotte Knott, Charles Johnson, Nancy Johnson, and Walter Macklin, you are and will forever be my inspiration.

To Elizabeth (Peterson) Lester, Montrell (Peterson) Ward, Crystal Brown, and Joyce (Johnson) Thompson, your due diligence and perseverance toward the completion of this project have been invaluable. To the steadfast board members of Friends of Hockessin Colored School #107C under the leadership of David Wilk and Ray Blackwell, my warmest regards.

To Lou Rosenberg, Eric Schmitt, Lisa Marine, Will Cooper, Erik Dressler, Madeline Fucile, and Dalia Banevicius of Mitchell Associates, I thank you. Special recognition to the staff of Hagley Museum and Library, including Angela Schad, Lucas Clawson, and Chloe Marine; the staff of the Delaware Public Archives under the leadership of Margaret Raubacher Dunham; and local historians Jean Nutter and Syl Woolford. Collectively, your expertise facilitated the excavation of materials and information integral to the completion of this project. I am eternally grateful for my lead research assistant Regina Smith, who played an integral role in seeing this project through from inception to completion. Your intelligence, keen eye, and love of history made the journey unforgettable.

Thank you to research team members Rovina Westbrook (North Carolina) and Yolanda Holbrook (Texas). Thanks to Bill and Cheryl Fisher (Kentucky), Michael and Tammie Shelton (Missouri), and Marsha Boyce and Harold Kirby (Delaware) for your support and encouragement.

To my Missouri family, especially my mother, Casandra; my sister Aariane; and my superhero, my daddy, Aaron T. Hendrix—you are my adorable Griswalds. I give special thanks to US senator Chris Coons (Delaware), US senator Tom Carper (Delaware), US representative Lisa Blunt Rochester (Delaware), and US representative Jim Clyburn (South Carolina), as well as Delaware governor John Carney, the Hon. Collins J. Seitz Jr., and New Castle County executive Matt Myers.

To the most courageous citizens of Delaware, our 46th President of the United States of America, Joseph Biden, and First Lady Dr. Jill Biden, thank you both for answering the call of duty. May this book remind you of your dedication to the revelation of truth and justice for the families of Hockessin. We humbly extend our appreciation and gratitude.

Unless otherwise noted, all images appear courtesy of Delaware Public Archives (DPA).

Introduction

According to the first US census, which was taken in 1790, there were 3,929,214 people living in the United States at that time. The most populous state was Virginia, with 747,610 inhabitants. Delaware had the lowest reported population, with 59,094 inhabitants. The census did not include native-born inhabitants of the land (Indians); however, colored residents were identified as "free others" or "enslaved."

Make no mistake—Delaware, home to patriots whose contributions solidified the foundation of our nation, became the proving ground for our republic. This remained the case from the ride of Caesar Rodney, who cast the deciding vote for independence, to the Bulahs' cry for equality. Holding the badge of honor as the first English colony to declare statehood by signing the document that unified the English-speaking subject states and the first state to desegregate Jim Crow public schools (in 1952), Delaware, the small wonder, met each challenge with compassion and courage. The bedrock of its foundation rested on the ability of its residents to overcome deeds and decisions that tested the content of its citizens' character. This is known as the Delaware Way.

Delaware's principles and values continued to reflect the growth of the nation. Consequently, at the nation's core was an unsettled issue of states' rights. After 13 states were united by a common cry for freedom, liberty, and the pursuit of happiness, separate philosophies on the preservation of democracy permeated the land. Although the state of Delaware was the first to declare its loyalty to the union, the common sense of citizenship, and the ideas of the republic, its inhabitants refused to outlaw the institution of importing and enslaving Africans to the United States as chattel. The inhumane treatment of enslaved descendants of Africans has been the dominant narrative of the history of persons of color living in America. As a result, the life experiences of free colored American citizens have been relegated to historical footnotes. Here in Delaware, the offspring of free colored citizens who resided in New Castle County, specifically in Mill Creek Hundred, were counted as such at the inception of the new nation.

In November 1860, Delaware remained true to its beliefs in support of slavery. That year, Delaware nominated as their presidential candidate John C. Breckinridge, a young congressman from Kentucky. Breckinridge was a lawyer and a slaveholder. Through the notoriety of his family's name and support from the Clay family, Breckinridge rivaled Stephen Douglas and Abraham Lincoln, both of Illinois, and John Bell of Tennessee in the election of 1860. Three years prior, at age 35, Breckinridge secured the seat of vice president of the nation under the 15th president, James Buchanan, who served from 1857 to 1861. Although Buchanan was from the neighboring state of Pennsylvania, his administration was plagued with widening rifts.

The Kansas-Nebraska Act of 1854 nullified the 1820 Missouri Compromise and gave way to a massive flood of European immigrants and refugees. Federal records from the 1830s indicate that the population of immigrants from Europe grew from 600,000 to over 2 million by the 1850s. Immigration, slavery, and the stability of the economy presented a challenge for the nation. The Buchanan administration's lines of allegiance began to splinter as the political ideology of the cabinet faltered. Vice President Breckinridge seized the opportunity to redirect the Democratic Party in favor of the Southern agenda. The young politician placed third in the popular vote and second in the electoral vote. Unwilling to accept defeat, delegates and leaders from deep Southern states viewed the newly elected president, Abraham Lincoln, as a leader of the abolitionists. By January 1861, South Carolina, Mississippi, Florida, Alabama, Georgia, Louisiana, Texas, Virginia, Arkansas, Tennessee, and North Carolina had seceded from the United States of America to form a Confederacy. Delaware did not declare secession, and neither did Kentucky, Missouri, or West Virginia. The election of 1860 became a canvas depicting the state of affairs in Delaware that stymied the narratives of its resilient colored communities. As a small state located between the corridors of other populous states, Delaware represented both Northern and Southern societal values. Delaware allowed both free and enslaved colored people to reside within its borders. Ultimately, it was Delaware's support to maintain state laws that created the unavoidable duplicitous conflict.

By the 1880s, at the onset of industrialization, manufacturing propelled the nation into the sphere of global powers. A larger workforce was needed to sustain productivity. Social norms were no longer based solely on social economic standing. Chimes of a new society echoed louder than the ringing of freedom. As European immigrants migrated to the United States, by the millions, they focused their hopes and dreams on acceptance, inclusion, and economic prosperity. In 1896, the US Supreme Court's *Plessy v. Ferguson* decision became the foundational case of federal separatism. Elements of the antebellum South took center stage with the full support of the country's legal system. Soon, all public facilities became segregated, with the idea of "whiteness" of skin being the deciding factor of citizenship and patriotism.

While some believe the truth is a new narrative, this is the narrative—free colored people created and maintained independent, self-sufficient societies prior to the American Civil War and the influx of non-natives. European immigrants benefitted from those efforts. The harmony of such existence was threatened as the tenor of the nation once united called for division. Segregation became nationally accepted as a cultural and societal norm.

By the start of the 20th century, Mill Creek Hundred encircled the American way as businesses, churches, and schools willingly separated. Much like the path taken by religious freedom-seekers, separatists in favor of Jim Crow laws and Black Codes carved a new trail. Public and private schools became segregated. In Delaware, residents of Yorklyn, Hockessin, Mt. Cuba, North Star, and Harmony built schools and provided services based on the new policy of separation.

It would take the efforts of a businessman—a leader hailing from the wealthiest family in Delaware—to change the tides. His name was Pierre S. duPont. As president of his family's multimillion-dollar company and president of General Motors, Pierre had great influence. He served as vice president of the state board of education from 1919 to 1921. For 20 years, he engaged in a campaign to improve the condition of education for Delaware students.

The Hockessin Colored School became a premier recipient of duPont's philanthropy. In 1920, Hockessin students transitioned from a wooden framed building on Grant Avenue to a newly constructed "duPont" brick schoolhouse. For over 30 years, the brick school remained the sole center of education for colored elementary students residing in Hockessin. This included the children of residents Fred Bulah. The Bulahs resided near the intersection of Limestone and Valley Roads. Together with his wife, Ida, Fred parented several children: Addie, Thomas, Emily, Ardella, Delma, Johnny, and Freddie, as well as one granddaughter, Hilda. In 1941, Ida Bulah died from health issues. After her death, Fred's brother Frank Bulah, a minister who resided in Pottsville, Pennsylvania, introduced him to a widow named Sarah. After agreeing to correspond for months, Fred and Sarah married on November 14, 1942. Following their nuptials, Sarah moved to Delaware. She did not have children. Upon moving to Hockessin, she became interested in adopting an abandoned female toddler. Little is known about the birth of the baby girl. Delaware public records indicate that in April 1945, at the approximate age of 10 months, the child was adopted and named Shirley Barbara Bulah. Her date of birth was declared as January 30, 1944.

Like the older Bulahs, who were no longer living at home, Shirley attended Hockessin Colored School #107C during her primary years. The school, located two miles from their home, did not offer bus transportation for its students. After two years of driving their daughter to school, the Bulahs sought bus transportation for Shirley. While a bus carrying white children passed by the Bulahs' home each day, Shirley was not permitted to ride. As mandated by state laws, school bus transportation was only provided for white students. The Bulahs wrote letters to the department of public instruction and the governor requesting bus transportation for their daughter. The state replied affirming that no bus transportation would be provided because colored children were not allowed to ride school buses that serviced white children. The Bulah family's long history of advocacy for children was about to change the nation's tapestry. A flag woven to embrace the tired, poor, and huddled masses yearning to breathe free and the wretched refuse of teeming shores struggled with the concept of liberty and justice for all of its citizens. A nation healing from wounds of self-inflicted discourse once again found its infrastructure tested by colored Americans. With the country's acceptance of exclusion, the lucid identity of citizens by mere skin tone relegated the nation's sight to black and white. Nevertheless, the Bulah family of Hockessin removed the nation's rose-colored glasses.

In the spring of 1951, after a letter-writing campaign that spanned six months, Sarah Bulah contacted attorney Louis Redding to pursue a legal remedy. At that time, Redding was the first and only colored lawyer in Delaware. Redding suggested the Bulahs petition to enroll Shirley in the whites-only Hockessin School #29. Redding set out to challenge racially segregated public schools by filing lawsuits regarding citizens in Hockessin and Claymont. The Hockessin case was filed using the names of Sarah and Fred Bulah on behalf of their daughter Shirley Barbara Bulah. One of the parents from the Claymont case, Ethel Lee Belton, filed on behalf of her daughter, Ethel Louise Belton.

The Bulah and Belton cases named 13 plaintiffs and the state board of education as principal defendants. The complaint specifically charged individual board members with violating the rights of colored students. The first name listed among board members was Francis B. Gebhart. With the assistance of attorney Jack Greenberg of New York, the resulting cases were filed as *Belton v. Gebhart* (July 13, 1951) and *Bulah v. Gebhart* (August 17, 1951).

On April 1, 1952, Chancellor Collins J. Seitz of the Delaware Court of Chancery directed the immediate admittance of plaintiff Shirley Bulah into Hockessin School #29 and Ethel Louise Belton, Elbert Crumpler, Richard Leon Davis, John Terrell Davis, Spencer Robinson, Styron Sanford, Almena Short, Myrtha Trotter, Carol Anderson, Joan Anderson, Merle Anderson, and Bernice Byrd into Claymont High School. On August 28, 1952, the Delaware Supreme Court consolidated both cases and affirmed the ruling of the lower court.

In the fall of 1952, third-grader Shirley Bulah of Hockessin became the first colored student to desegregate public grade schools and school buses in the state of Delaware. Although it was a victory for children in the Bulah and Belton cases, the state courts' decisions did not apply broadly throughout Delaware—the ruling pertained solely to the named plaintiffs and schools in Hockessin and Claymont. Unfortunately, the ruling of the case came too late for Ethel Belton, who reached her senior year of high school in the fall of 1953. She graduated with the Howard High School class of 1954 within days of the US Supreme Court's decision regarding segregated schools. On May 17, 1954, the court ruled 9–0 in favor of the plaintiffs in *Brown v. Board of Education*. Ethel Belton was quoted 10 years after the decision as saying, "Even though I did not reap the benefits of my efforts, I felt kind of great. It wasn't everybody who took a stand like my mother and me. Schools are open now because we took a stand. I'm glad I helped start the change in Delaware. The only hurting part is that I didn't get a chance to go to Claymont, but it helped my children and others."

In 1954, the US Supreme Court rendered the decision that struck down school segregation. The integration of Hockessin #29 began with the transfer of the first grade from Hockessin #107C. One grade per year was allowed to transfer into Hockessin #29. It took five years to complete the transfer of all #107C students. Under the leadership of Dr. J. Fletcher Walker, both Hockessin Schools #29 and #107C consolidated with Alexis I duPont Secondary School District. In 1951, there were 46 students enrolled at #107C, but by June 13, 1957, at the end of the school year, the school building closed with 10 students enrolled. Local philanthropists, community activists, and academic stakeholders (such as Lillian C. Mitchell, K.L Berry, Dr. Howe, and attorney Carroll Poole) collaborated to conceptualize alternative options for usage of the newly closed school. On September 30, 1959, the property was transferred to Chippey Chapel Board of Trustees and became the Hockessin Community Center. Chippey Chapel, a Methodist church adjacent to #107C, is a pillar in the community and played an integral role in the formation of the original Hockessin Colored School.

The Hockessin Community Center operated for over 30 years with Roslyn Smith as its executive director. After her departure, efforts were put in place to gain recognition for the role the schoolhouse played in the historic *Brown v. Board of Education* decision. On May 17, 2004, the Hockessin Community Center secured the approval for the installation of a historical marker at the main entrance of the school. Not long after the marker was installed, Hockessin Community Center ceased to render services to the community, and the building subsequently closed. In the spring of 2011, the dormant structure was slated for demolition. On November 11, 2011, a group of concerned citizens known as the Friends of Hockessin Colored School #107C mounted a last-ditch effort to save the building. Spearheaded by the efforts of Judge Lenny Williams, Bill Allen, husband-and-wife Joshua and Cynthia Martin, and a coalition called the Friends of Hockessin Colored School (FOHCS), along with a separate group known as the African American Empowerment Fund of Delaware, forged ahead with a plan of action. On January 9, 2012, one day before the scheduled sale, FOHCS and the African American Empowerment Fund of Delaware procured resources to acquire and repurpose the facility. For nearly a decade, the coalition bore the financial responsibility of the premises and successfully sustained the property. In 2019, with support from federal, state, and local entities, plans for renovations of the schoolhouse were finalized. A ground-breaking ceremony occurred on December 14, 2021. Exactly one year later, on December 14, 2022, FOHCS celebrated the restoration of the little brick schoolhouse by walking through the doors again as the newly renovated school opened as the Hockessin Colored School #107C Center for Diversity, Inclusion, and Social Equity.

While some believe this truth is a new narrative, this is the narrative—colored and white people in Delaware and throughout the nation were indeed integrated, and when they were not, colored people still thrived. This is the narrative—if the Union was already totally segregated, why was there such an institutional push to make things segregated almost 200 years after Africans were forced into slavery in the Americas? There is no denying it. That happened; that is true, but it did not take 400 years for those same descendants to make their own mark on American education—a mark that somehow continues to remain in historical footnotes.

One

"C" Is for Colored

The Historical Origins of #107C

Colored families enjoyed the privilege of their children attending "integrated schools" before and decades after the Civil War. Prior to 1880, most children received instruction according to their family's social economic status.

Unbeknownst to many outside of the Hockessin community, during this time period, colored children residing in Mill Creek Hundred received a formal integrated education. Schooling in the region required the payment of tuition. Those who could afford it obtained it. Those who could not conspired against the uppity. Cloaked in aspirations, the desires of the downtrodden aimed to subvert the balance of power within the system. In 1896, their efforts were championed by the US Supreme Court's ruling in *Plessy v. Ferguson*.

After the nation embraced the philosophy of segregation, the separation of public facilities, including schools, was enforced by law. At their inception, colored schools were operated and maintained by colored communities. Although newly enacted segregation laws prohibited interactions of people based on the most rudimentary system of separation, colored residents of Hockessin enjoyed the true essence of their freedom as independent, self-sufficient contributors to society. Their minds were well-versed in maneuvering a system controlled by white citizens seeking economic and political dominance in the name of self-preservation.

Beyond the national condition of second-class citizenship, the colored residents of Hockessin were seldom relegated to their skin pigmentation. The pride of their ancestors' patriotism ran warm through their veins. They embraced degrees of onyx clandestine beneath their dermis of treasures. They understood that unity and harmony strengthened their humanity. They knew themselves to be conciliatory agents of change who epitomized charity, compassion, and courage, yet to others, "C" stood for colored.

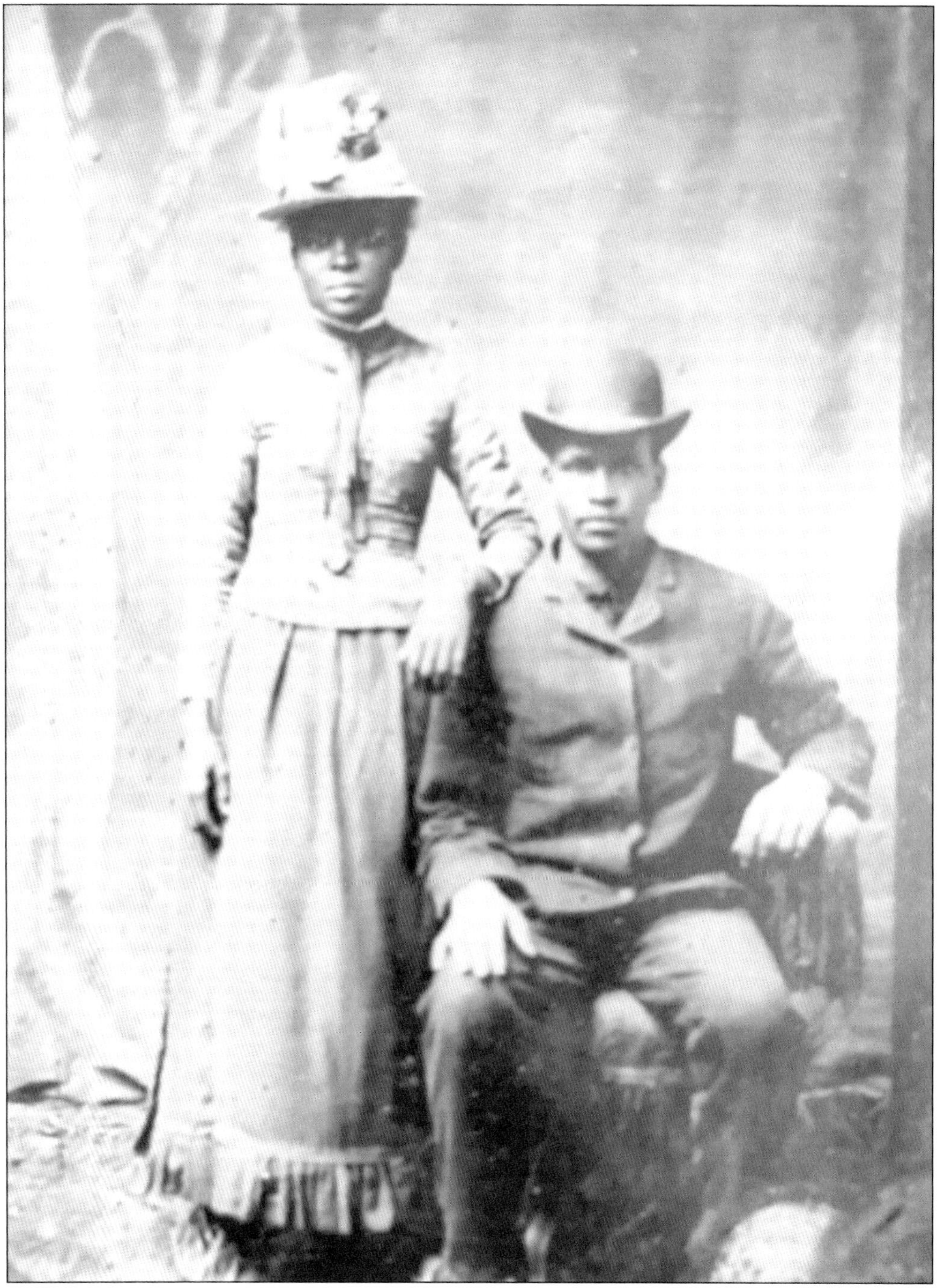

As established contributors to the sustainability of their home and community, the Petersons were among the earliest colored families that settled in Mill Creek Hundred. The Peterson family, descendants of the Carter family from Chester County, Pennsylvania, worked as caretakers and laborers for prominent white families in Chester County. They established roots in Hockessin after securing permanent employment with the Marshall family, who owned several industrial mills. This picture shows Joseph and Sarah Carter in 1910. (Elizabeth Lester.)

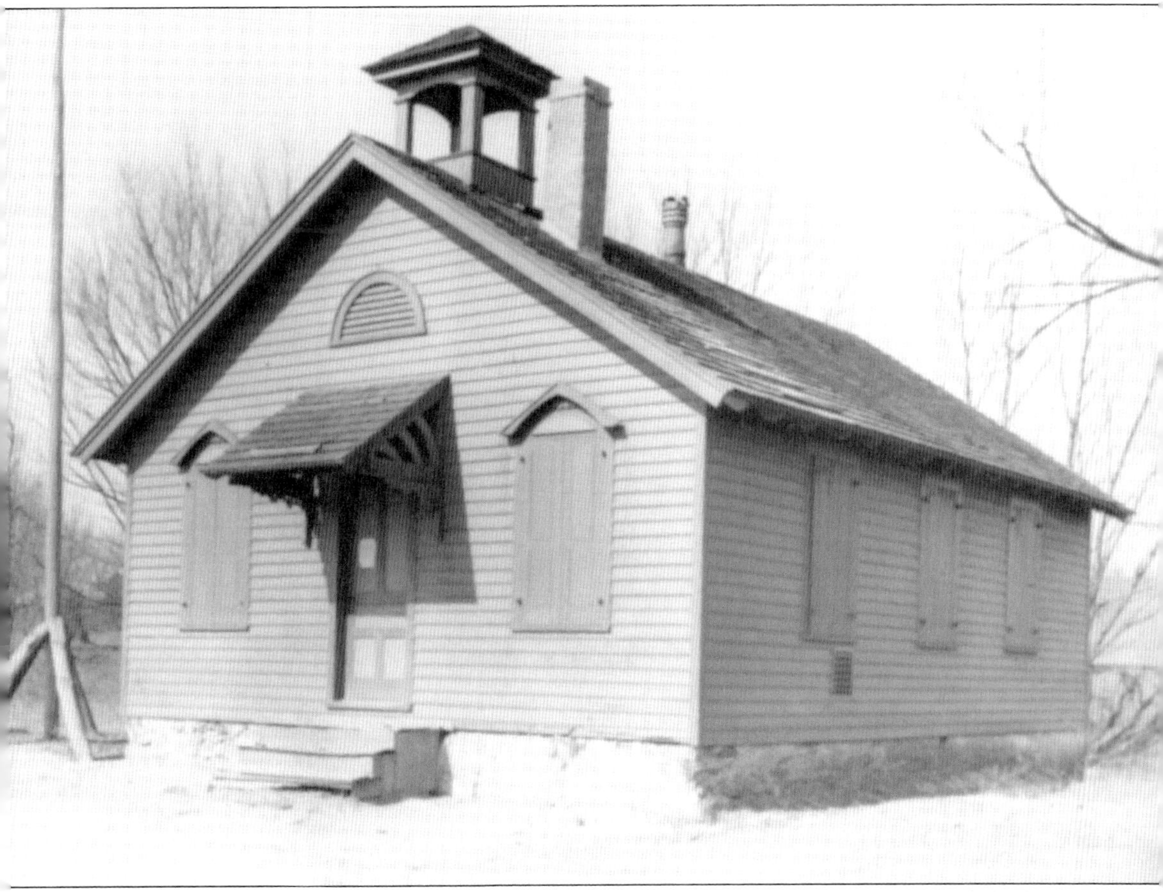

Built in 1878 as a wooden framed one-room schoolhouse, the original school was established as colored school three (#3C-Hockessin). Both structures were primarily sustained by the contributions of Hockessin colored citizens and a "society of friends." (Hagley Museum and Library.)

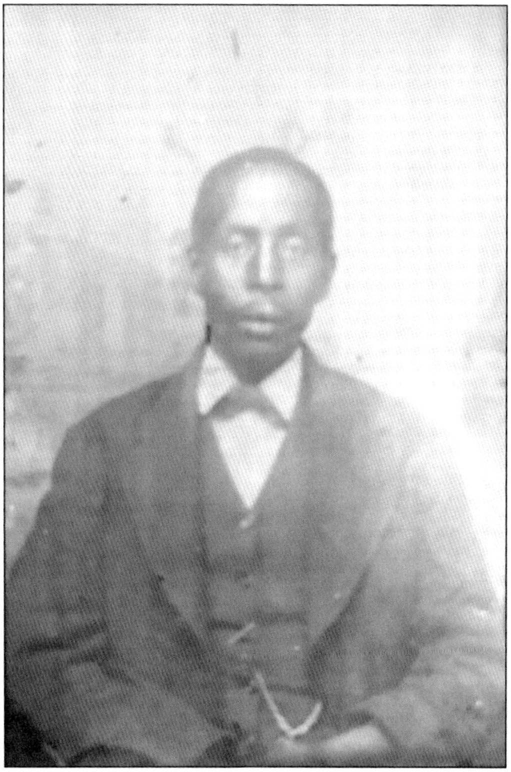

Abe Peterson (left) was among the colored laborers who became well-versed in agriculture, mill operations, maintenance of structures, and animals. Generations of his offspring followed in his footsteps and continued the tradition of ingenuity. These pictures were taken around 1908 as part of a series of photographs of individuals and couples who were members of the Peterson and Carter families. Abe is pictured below with his wife, whose first name is not known. (Both, Elizabeth Lester.)

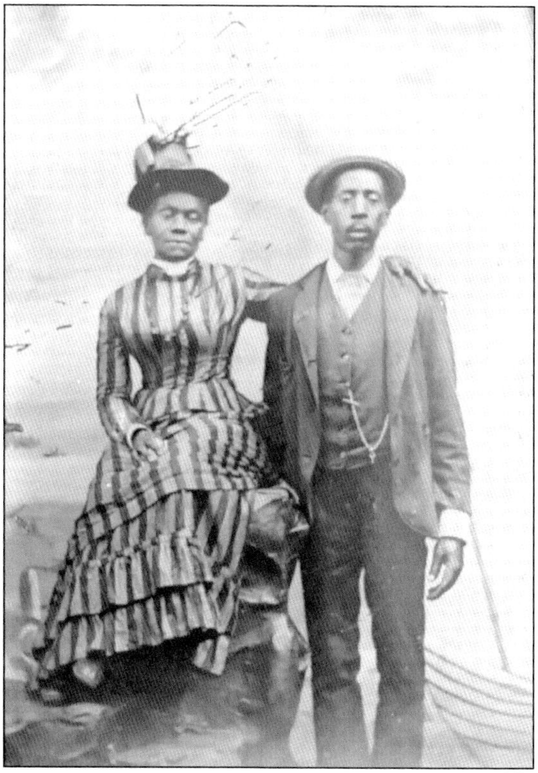

In Hockessin, churches were the earliest centers of education. Colored citizens' gatherings were held at three local churches: Pleasant Grove, St. Luke Methodist Episcopal, and Chippey African Union Methodist Protestant (AUMP). Chippey AUMP Church was established on September 24, 1886. A lot located at Grant Avenue and Mill Creek Road was purchased from D.H. Kent. On March 27, 1897, the title for the property was issued to members of Chippey Church. On December 8, 1897, H.V. McVaugh sold an additional dwelling to the Chippey congregation that became the site of the Hockessin Colored Union Hall. By 1912, three Hockessin buildings—Colored School #3, Chippey AUMP Church, and the Hockessin Colored Union Hall—had become the societal pillars of the Hockessin colored community. The church, pictured here around 1930, remains at its original site at 4272 Mill Creek Road. (Chippey AUMP Archives.)

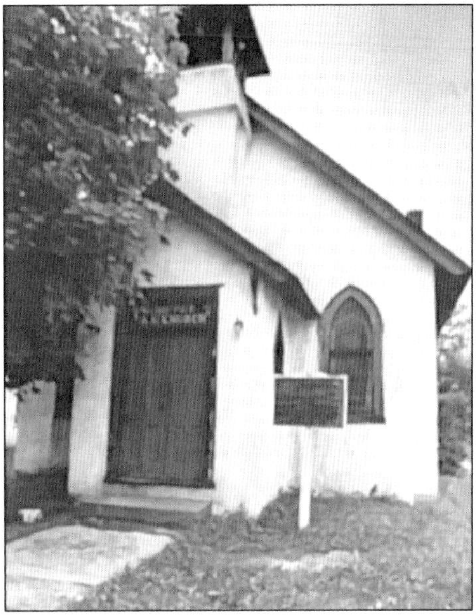

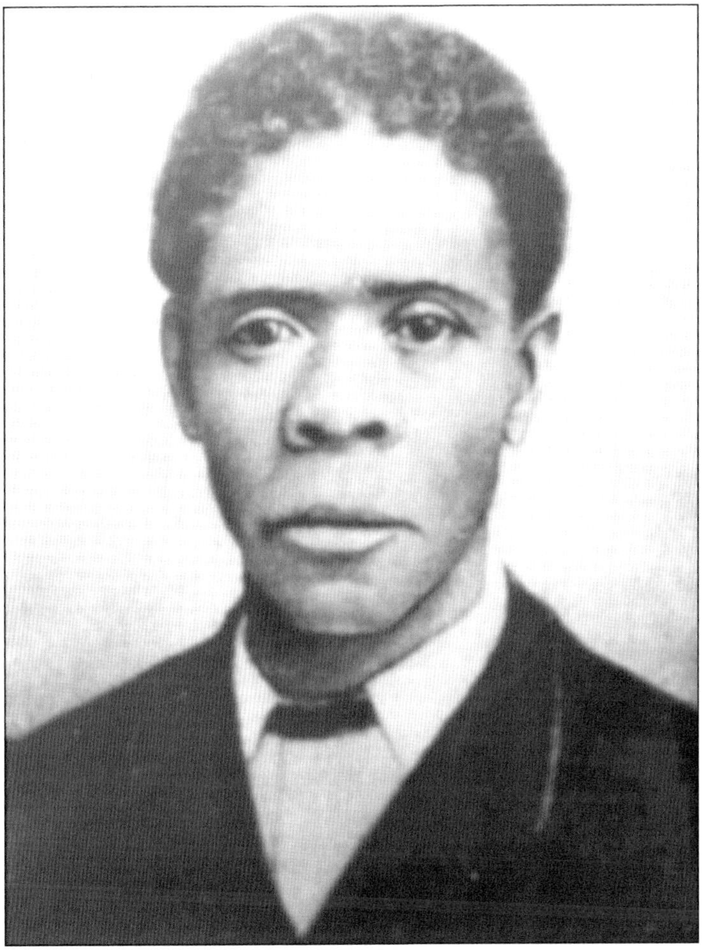

Rev. Edward H. Chippey (1825–1900) was the founder of St. Peter's African Union Methodist Protestant (AUMP) Church in Wilmington, Delaware. The building was established in 1870. In 1873, he built a second church that included a Sunday school and a day school. The facility became the first public school created for colored children in the state of Delaware. A descendant of Rev. Moses Chippey, a founding father of the AUMP faith, Edward dedicated over 50 years of his life to serving the colored people of Delaware.

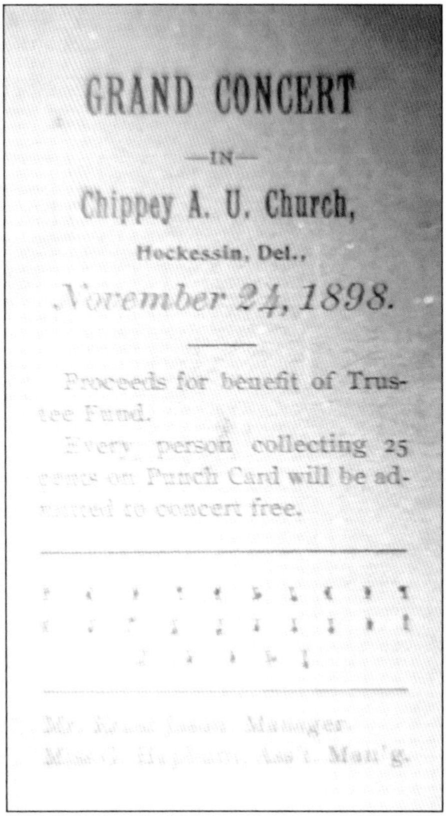

A "Grand Concert" was held at Chippey AUMP Church on November 24, 1898. Punch cards were sold as a means of financial support, with proceeds benefitting the trustee fund managed by overseers of the church and the school. This image is an original 25¢ punch card used as a primary source of fundraising for this event. Each punched hole was equivalent to one cent. A fully punched card granted the cardholder free admission to the concert. (Elizabeth Lester.)

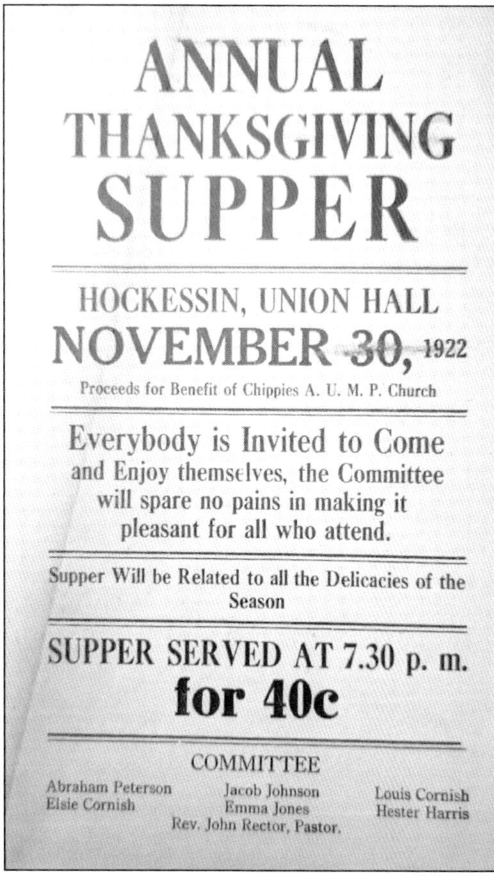

A successful local strategy to record the amount of financial support raised by colored residents for their school was implemented with the assistance of their clergy. Rev. Edward H. Chippey maintained a separate log for marriages, identifying them by location and school. Utilizing this method of calculation, fees paid to the state education fund earmarked for colored schools were easily verified. In Hockessin, these efforts were combined with fundraisers to support the needs of the community hall, church, and school. This flyer is an advertisement for the Chippey AUMP Church's annual Thanksgiving supper. Proceeds were collected by church committee members who served as trustees of the board of education for the old frame school. Although it may have appeared to outsiders as a mere harvest celebration, the annual gathering had greater implications. The tradition of the supper gathering lasted into the 1980s, excluding wedding nuptials. (Elizabeth Lester.)

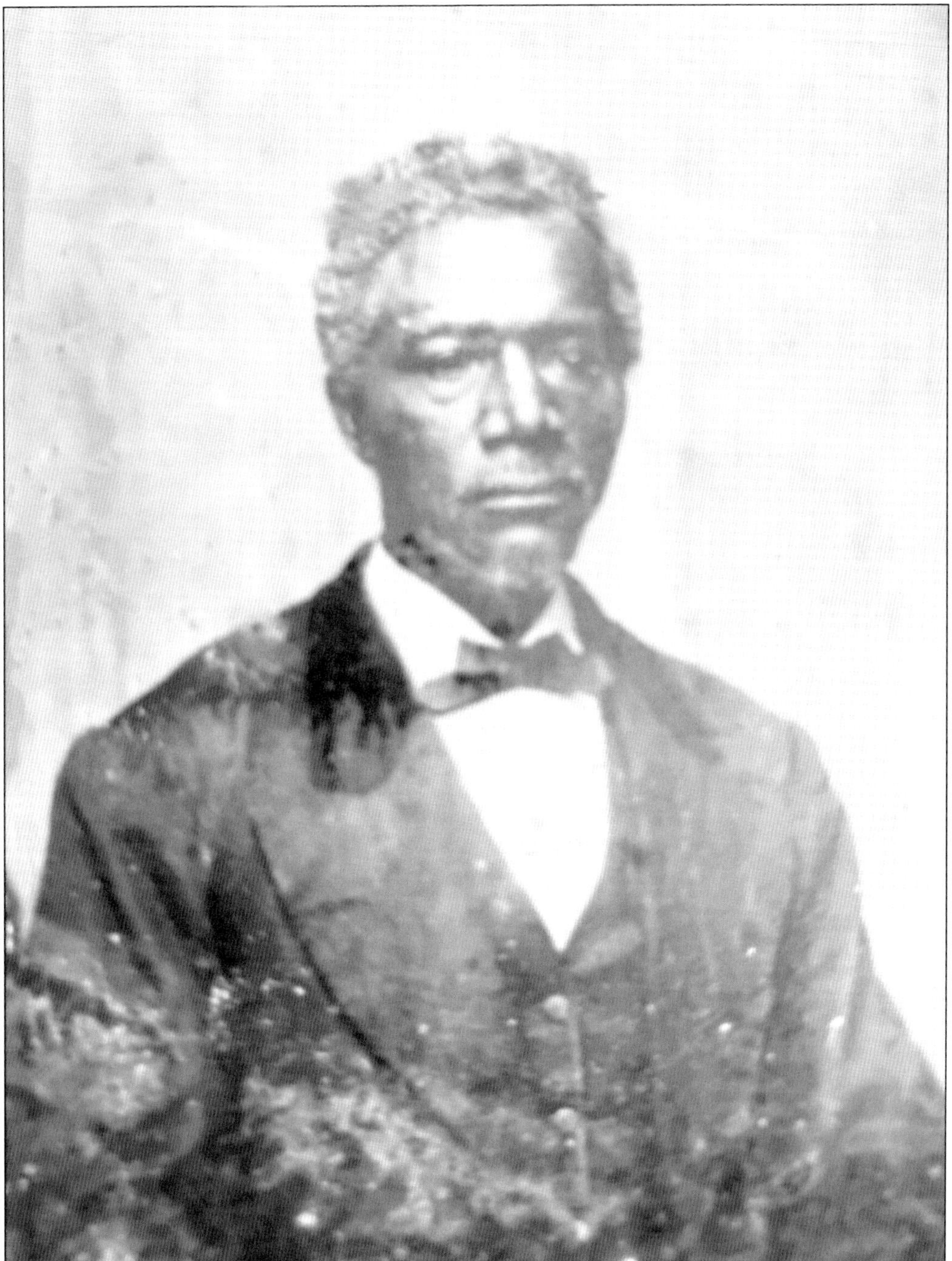

This is Abraham Peterson, a colored landowner in Hockessin. The Petersons were staunch advocates and financial supporters of education for colored children. Abraham was born on July 29, 1850. He married Eliza Jane Bradley on November 25, 1875, and their marriage ceremony was performed by Rev. Edward H. Chippey. (Elizabeth Lester.)

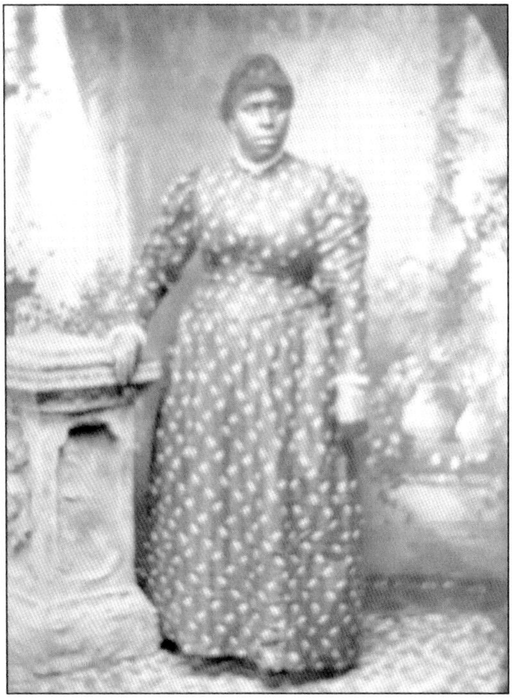

Letitia Calhoun Peterson is pictured in her finery, as was the custom in the colored community when being photographed. She was born around 1835 in Kent County, Delaware, near the town of Smyrna. Her grandchildren were in the inaugural class of students who attended Hockessin Colored School #3. (Elizabeth Lester.)

This is a copy of the deed to the St. Peter's Cemetery plot for Abraham Peterson and his heirs. The Petersons were landowners and prominent citizens in the Hockessin colored community. This policy was established on June 24, 1889, for the amount of $15.37. Proceeds from the policies supported St. Peter's Church and a local private colored school. (Elizabeth Lester.)

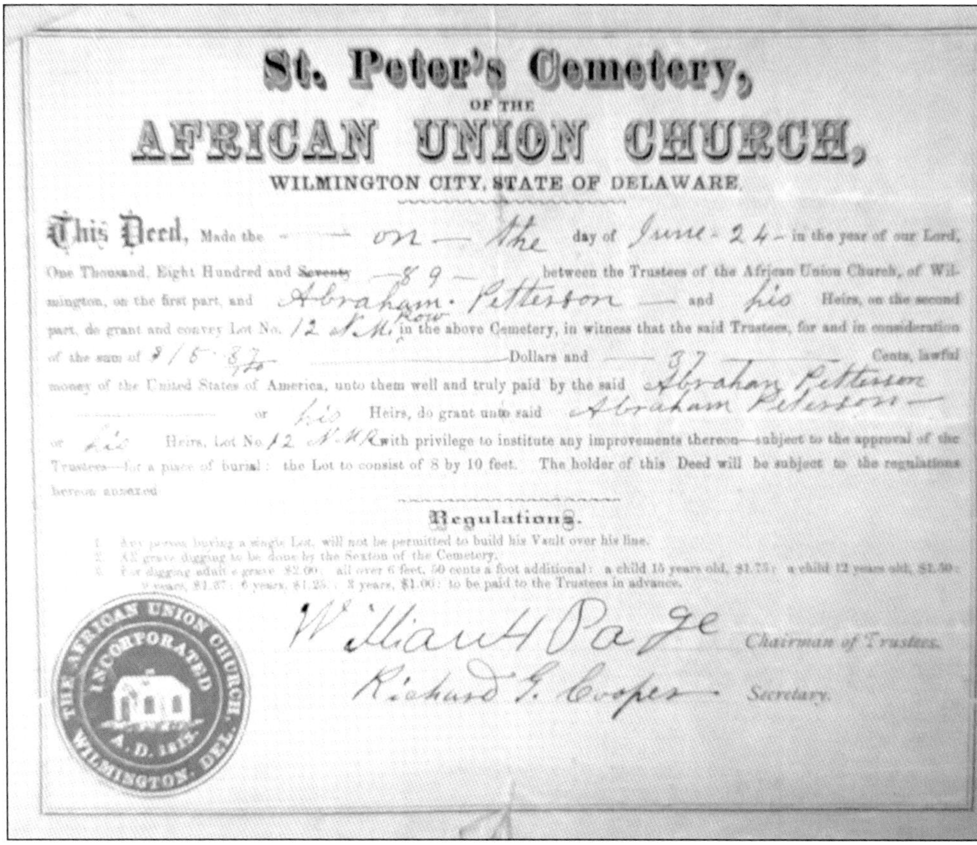

St. Peter's Cemetery,

OF THE

AFRICAN UNION CHURCH,

WILMINGTON CITY, STATE OF DELAWARE.

This Deed, Made the on the day of June 24 in the year of our Lord, One Thousand, Eight Hundred and ~~Seventy~~ 89 between the Trustees of the African Union Church, of Wilmington, on the first part, and Abraham Petterson and his Heirs, on the second part, do grant and convey Lot No. 12 N. M. Row in the above Cemetery, in witness that the said Trustees, for and in consideration of the sum of $15.37/100 Dollars and 37 Cents, lawful money of the United States of America, unto them well and truly paid by the said Abraham Petterson or his Heirs, do grant unto said Abraham Peterson or his Heirs, Lot No. 12 N. M. R. with privilege to institute any improvements thereon—subject to the approval of the Trustees—for a place of burial: the Lot to consist of 8 by 10 feet. The holder of this Deed will be subject to the regulations hereon annexed.

Regulations.

1. Any person buying a single Lot, will not be permitted to build his Vault over his line.
2. All grave digging to be done by the Sexton of the Cemetery.
3. For digging adult's grave $2.00; all over 6 feet, 50 cents a foot additional: a child 15 years old, $1.75; a child 12 years old, $1.50; 9 years, $1.37; 6 years, $1.25; 3 years, $1.00; to be paid to the Trustees in advance.

William Page Chairman of Trustees.

Richard G. Cooper Secretary.

The opening of a new hall in Hockessin created quite a stir, as colored people from neighboring towns were invited to the grand celebration. The event was declared a monumental community accomplishment for colored residents. Admission prices were set at 20¢ for adults and 10¢ for children (equivalent to around $6.50 and $3.25 today, respectively). This concert flyer announced the grand opening and christening of a new hall on March 23, 1911. The featured attraction was a performance by the Colored Band of Kennett Square from Pennsylvania. (Elizabeth Lester.)

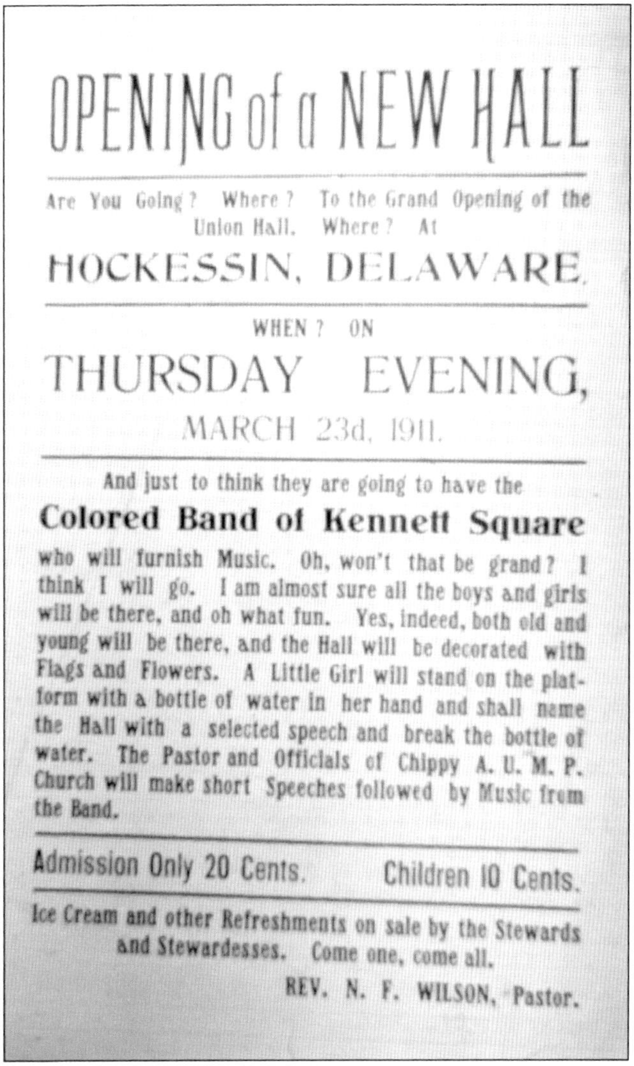

OPENING of a NEW HALL

Are You Going? Where? To the Grand Opening of the Union Hall. Where? At

HOCKESSIN, DELAWARE.

WHEN? ON

THURSDAY EVENING,

MARCH 23d, 1911.

And just to think they are going to have the

Colored Band of Kennett Square

who will furnish Music. Oh, won't that be grand? I think I will go. I am almost sure all the boys and girls will be there, and oh what fun. Yes, indeed, both old and young will be there, and the Hall will be decorated with Flags and Flowers. A Little Girl will stand on the platform with a bottle of water in her hand and shall name the Hall with a selected speech and break the bottle of water. The Pastor and Officials of Chippy A. U. M. P. Church will make short Speeches followed by Music from the Band.

Admission Only 20 Cents. Children 10 Cents.

Ice Cream and other Refreshments on sale by the Stewards and Stewardesses. Come one, come all.

REV. N. F. WILSON, Pastor.

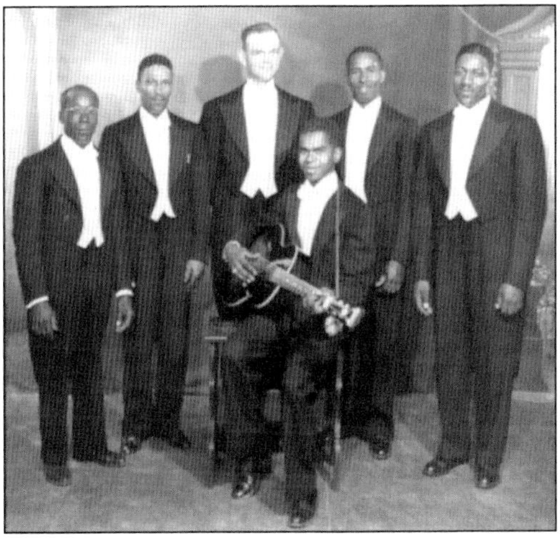

The Harmony Singers from Sussex County, Delaware, were among those who toured the region providing entertainment for audiences at churches and charitable events, including at the famous Rosedale Beach Hotel in Millsboro. This establishment was a favorite among influential colored entertainers during segregation. Swing and jazz bands featuring Louis Armstrong, Count Basie, Cab Calloway, Duke Ellington, and Ella Fitzgerald enjoyed on-site hotel accommodations—a rarity during the 1930s and 1940s. Calloway and members of the Harmony Singers became permanent residents of Hockessin. Their contributions were beacons of hope and inspiration for local citizens.

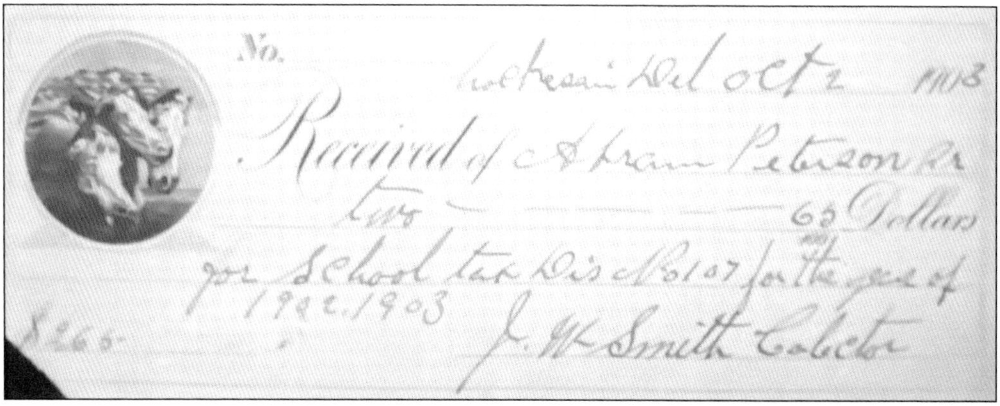
No. Hockessin Del Oct 2 1903
Received of Abram Peterson Sr
Two — 65/100 Dollars
for School tax Dis No 107 for the year of 1902.1903
$2.65 J. W. Smith Collector

State funding for schools was distributed disproportionately in favor of public schools attended by white children. This practice became the foundation of disparity for colored children, causing extreme inequities among the separated entities. This is a school tax receipt signed by the Collector of Revenue for taxes paid by Abraham Peterson. The receipt—dated October 2, 1903, in the sum of $2.65—covered assessed taxes for the 1902–1903 school year in District 107. The amount of the apportionment issued to colored schools in comparison to the amount of taxes paid by colored citizens was so minuscule that it barely equated to one cent on the dollar. (Elizabeth Lester.)

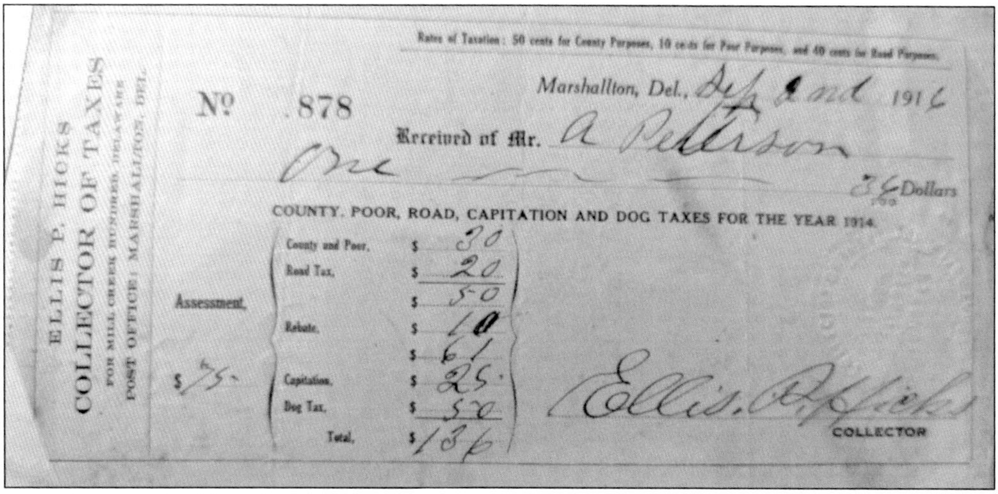
Rates of Taxation: 50 cents for County Purposes, 10 cents for Poor Purposes, and 40 cents for Road Purposes.
ELLIS P. HICKS
COLLECTOR OF TAXES
FOR MILL CREEK HUNDRED, DELAWARE
POST OFFICE: MARSHALLTON, DEL.
No. 878 Marshallton, Del., Sep 2nd 1916
Received of Mr. A Peterson
One — 36/100 Dollars
COUNTY, POOR, ROAD, CAPITATION AND DOG TAXES FOR THE YEAR 1916

	County and Poor,	$ 30
	Road Tax,	$ 20
Assessment,		$ 50
	Rebate,	$ 10
		$ 61
$ 75	Capitation,	$ 25
	Dog Tax,	$ 50
	Total,	$ 1 36

Ellis P. Hicks
COLLECTOR

As early as 1875, although colored citizens in Hockessin paid public school taxes, their monies were placed into a general fund for all schools. It was not until 1881 that the state of Delaware began disseminating state funds equally amongst schools. This is a copy of a county tax receipt issued on September 2, 1916, to Abraham Peterson. According to Peterson family records, only a small portion of the rebate taken from the total collection of county tax (50¢), poor tax (10¢), and road tax (40¢) was considered by question, if asked, for donation to local colored schools. Such practices led to the widespread belief that colored residents lacked the financial resources to fund their independent school districts. (Elizabeth Lester.)

Two

The Former Students of #107C

A Community of Learners

Colored families were obligated to adhere to societal practices of isolation and exclusion based on national perceptions of ethnicity. Public records and private collections indicate that from 1829 to 1919, colored families residing in Mill Creek Hundred established schools for their children. These buildings were located in the same vicinity along Grant Avenue between Evanson Road and Mill Creek Road.

After the Civil War, schools in Delaware were organized as independent districts. By the 1880s, colored districts were collectively referred to as penny hill schools. Among those located in New Castle County were Penny Hill (Claymont) #1C, Newport (Belvedere) #2C, Hockessin #3C, Marshallton #4C, Christiana #5C, Iron Hill #6C, Williamsville #7C, Bethesda #8C, Kirkwood #9C, Summit Bridge #10C, Saint Georges #11C, and Delaware City #12C.

Colored children living in these communities were prepared at early ages to anticipate their entry into first grade. They remained at their community school until the completion of sixth grade. Teachers were expected to be proficient in the basic subjects of reading, writing, and arithmetic. As for Hockessin, many of their colored educators obtained teaching degrees from prestigious historically black collegiate institutions with teacher colleges such as the State College for Colored Students (now Delaware State University), Ashman Institute (now Lincoln University), the African Institute for Colored Youth (now Cheyney University of Pennsylvania), Hampton Institute, and Howard University.

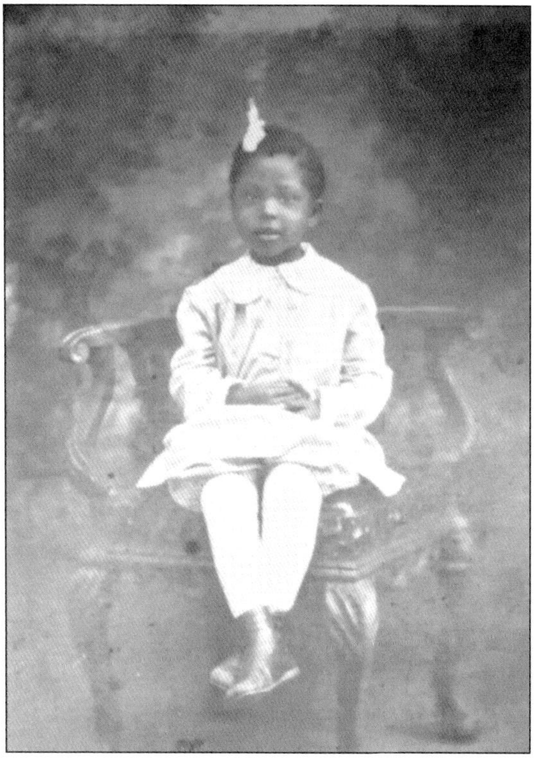

Pictured on this page are Hockessin toddlers Bettye Peterson (left) and Charlotte Knott (below). Charlotte and Bettye were the youngest members of two large colored families with ties to the Mill Creek area that extended beyond three generations. With great anticipation, in the late 1920s, as the youngest sibling of four older students, Bettye entered first grade at the brick #107C schoolhouse. She became a dear classmate of Hilda Octavia Bulah, the youngest member of the Bulah family. Charlotte entered first grade at the brick #107C in 1950 with Shirley Bulah, an adopted member of the Bulah family, whose educational journey became the focal point of a national movement. The girls enjoyed recreational activities and social endeavors during their primary years at Hockessin Colored School #107C. (Left, Elizabeth Lester; below, Charlotte Knott.)

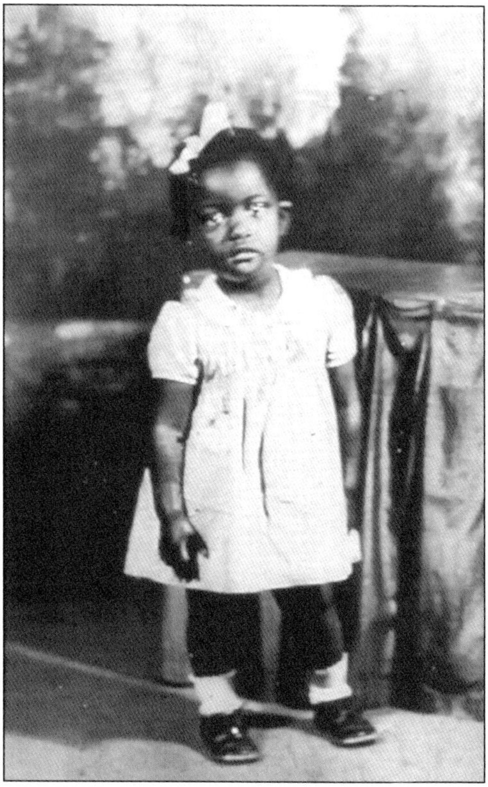

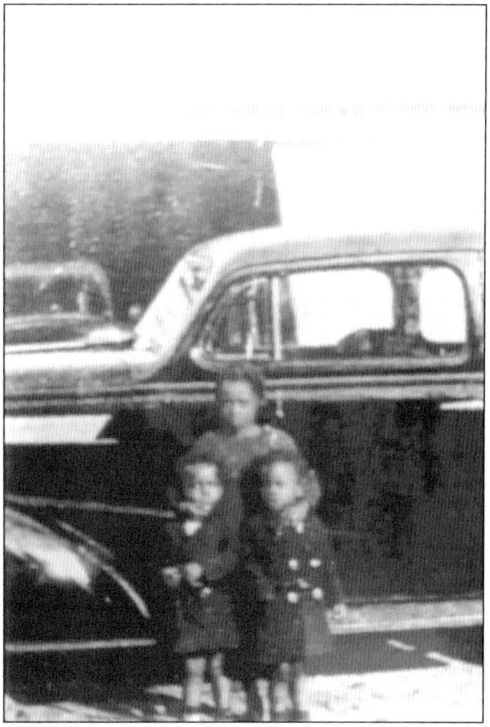

These photographs depict scenes of little ones actively discovering the boundaries of their neighborhood. The photographs epitomize the uninhibited nature of the rural lifestyles experienced by the youngest colored residents of Hockessin. The Johnson children are standing next to an automobile in the image at right, while members of the Bulah family are pictured below sitting on tricycles in their backyard. (Right, Walter Macklin; below, Hilda Bulah Morris.)

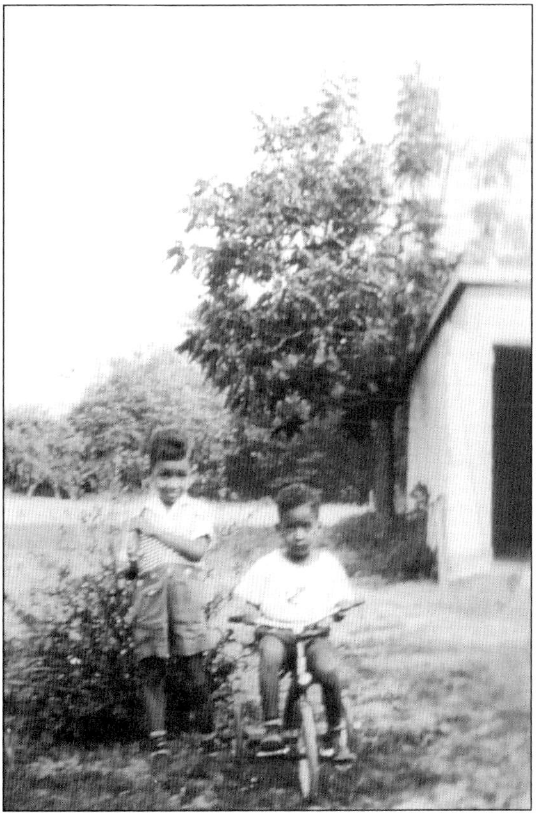

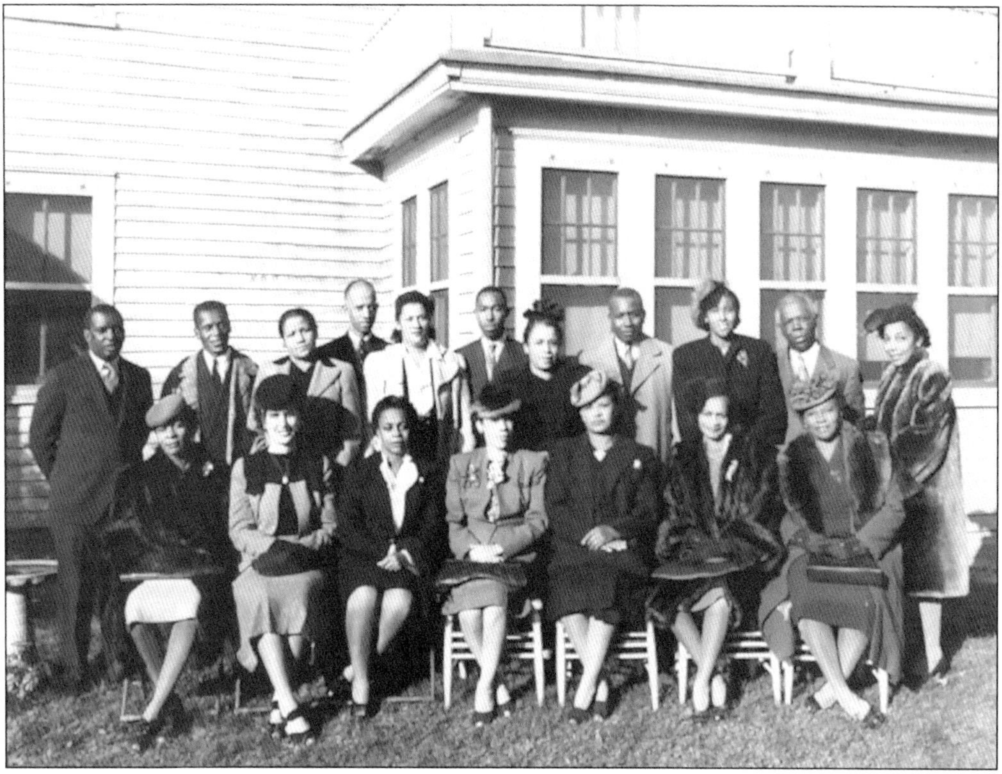

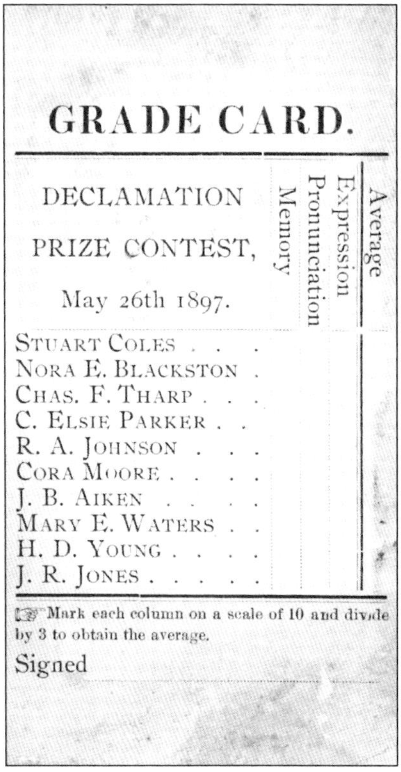

GRADE CARD.

DECLAMATION PRIZE CONTEST, May 26th 1897.

	Memory	Pronunciation	Expression	Average
STUART COLES . . .				
NORA E. BLACKSTON .				
CHAS. F. THARP . . .				
C. ELSIE PARKER . .				
R. A. JOHNSON . . .				
CORA MOORE				
J. B. AIKEN				
MARY E. WATERS . .				
H. D. YOUNG				
J. R. JONES				

☞ Mark each column on a scale of 10 and divide by 3 to obtain the average.

Signed

At its inception on May 15, 1861, the general curriculum of the State College for Colored Students was solidified. However, coursework was added to address the academic needs of a growing colored population. By 1897, changes included the addition of a three-year normal course, resulting in a teacher's certificate. The State College for Colored Students graduated its first class of degreed candidates in May 1898. By 1911, the teacher education program had been extended to a four-year degree—a bachelor's of pedagogy awarded upon satisfactory completion of the curriculum. This group of teachers gathered on the campus of the school (renamed Delaware State College) in Dover, Delaware, in 1945.

Oratorical grade cards, end-of-the-year audit cards, school ledgers, and grade books were standard instructional materials for colored teachers. This oratorical grade card is dated May 26, 1897. Oratorical contests were held to exhibit students' educational prowess and as a measurement of academic progress. Scoring and calculation instructions, accompanied by a judge's signature, provided feedback for participating students. Declamation as a rhetorical exercise included memory, pronunciation, and expression. Students scored high marks for passionate deliveries of poems, sonnets, soliloquies, and speeches. (Elizabeth Lester.)

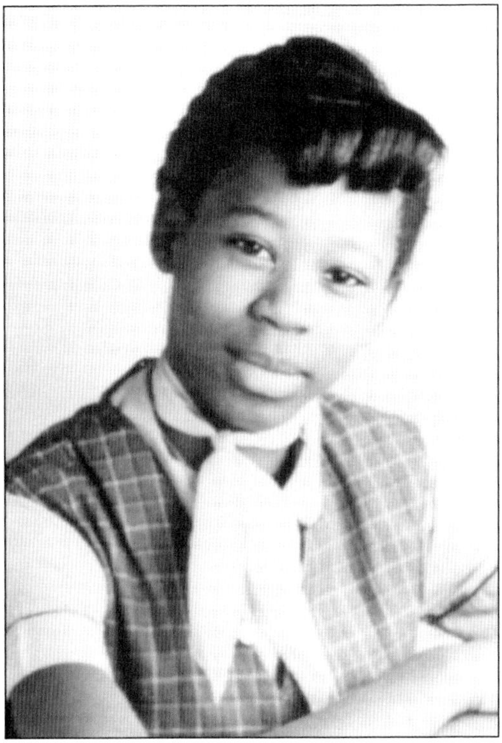

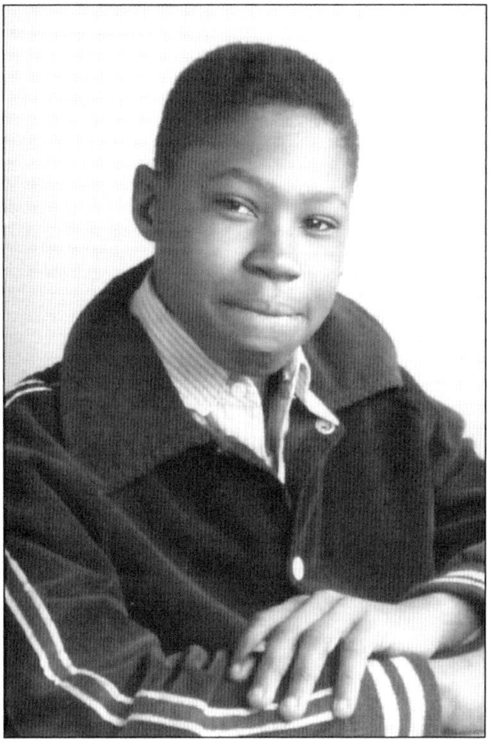

Blanche Knott (left) attended Hockessin Colored School #107C from 1945 to 1950. James Henry Knott (right), an older brother of Blanche, attended Hockessin Colored School #107C from 1943 to 1948. Blanche's fondest memories included being a member of the checkered socks club and the school's Girl Scout troop No. 55 under the leadership of Ruby Copper. (Both, Blanche Knott.)

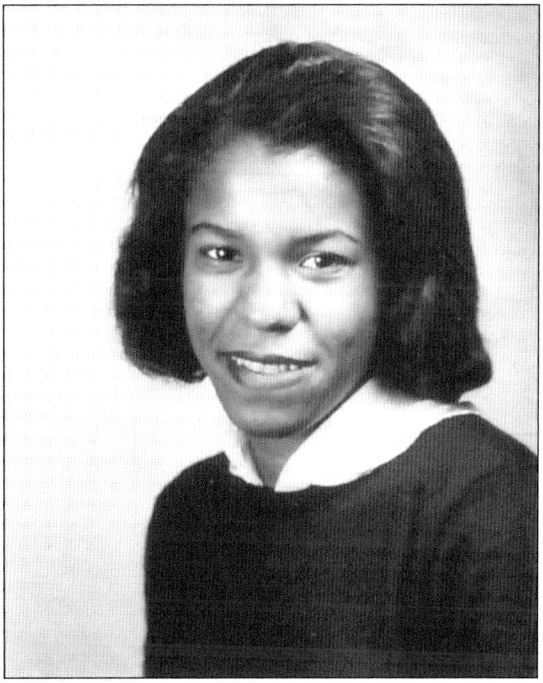

Laura Bantum enjoyed attending Hockessin Colored School #107C with her older sisters June and Maryann Bantum. She considered her six years of schooling at #107C a family affair. According to many former #107C students, being in the company of siblings and relatives bolstered their confidence and enthusiasm for learning. In the case of Laura, her cousins James Henry Knott and Blanche Knott provided her with that sense of comfort. (Blanche Knott.)

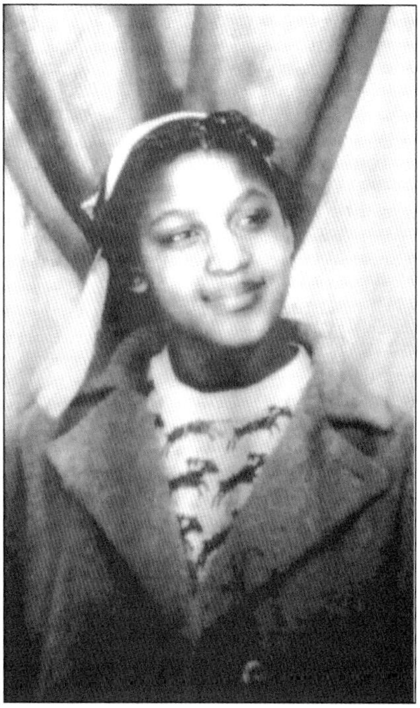
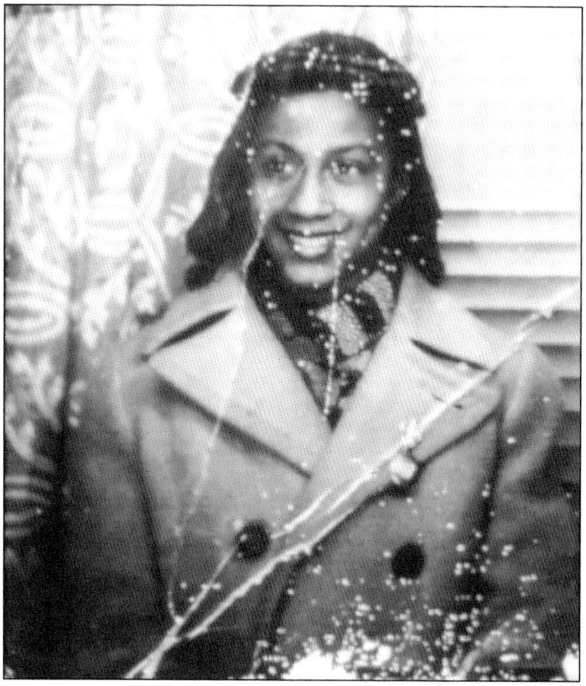

Ethel Carter (left) attended Hockessin Colored School #107C with classmates Gwendolyn Peterson, James Sonny Knott, and Isaiah Watters from 1935 to 1940. Ethel's younger sister Mary and younger brother Joseph Thomas both attended Hockessin Colored School #107C from 1945 to 1950. At right, Mary is pictured wearing her favorite double-breasted coat. Mary was an enthusiastic member of the #107C checkered socks club. (Elizabeth Lester.)

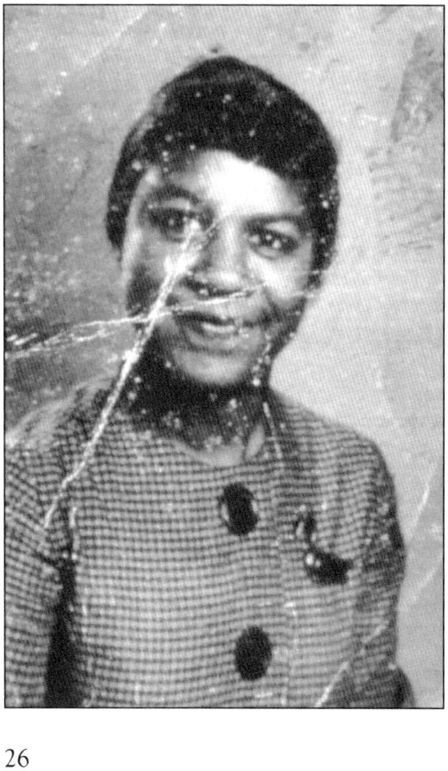

Rosetta Johnson attended Hockessin Colored School #107C in the 1950s. She represented the fourth generation of Johnson females to attend at Hockessin Colored Schools. (Charles Johnson.)

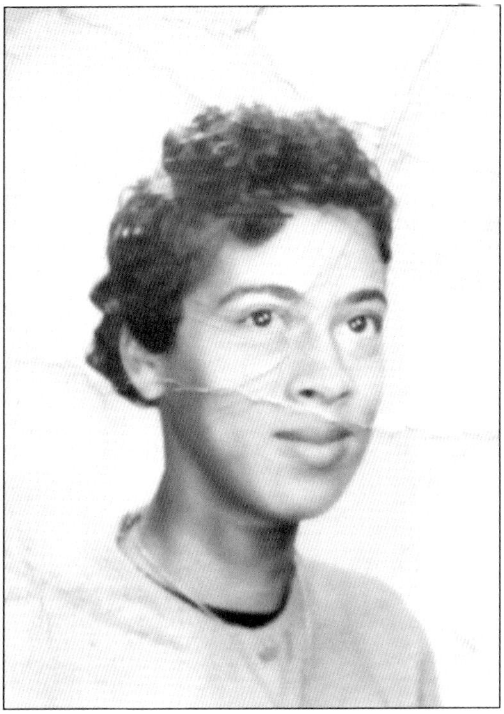

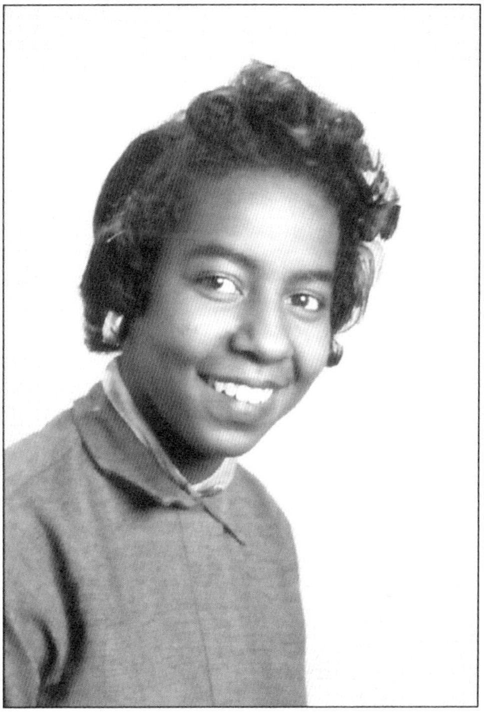

Carol Ann Jackson (left) attended Hockessin Colored School #107C from 1950 to 1954. Affectionately known as Annie, she was a descendant of the early families that settled in Hockessin at the turn of the 20th century. Dorothy Gasby (right) attended Hockessin Colored School #107C from 1950 to 1954. Members of the Gasby, Jackson, and Peterson families were among the first colored people to work in the mill industries located throughout Mill Creek Hundred. (Both, Charlotte Knott.)

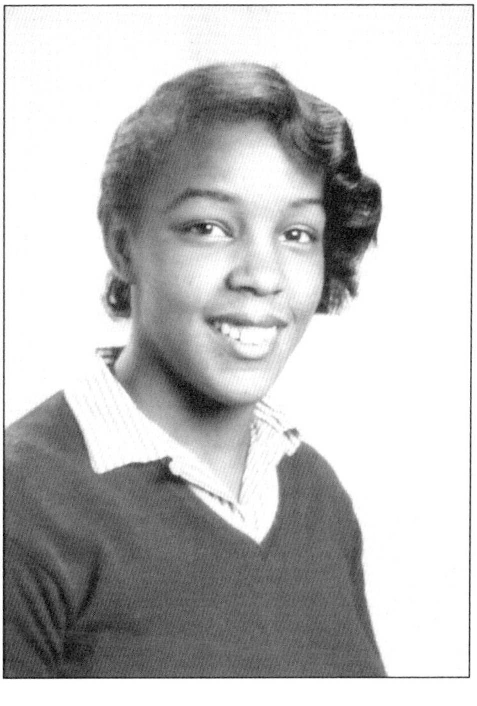

Bertha Smith attended Hockessin Colored School #107C from 1952 to 1957. Bertha lived across the street from the school. She remembered sitting in the comfort of her home waiting for the school bell to ring before dashing out the front door and into her school seat in a matter of seconds. Although Bertha did not attend Hockessin School #29, prior to desegregation, her mother was the only colored female janitor employed on staff at the segregated school. (Charlotte Knott.)

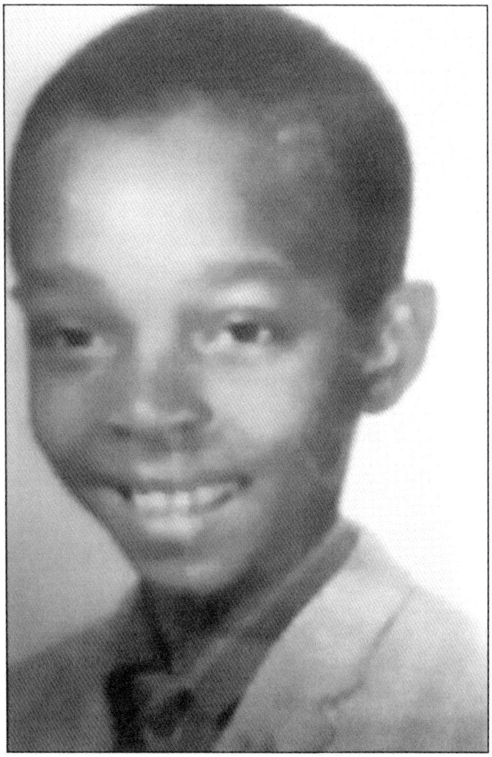

Alan Peterson, locally known as Skippy, attended Hockessin Colored School #107C in the 1950s. His younger siblings were among the first students to enter Hockessin #29 and Alexis I. duPont Junior High School after the national implementation of *Brown v. Board I* and *II*–with deliberate speed. (Elizabeth Lester.)

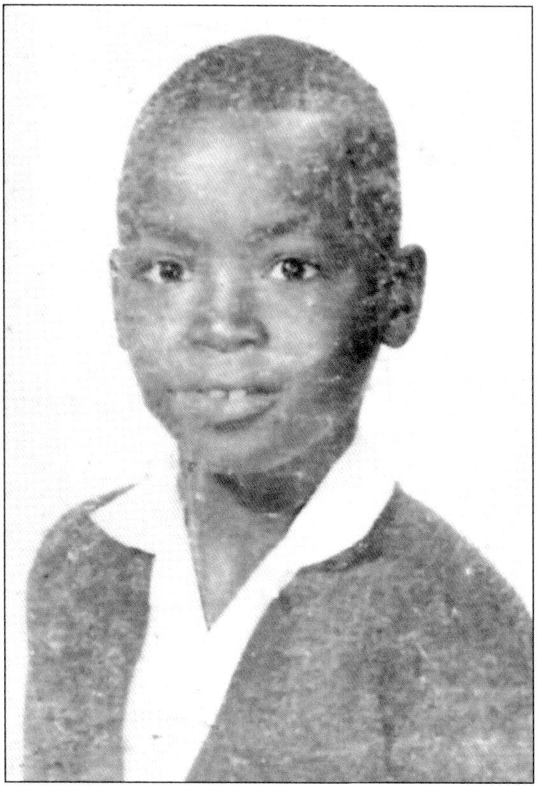

Walter Macklin is pictured in his primary years at Hockessin Colored School #107C, which he attended from 1954 to 1959. Affectionately known as Mack, he was in the last class of students educated by S. Constancia Beaujon in the #107C brick schoolhouse. The class had the distinction of being the last pupils to transfer into the newly desegregated Alexis I. duPont Junior High School. His forever classmates were Stanley Gray and Pia Peterson. (Walter Macklin.)

RULES AND REGULATIONS

The following rules and regulations established by the State Board of Education must be observed in making the contract on the other side of this sheet.

All white schools are to open the second Monday in September.

All colored schools are to open the first Monday in October.

The days of the Annual Institute are not to be counted as days taught, but teachers are to be paid for attendance at the Institute at the rate of salary mentioned in the teacher's contract.

SCHOOL HOLIDAYS

The following holidays, with full pay to teachers, are hereby established.

1. Thanksgiving Day and the day following.
2. Christmas holidays, including the day before Christmas and New Year's Day.
3. Good Friday and Easter Monday for all teachers whose contracts call for a school year of nine or ten months.
4. Such days, as Columbus Day, Lincoln's Birthday, Washington's Birthday, Arbor and Bird Day, Memorial Day and Flag Day, are not school holidays, but special days, set apart for a specific purpose. Teachers are urged to emphasize the importance of these days with appropriate exercises in the schools.

SERIOUS ILLNESS OF TEACHERS WHILE IN SERVICE.

1. In case of illness during the school year a teacher shall be allowed half pay for the first week, full pay for the second and third weeks, and half pay for the fourth week. After four weeks no pay shall be allowed.
2. During the time a teacher is ill a substitute teacher shall be provided for the school at the expense of the local school board.
3. The salary of a qualified substitute teacher shall be 90% of the regular teacher's salary.

PAY FOR TEACHERS WHEN SCHOOLS ARE UNAVOIDABLY CLOSED.

Teachers shall receive full pay for any length of time schools may be closed on account of contagious or infectious diseases, or for any other reason over which the teacher has no control.

Rules and regulations established by the State Board of Education were different for colored educators and white educators. Whereas white schools opened on the second Monday of September, all colored schools opened on the first Monday in October. The days of the annual institute included school holidays: Thanksgiving Day and the day after; Christmas holidays, including Christmas Eve and New Year's Day; and Good Friday and Easter Monday for all teachers on nine- or ten-month school-year contracts. If a primary teacher had an illness, the services of a substitute teacher were enlisted at the expense of the local school board.

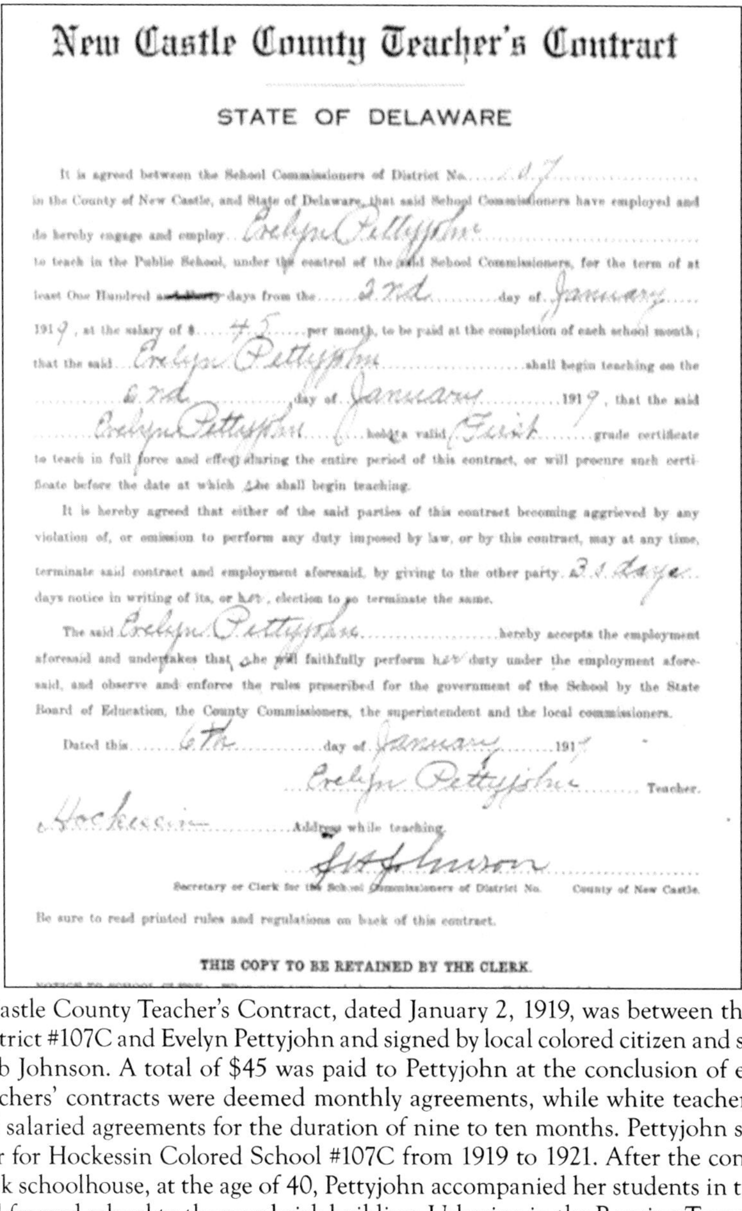

New Castle County Teacher's Contract

STATE OF DELAWARE

It is agreed between the School Commissioners of District No. 107 in the County of New Castle, and State of Delaware, that said School Commissioners have employed and do hereby engage and employ Evelyn Pettyjohn to teach in the Public School, under the control of the said School Commissioners, for the term of at least One Hundred and ~~eighty~~ days from the 2nd day of January 1919, at the salary of $ 45 per month, to be paid at the completion of each school month; that the said Evelyn Pettyjohn shall begin teaching on the 2nd day of January 1919, that the said Evelyn Pettyjohn holds a valid First grade certificate to teach in full force and effect during the entire period of this contract, or will procure such certificate before the date at which she shall begin teaching.

It is hereby agreed that either of the said parties of this contract becoming aggrieved by any violation of, or omission to perform any duty imposed by law, or by this contract, may at any time, terminate said contract and employment aforesaid, by giving to the other party 30 days days notice in writing of its, or her, election to so terminate the same.

The said Evelyn Pettyjohn hereby accepts the employment aforesaid and undertakes that she will faithfully perform her duty under the employment aforesaid, and observe and enforce the rules prescribed for the government of the School by the State Board of Education, the County Commissioners, the superintendent and the local commissioners.

Dated this 6th day of January 1919

Evelyn Pettyjohn Teacher.

Hockessin Address while teaching.

J H Johnson

Secretary or Clerk for the School Commissioners of District No. County of New Castle.

Be sure to read printed rules and regulations on back of this contract.

THIS COPY TO BE RETAINED BY THE CLERK.

This New Castle County Teacher's Contract, dated January 2, 1919, was between the Hockessin Colored District #107C and Evelyn Pettyjohn and signed by local colored citizen and school board trustee Jacob Johnson. A total of $45 was paid to Pettyjohn at the conclusion of each month. Colored teachers' contracts were deemed monthly agreements, while white teachers' contracts were annual salaried agreements for the duration of nine to ten months. Pettyjohn served as the head teacher for Hockessin Colored School #107C from 1919 to 1921. After the construction of the new brick schoolhouse, at the age of 40, Pettyjohn accompanied her students in transitioning from the old framed school to the new brick building. Ushering in the Roaring Twenties in a new facility with state-of-the-art instructional materials did not result in a pay increase for the veteran educator. Much like a conductor, Pettyjohn skillfully guided Hockessin students through one of the most horrific epidemics in the United States—the Spanish flu, commonly known as the Great Influenza, which peaked in 1919. Despite an increase in the mortality rate among young colored children, Pettyjohn continued to hold a standard of academic excellence that connected the legacy of the old school to the promise and vision of the new. Special recognition goes to the former head teachers of Hockessin Colored School #107C (the years they served as head teacher are indicated in parentheses): Evelyn Pettyjohn (1919–1921), Minnie Greene (1921–1922), Ella Saunders (1922–1924), Amanda Pierce (1924–1925), Eleanor Montague (1925–1926), Edna Smith (1926–1927), Meta Boddy (1927–1930), Anna Russum (1950–1952), Marian Beaujon (substitute teacher, 1930–1950), and Sarah Constancia Beaujon (1930–1959).

Three

From Whence We Have Come

A Community of Workers

According to the first US census, which was taken in 1790, there were 3,929,214 people living in the 13 United States at that time. The most populous state was Virginia, with 747,610 inhabitants. Delaware had the lowest reported population, with 59,094. The census did not include native-born/Indigenous people, commonly referred to as Indians. The census did identify colored residents as "free others" or "enslaved."

By the start of the 19th century, migrants, including colored settlers, made the small state of Delaware their permanent domain. In 1804, county records indicated 463 taxable persons were property owners residing in Hockessin, and 7 of those persons were colored men. By 1860, the US census identified 21,627 permanent colored Delaware residents. A small population of those colored residents, 268 free and 4 enslaved, called the little village of Hockessin their home. Contending with a new form of exclusion, black codes established degrees of ethnicity. As Pythagoras would have it, *a* plus *b* equaled *mulatto*, a leg of its own.

Before and after emancipation, Hockessin's colored residents worked to solidify their presence in the community. The majority of colored residents in Hockessin were hired by prominent white families with names like Marshall, Mitchell, Jackson, Dixon, Pierson, and Wilson. Familiar names of colored workers included Gasby, Harris, Hunter, Jackson, Johnson, Lewis, Knott, Peterson, Poindexter, Reed, Washington, Williams, and Smith—these names remain in the community to this day. Descendants of those colored families pooled their resources to create learning experiences for their children, promote wholesomeness and charity toward their neighbors, and embrace camaraderie through communal social interaction. These were the core values that were taught at Hockessin Colored School #107C.

Keeping in step with tradition, the children who became students of #107C learned to appreciate the sacrifices made by their forefathers. Thankful for the promise of new opportunities, they grew to understand the community mantra—from whence we have come.

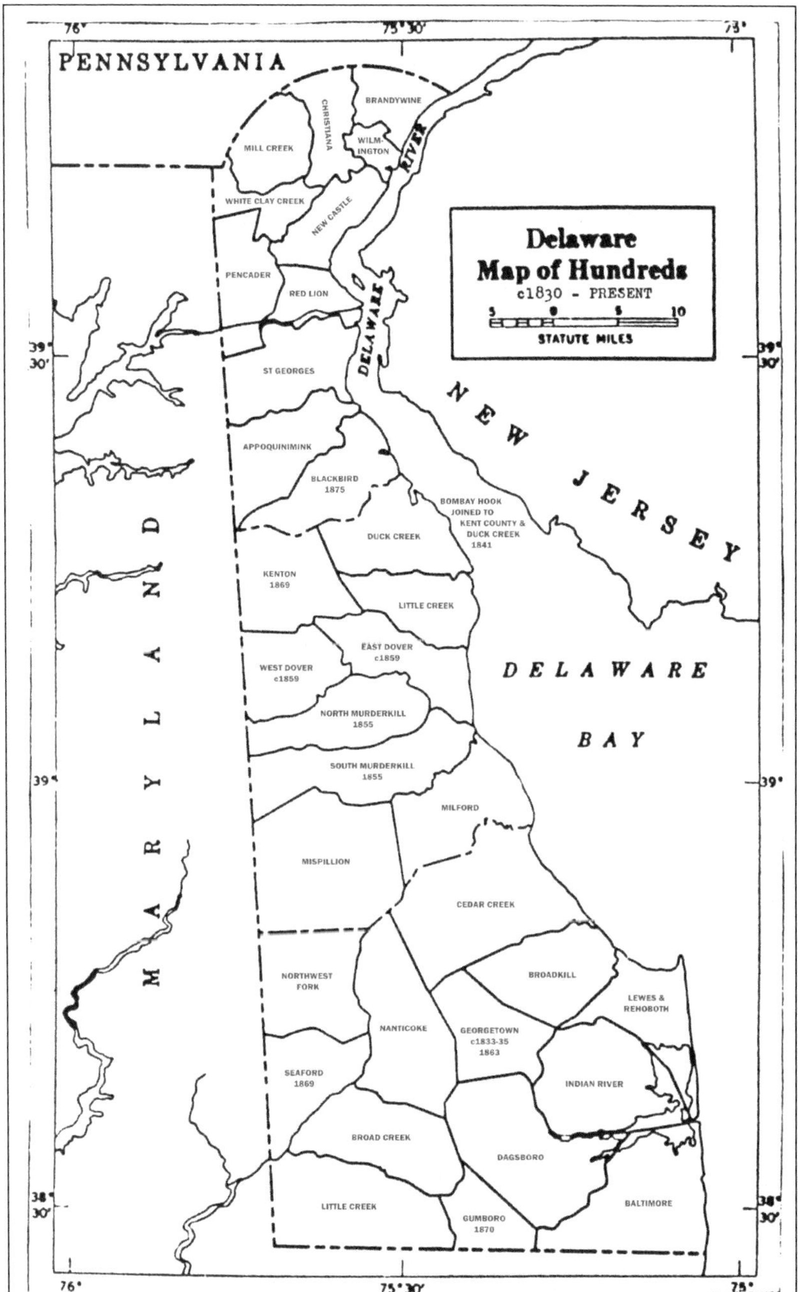

The state of Delaware is divided into three counties; New Castle (in the north), Kent (in the central part of the state), and Sussex (in the south). In addition to the three counties, Delaware is divided into lands known as hundreds. The term "hundreds" originated during the colonial era, when Delaware was under English rule. Divisions were made by increments of 100, usually by farms, families, and males of at least 16 years of age who were able to bear arms. This map identifies the geographical separation of Delaware among the three counties in 1830. Mill Creek Hundred was located in the northwest region of Delaware. Among the settlements established in Mill Creek Hundred was the small village of Hockessin, founded in 1688. (Hagley Museum and Library.)

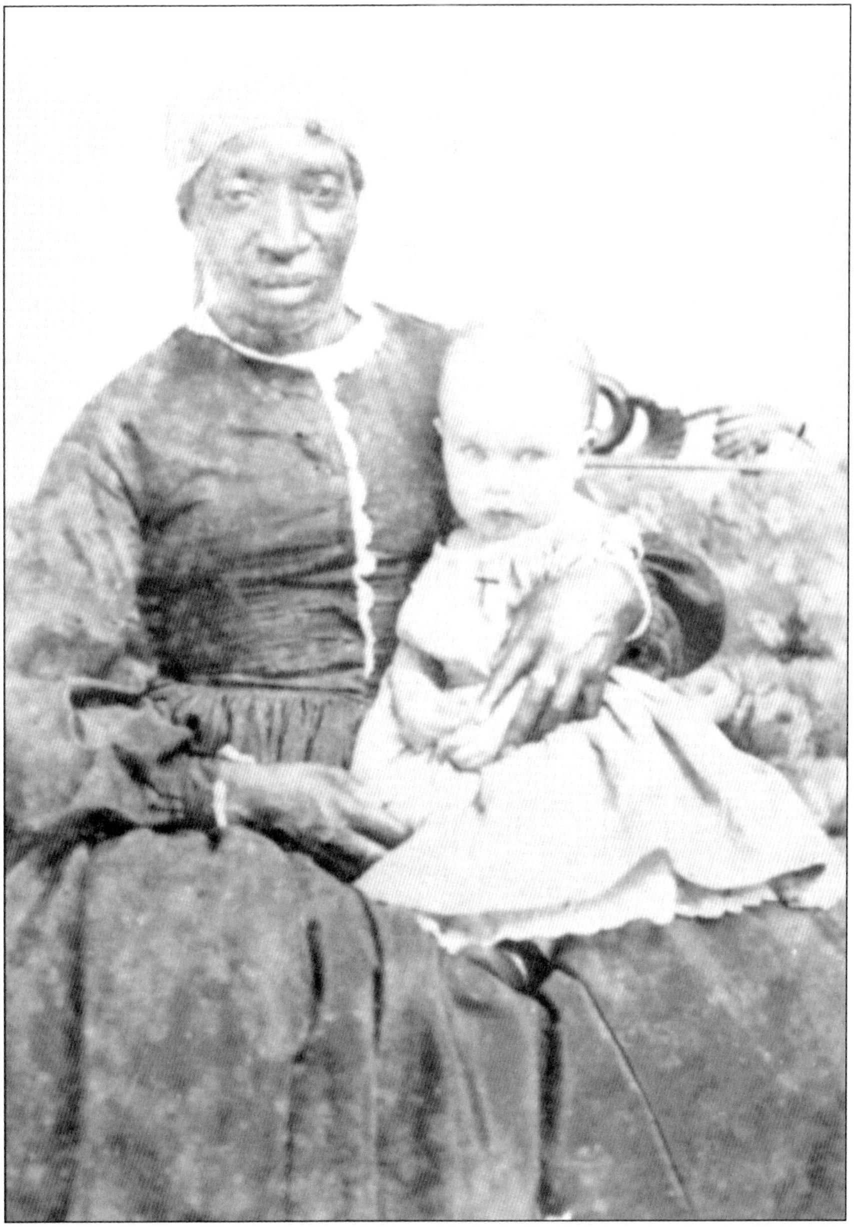

The 1860 US census identified 21,627 colored Delaware residents; 1,797 were identified as enslaved, and 1,341 of those persons were in Sussex County. Ten percent of those enslaved in Sussex County were listed on the 1860 slave schedule for Broadkill Hundred. At that time, James Anderson was the largest slaveholder in Broadkill Hundred. Among his slaves were two females; the younger of the two was identified by the name of Jints. It is presumed that Jints was the caretaker for many of Anderson's offspring. Other slaveholders in the state included James Ponder, David Hazzard, and Samuel Paynter—all of whom held the office of governor of Delaware at one time. This photograph shows infant Hannah Stockley (approximately 16 months of age), granddaughter of James Anderson, sitting on Jints's lap in 1860. Hannah was born in 1858. Hannah's father Charles Clark Stockley served as governor of Delaware from 1883 to 1887 (post-Reconstruction era). Hannah was 25 years old when her father took office. (Hagley Museum and Library.)

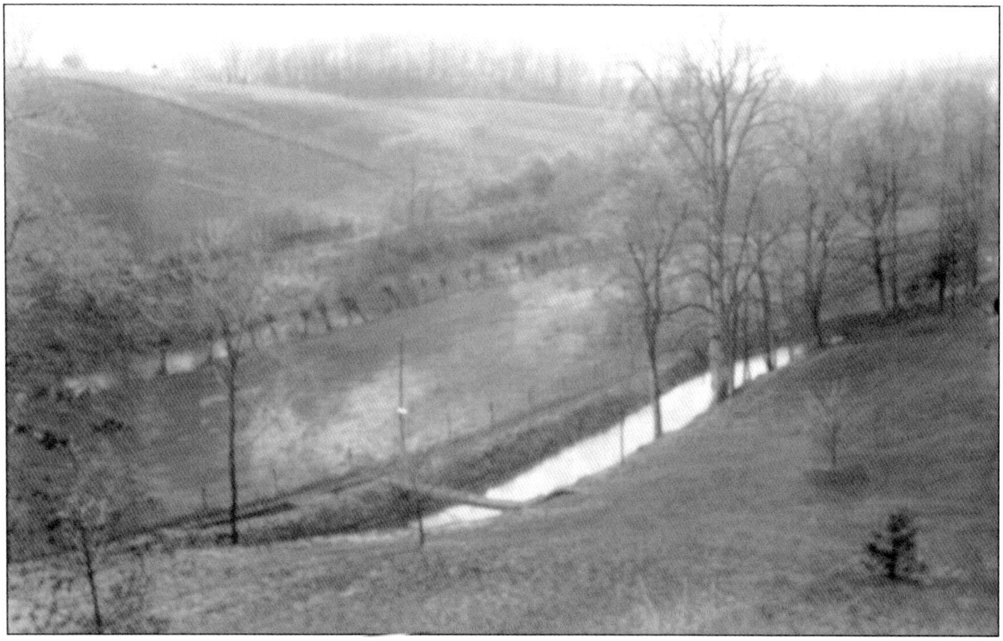

The fabric of the nation was woven together through commerce stemming from agriculture and industrialization. The intersecting of these industries facilitated the evolution of lifestyles for the Native Americans, European settlers, and colored people of Mill Creek Hundred, with its abundance of valleys and waterways. European settlers established villages on land once inhabited by Native Americans in the region who identified themselves as the people of Lenni-Lenapi. In later years, much like Hockessin Colored School #107C, in Delaware, schools for Native American children, like Cheswold School #143, received the controversial identification of "C" for colored. These pictures show the expansive nature of land in Delaware that became home to over 50 colored schools by 1925. Identified as part of the 15,000 acres of land given to Leticia Penn by her father, William Penn, this area ranged from the southeastern region of Chester County, Pennsylvania, to northern Mill Creek Hundred, Delaware. The towns of Hockessin, Yorklyn, and North Star became prime real estate for mills and industrial factories. The emergence of industrialization in the region brought about the need for a literate workforce. Few laws prohibited the utilization of child labor in mills and factories, resulting in a third-tier workforce often excluded from integrated schools. Just as colored schools were being established by the late 1800s, public schools for the newly declared "white " society began consolidating, as was the case for Hockessin #29 and Auburn #91. (Both, Hagley Museum and Library.)

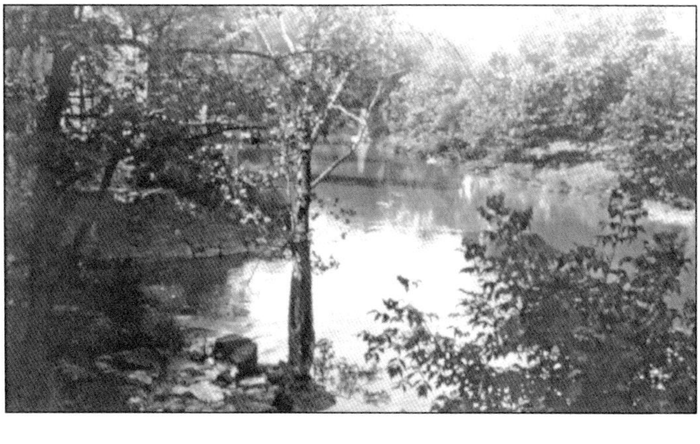

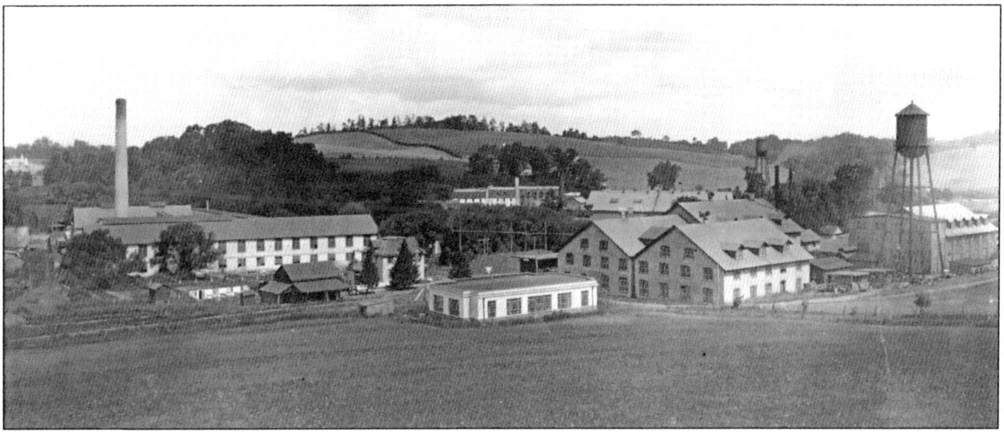

Pre-Civil War southern Delaware consisted mainly of farmlands. Sussex County depended on agriculture, which utilized enslaved labor. Northern Delaware employed free and manumitted colored workers—residents of New Castle County—to maintain a growing number of factories and mills. The Garrett Snuff Mill and the Yorklyn Mill were among the numerous factories that decorated the landscape in Mill Creek Hundred. Colored adult workers residing in Hockessin received weekly compensation for their labor. Revenue generated from their wages paid for the upkeep of Hockessin Colored School #107C. (Hagley Museum and Library.)

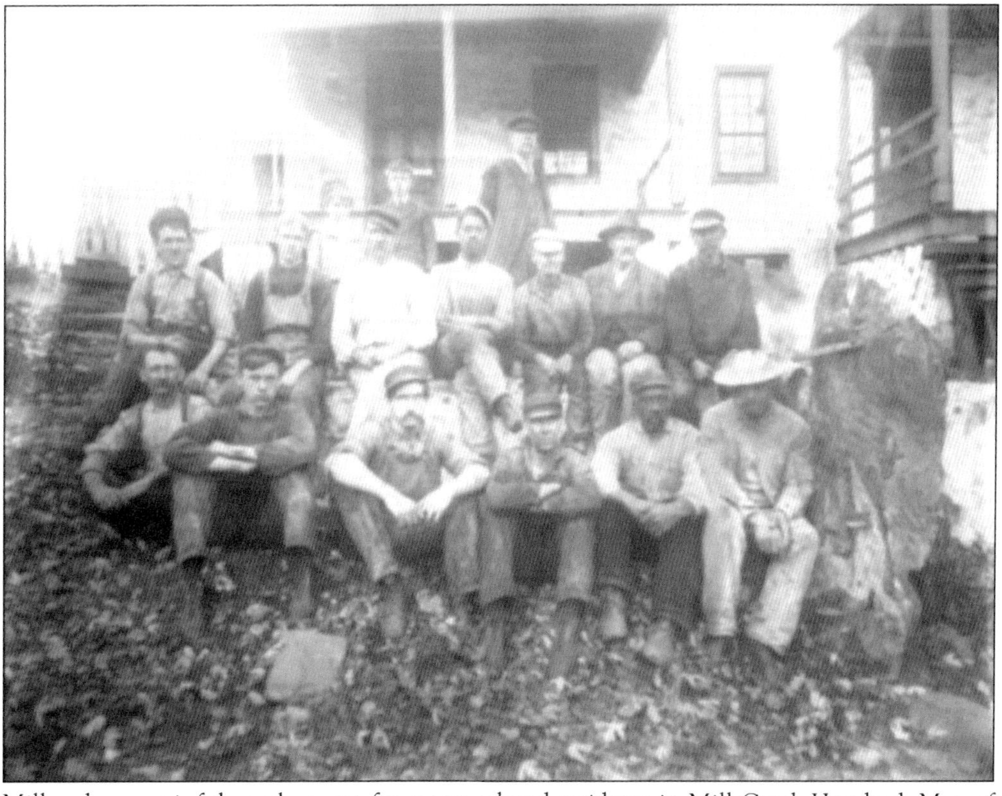

Millwork was gainful employment for many colored residents in Mill Creek Hundred. Men of various ethnicities and backgrounds worked together in the mills. This 1908 picture offers a peek into the labor force employed at the Garrett Snuff Mill and Marshall Brothers Mill in Yorklyn. (Hagley Museum and Library.)

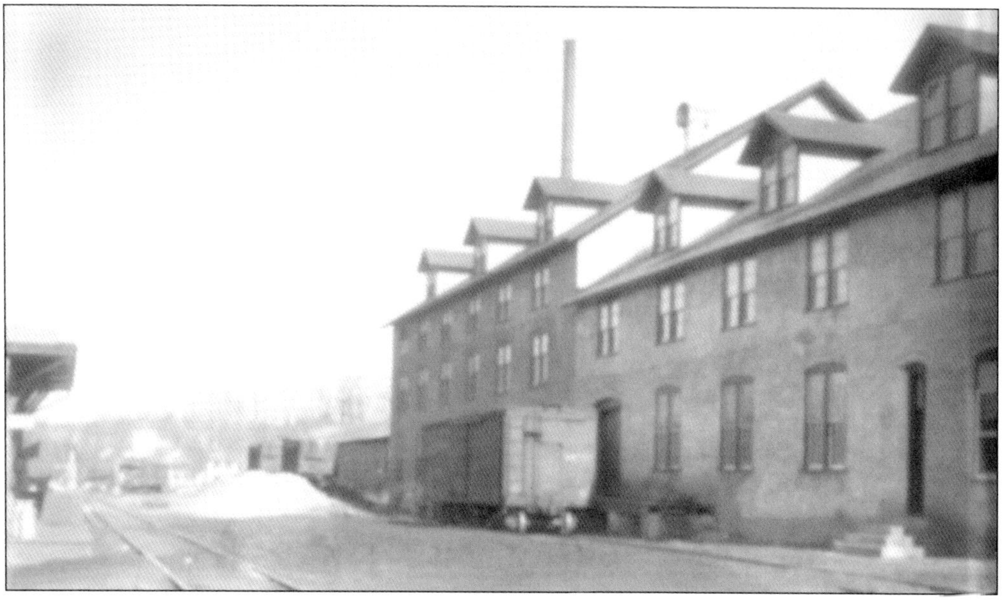

Shown here are mill buildings, some of which are situated parallel to railroad tracks. Mills were structured to take advantage of the natural placement of waterways and stream paths. These mills were fortified by the usage of railroads as their primary source of transporting products. Railroad cars were often found on the grounds of mills. This mill is a prime example of a place for the production of textiles, which were loaded onto railcars of the Western, Wilmington, and Baltimore & Ohio (B&O) Railroads. (Hagley Museum and Library.)

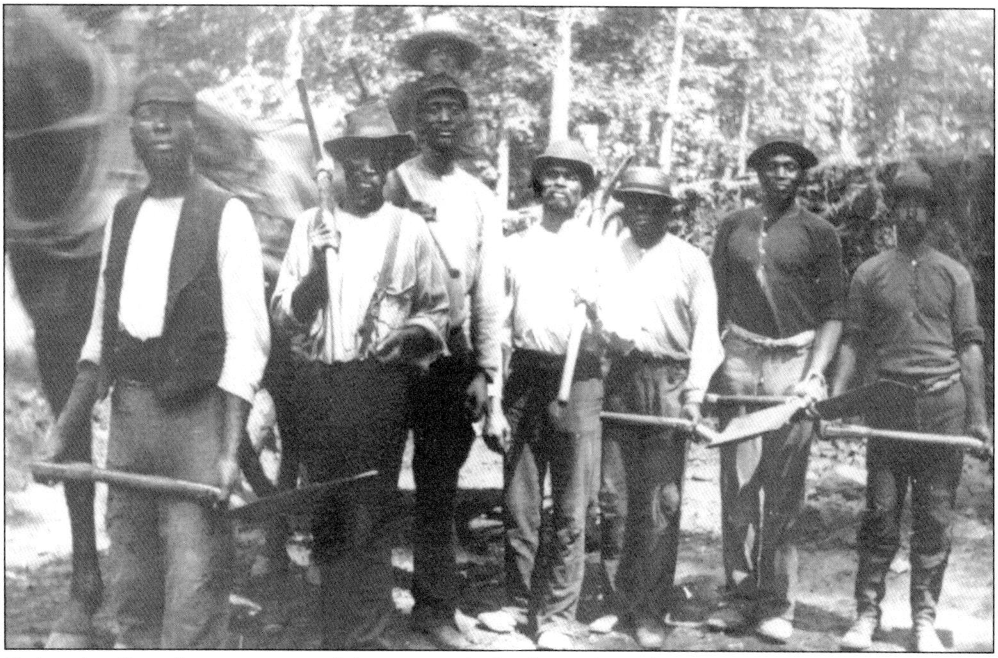

Colored mill workers were given laborious tasks both inside and outside of mill facilities. A major part of their daily work schedules included using shovels for product and pile removal. Shown here are colored workmen—employed by Pierre S. duPont—who worked on railroads and stations throughout the area, including at Hockessin and Yorklyn, Delaware. (Hagley Museum and Library.)

Auburn Heights was the home of the Marshall family, who were among Mill Creek Hundred's early English settlers. This photograph of the Marshall estate was taken in 1890. It was an integral part of family interaction and socialization as well as an essential component for entertaining other affluent and influential members of society. (Hagley Museum and Library.)

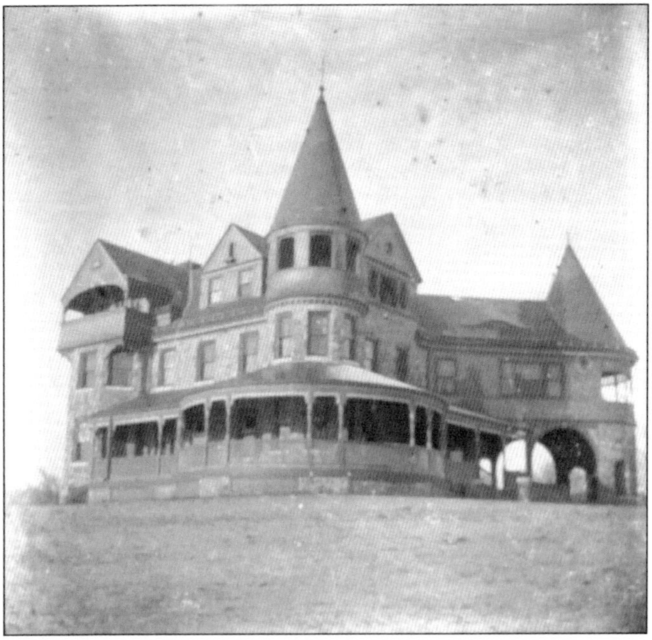

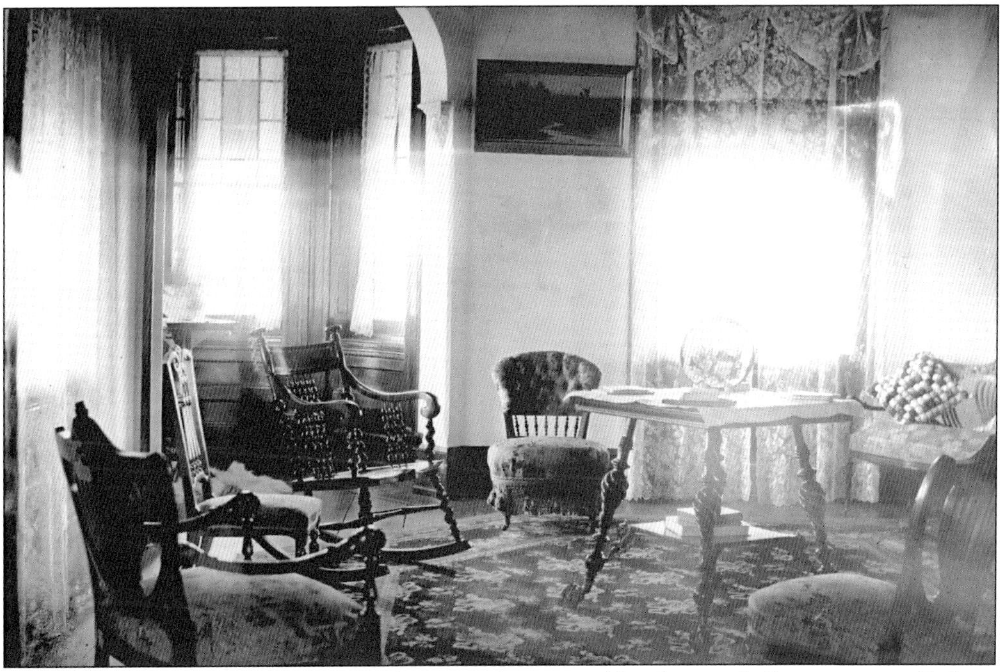

For nearly a century, the Marshall family amassed great wealth. The Marshalls were originally from Kennett Township, Pennsylvania, where they operated a gristmill and sawmill. They subsequently moved to Yorklyn, Delaware, and changed their operations to paper mills. Their mills employed many people in Yorklyn and the surrounding areas, including several members of the Hockessin colored community. This 1903 picture of the Marshall family parlor shows a table, multiple cushioned chairs, long stained-glass windows with curtains, and an alcove. This décor was typical of upscale homes of the era. The plush space was one of the areas that Martha Peterson, a colored resident of Hockessin, was personally responsible for maintaining. (Hagley Museum and Library.)

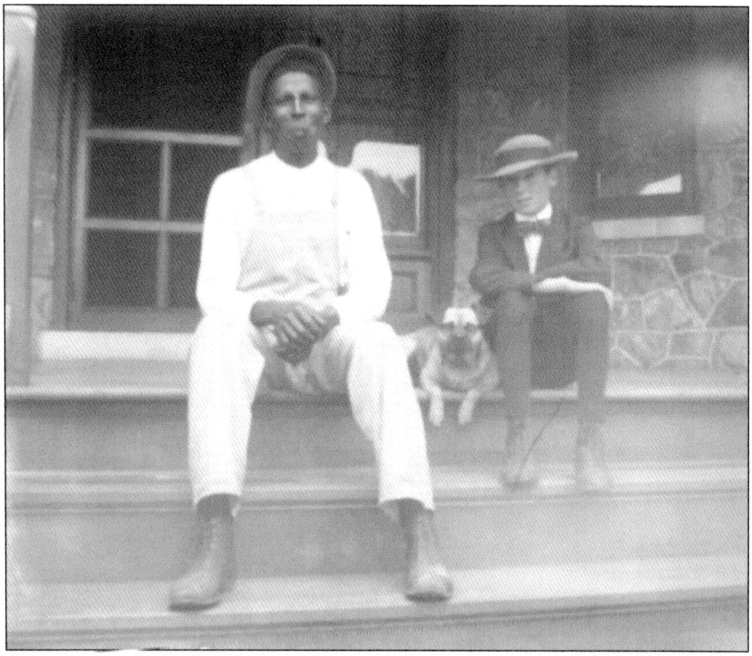

By the mid-1800s, the term "colored" was used in the US federal census to identify free-born descendants of Africans in America. In Delaware, freeborn colored people secured employment as laborers on farms and in mills. This 1900 photograph shows Peterson (left), a farmworker, sitting with a young male member of the Marshall family at Auburn Heights. (Hagley Museum and Library.)

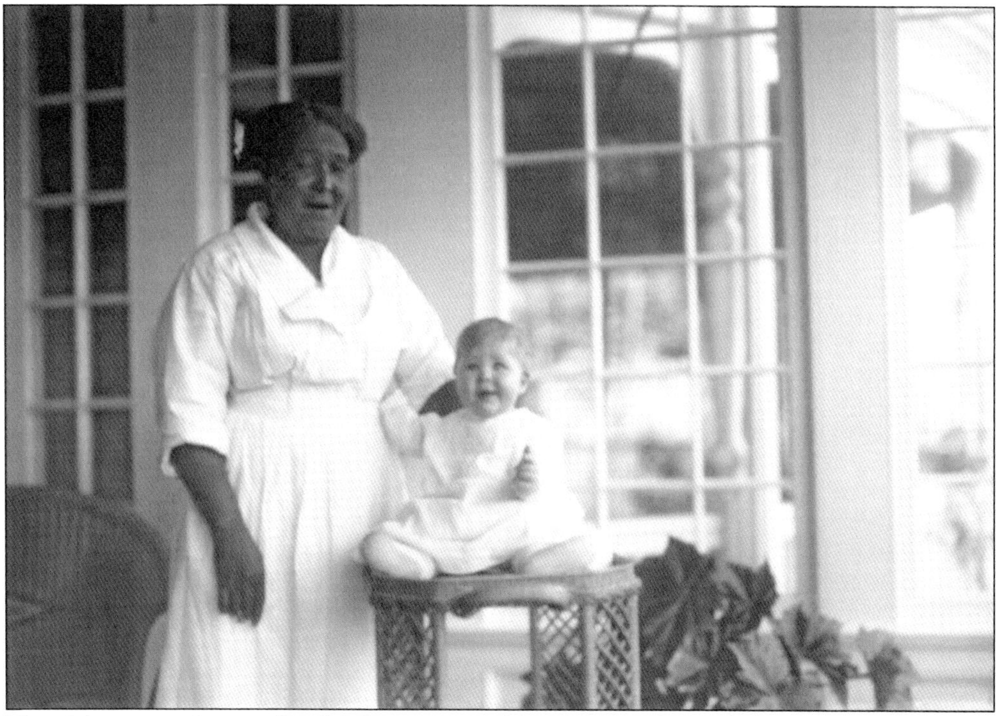

Mary Johnson, a relative of Jacob Johnson, was a domestic caretaker with the Marshall family. She is pictured with Thomas Clarence Marshall Jr., who was 10 months old at the time. The faces of baby Thomas and Mary are filled with joy.

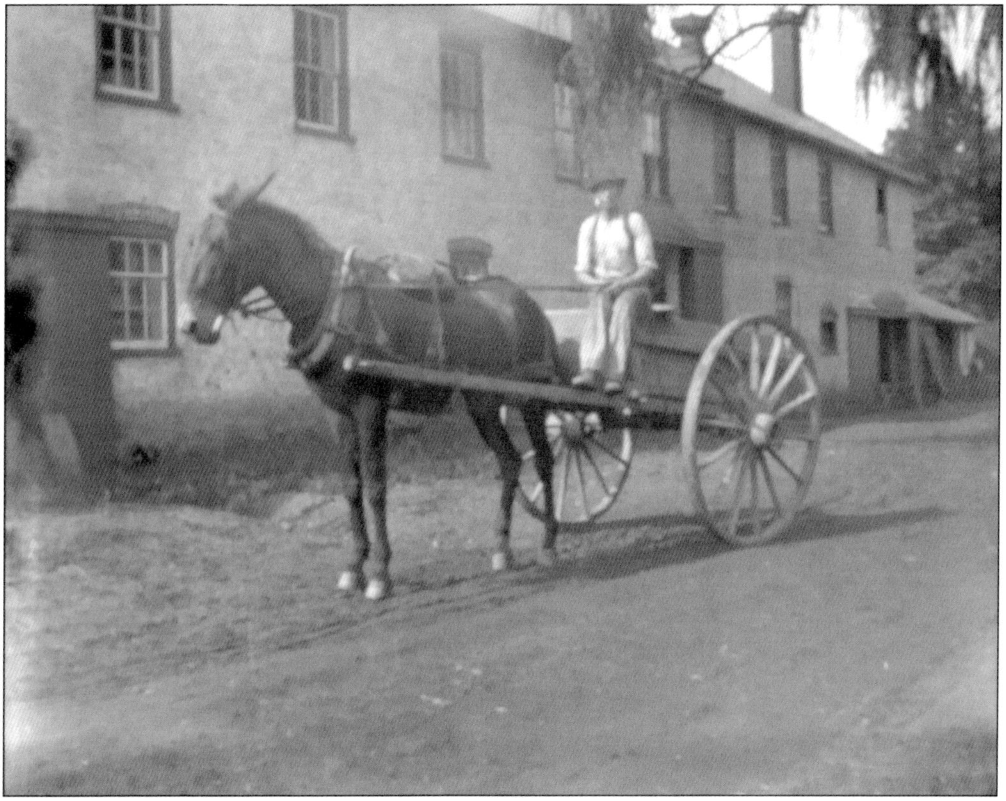

Dorsey Peterson was a mill worker and wagon driver for the Marshall Brothers mills. Dorsey's day included many hours at the carriage house. As a coachman, Dorsey attended to the Marshall family horses and wagons. Being a coachman was a typical occupation for colored males in the region. (Hagley Museum and Library.)

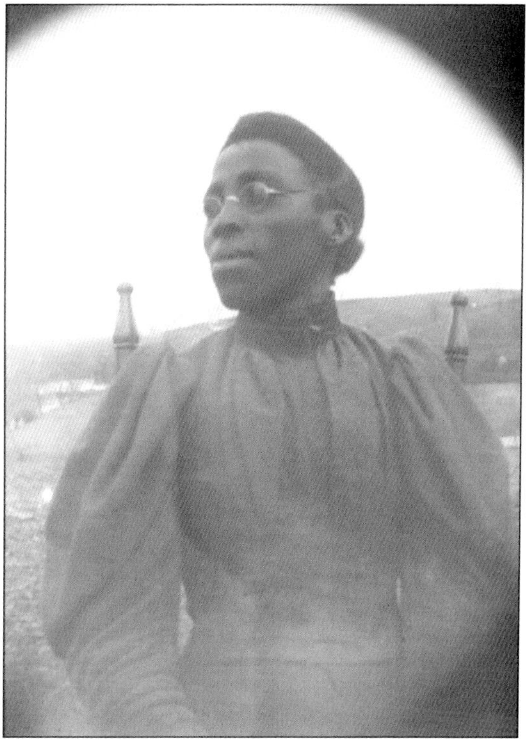

Martha Peterson was married to Dorsey Peterson. Both Martha and Dorsey worked for the Marshall family at Auburn Heights. Martha was the head domestic worker entrusted with taking care of household affairs. Martha is pictured here in 1908 in front of Auburn Heights, the Marshall Estate homestead. (Hagley Museum and Library.)

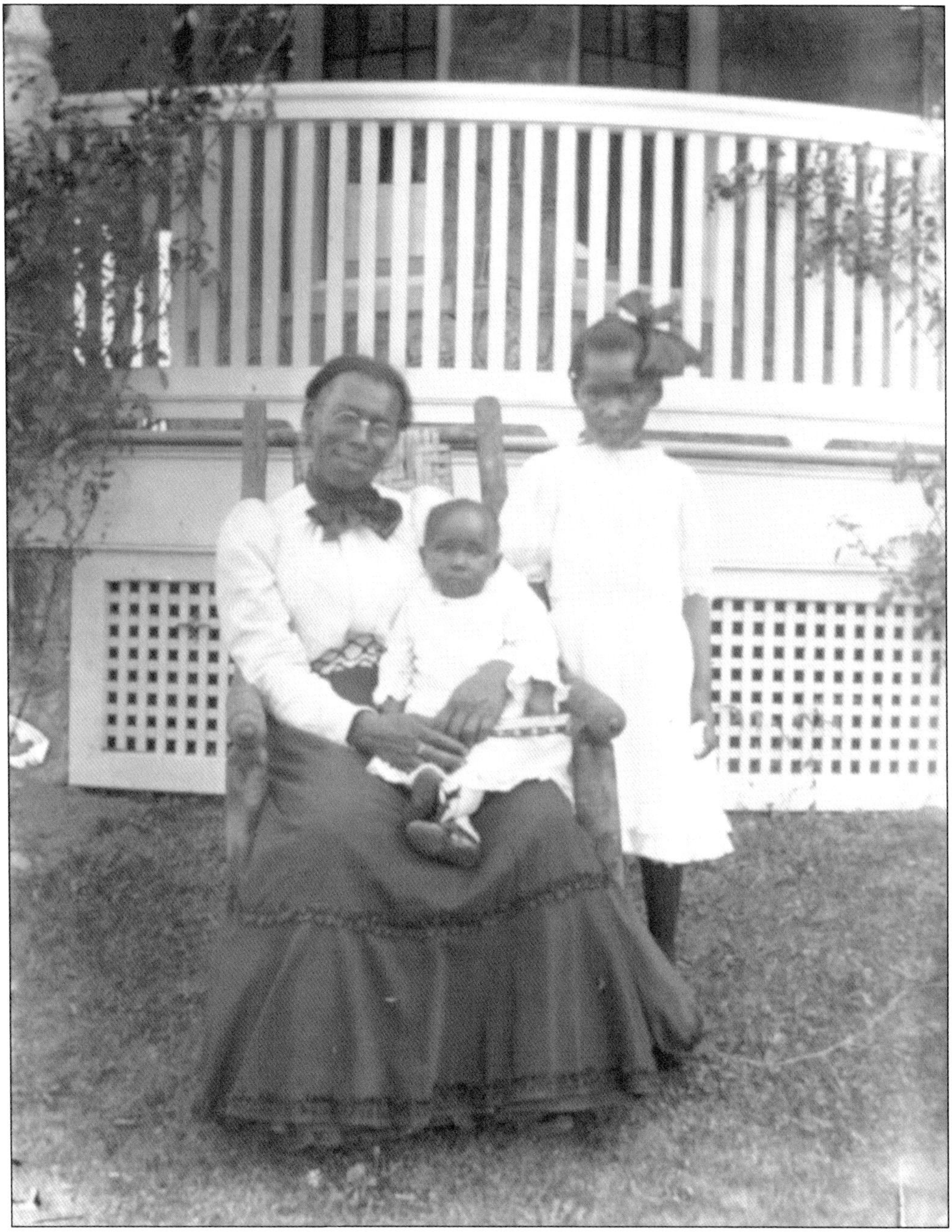

This 1908 photograph features Martha Peterson with two of her children, Eliza and Samuel (on her lap). Although he was present at Auburn Heights at the time of the photograph, her eldest child, preteen Dorsey Peterson Jr., is not shown. (Hagley Museum and Library.)

Four

Wholeness of Heart
A Community of Families

In Mill Creek Hundred, nestled in the northwestern corner of New Castle County, the livelihood of families revolved around three major elements; employment, education, and spirituality. Hockessin enjoyed the fruits of labor and synergy from its residents. An epitome of the nation's conceptualized theory of the land of opportunity and the great American melting pot, Hockessin's 10 square miles provided a refuge for people of all backgrounds. For nearly 150 years (from 1820 to 1970), it became home to a growing population of European immigrants seeking to escape poverty, political oppression, and the deplorable inhumane living conditions of their homelands.

While many families trace their roots to the adventurous spirits of immigrant ancestors, it has been standard practice in America to associate the ancestry of descendants of Africans living in America with chains of slavery. Descendants of Delaware's free colored citizens lived and thrived in the Mill Creek Hundred area. Whereas many contemporary scientific measures are capable of connecting DNA sequences to the shores of Europe, Africa, Asia, and the like, colored residents of Hockessin share a unique bond with their community. Some are descendants of more than 10 generations of colored ancestors who were present on the land prior to industrialization.

As the nation wrestled with methods of tolerance and citizen apportionment, the colored people of Hockessin organized the components of their day-to-day routines. Images in this chapter will introduce the reader to the descendants of those families who built and funded schools for their children. These photographs, which feature former students who attended Hockessin Colored School #107C, depict life's circumstances that contributed to their accomplishments and the survival of their posterity.

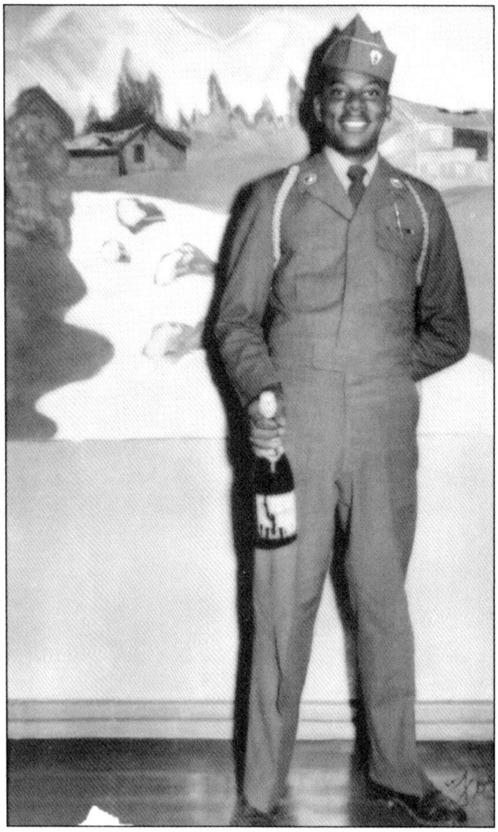

Celebrating the completion of his tour of duty with the US Army, Pfc. James Sonny Knott flashes a smile for the camera in this c. 1954 picture. After graduating from Howard High School with the class of 1945, Knott enlisted in the military. He completed basic training at Fort Gordon, Georgia, and Camp Chaffee in Arkansas. Knott served his country for years. Stationed in cities both domestic and abroad, he never lost sight of his love for home and humanity. (James Knott.)

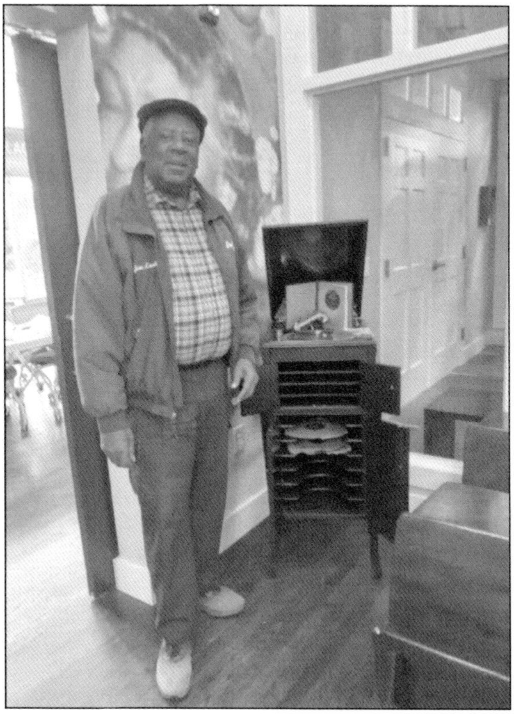

"Oh, happy day," James Sonny Knott declared as he stood in the renovated classroom of Hockessin Colored School #107C next to a replica of the old 1920 school-issued Victrola on December 12, 2022. Pictured here at age 92, Knott reminisced about his first day of school. He recalled walking through the doors of the school as a second grader in 1937. (Regina Smith.)

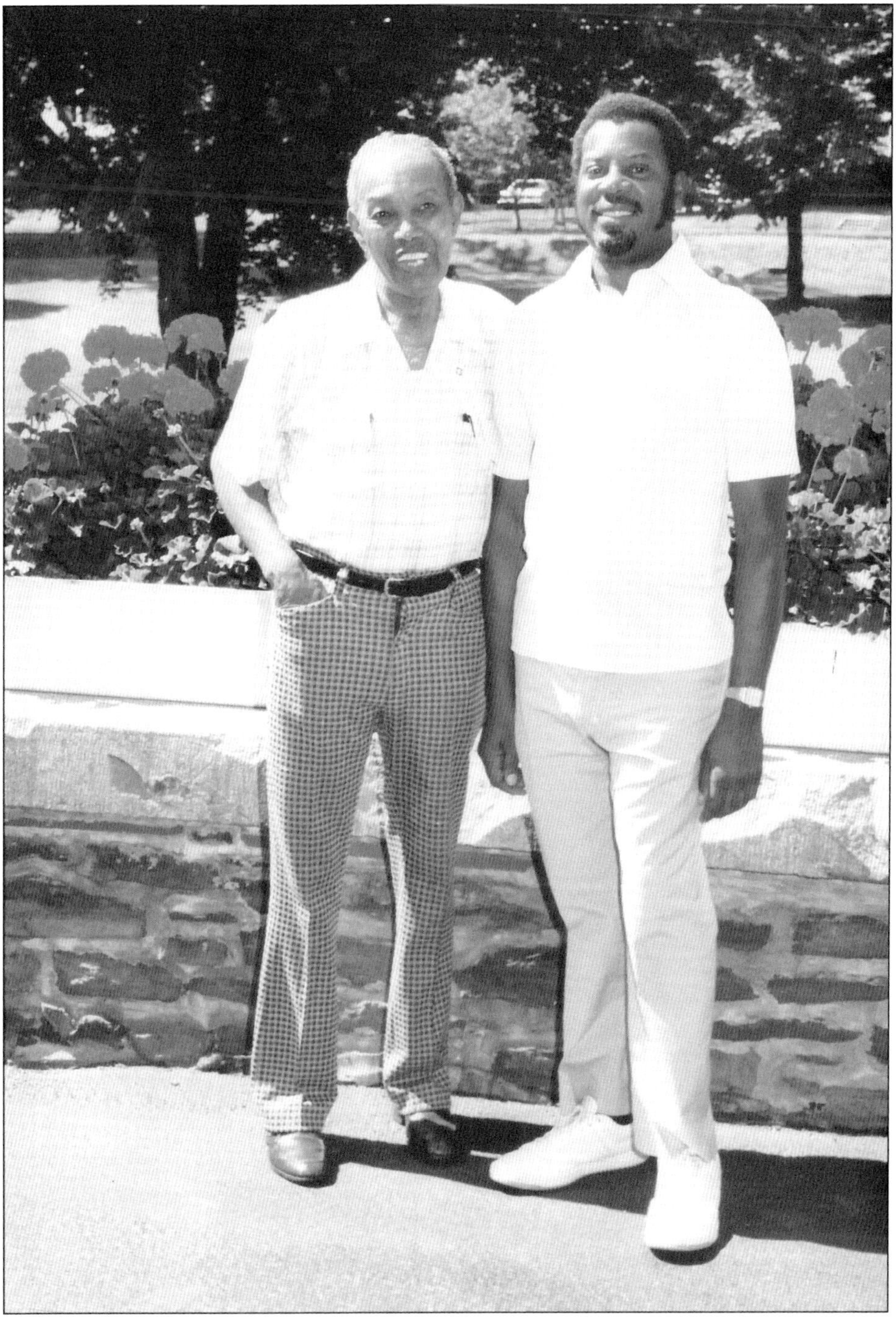

James Sonny Knott (right) is pictured with his mentor, William Julius Johnson. After receiving an honorable discharge from the US Armed Services, Knott sought employment opportunities. He was hired as a security specialist with Mullins, a local clothier. It was at this department store that he was paired with Johnson, affectionately known as Judy. But at first, Knott was unaware of Judy's past—he was none other than 1975 Baseball Hall of Fame inductee Judy Johnson, professional third baseman and scout manager. (James Knott.)

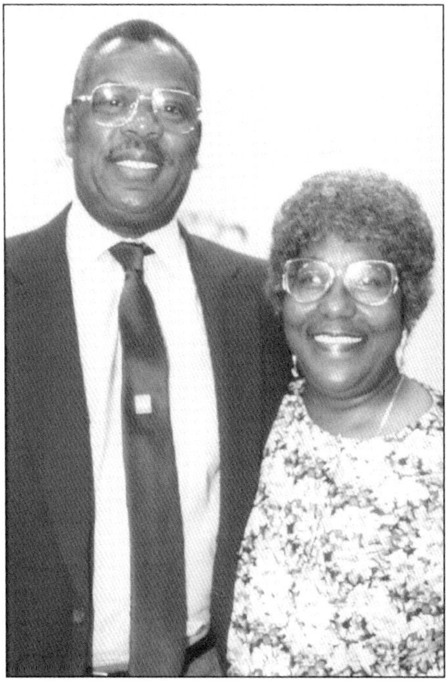

James Sonny Knott, a resident of Hockessin, met Elizabeth "Betty" Heyward, a resident of Belvedere, while attending Howard High School. The students at Hockessin Colored School #107C socialized with students from Newport Colored School (located in Belvedere) and other colored schools in surrounding areas. Generations of students from colored elementary schools became classmates, lifelong friends, and spouses as a result of meeting at Howard High School. (James Knott.)

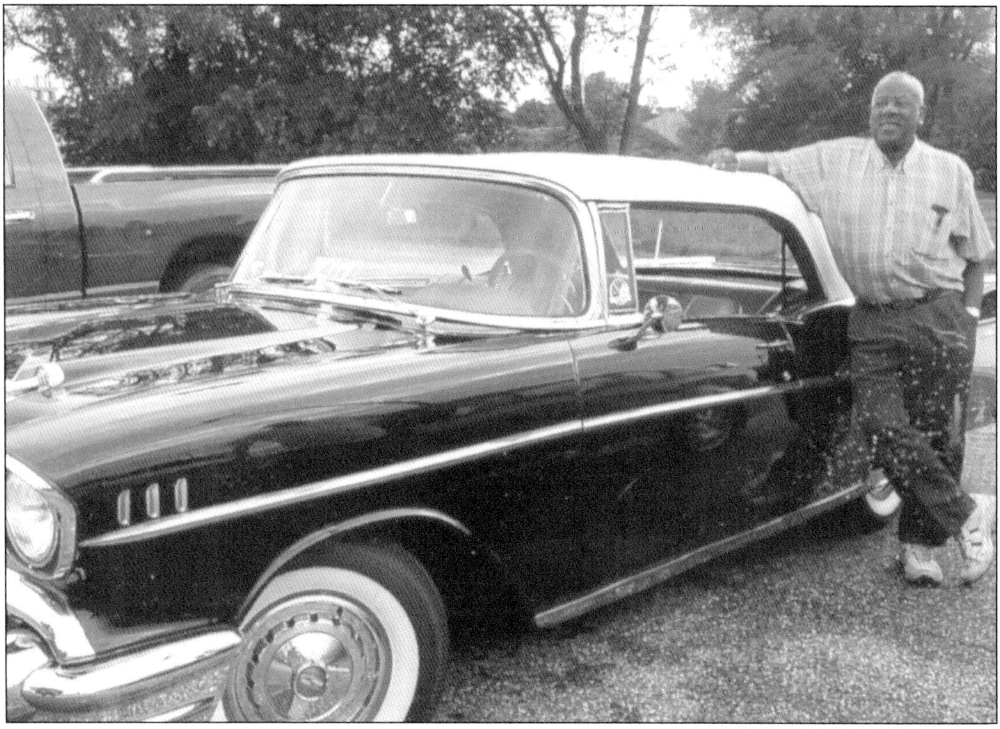

James Sonny Knott took pride in working with and for the community. Pictured here with his black 1957 Chevy Bel Air, he entered many car shows. Dedication and attention to detail afforded him top honors in 12 states. In 2021, he was named the first official marshal of Brown Day. Brown Day–Bulahthon is a commemorative two-mile parade held in recognition of the Bulah family members who walked two miles to attend Hockessin Colored School #107C. (James Knott.)

On December 12, 2022, Charlotte (left) and Blanche Knott rejoiced in the reopening of their beloved Hockessin Colored School #107C. These cousins are the best of friends and gladly shared their cherished memories of attending #107C from the late 1940s to the early 1950s. They reminisced about community and school volunteers like Velma Johnson and Madeline Williams, who sponsored the checkered socks club. Charlotte and Blanche cheerfully toured the new #107C facilities with great anticipation. They are among the last living #107C classmates of Shirley Barbara Bulah. (Regina Smith.)

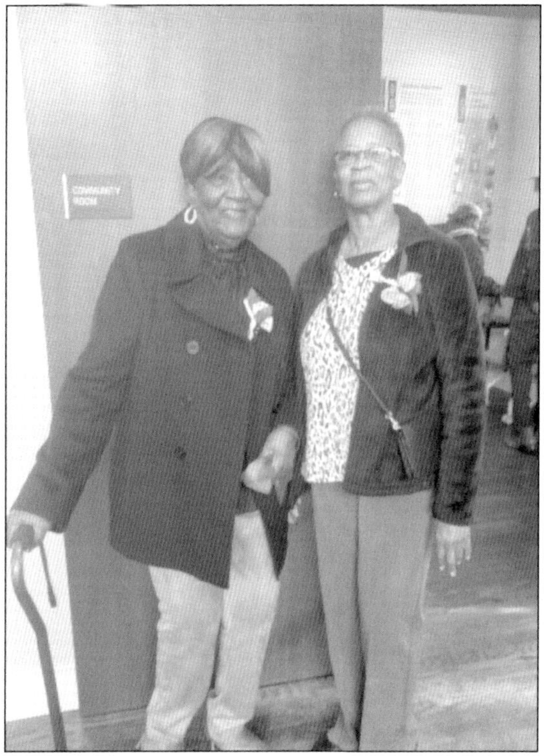

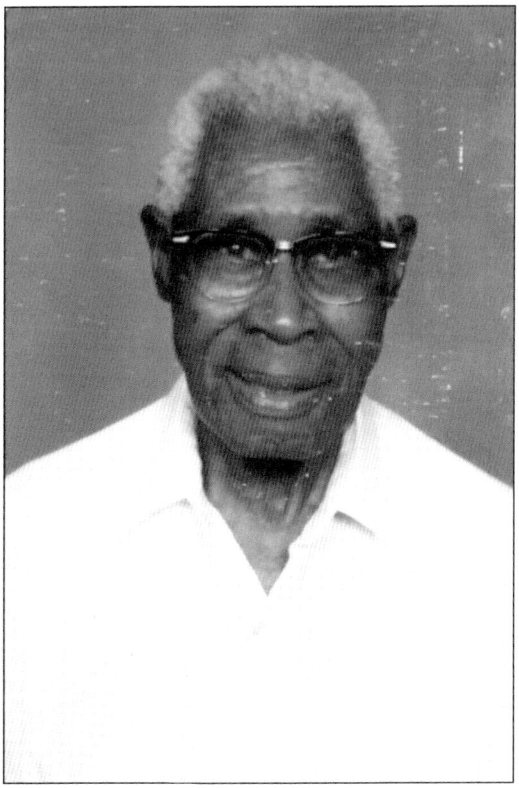

John Knott, the father of Blanche and James Henry Knott, was the surrogate father of Laura, Maryann, June Bantum, and Joseph Thomas after the death of their parents. John and his wife, Clara, nurtured and cherished their extended family. The Knott family was well acquainted with their neighbors the Bulahs and frequently shared Sunday evening meals with them. Homemade pound cake and fruit cocktail were the after-dinner treats for Blanche, James, Charlotte, and Shirley. (Blanche Knott.)

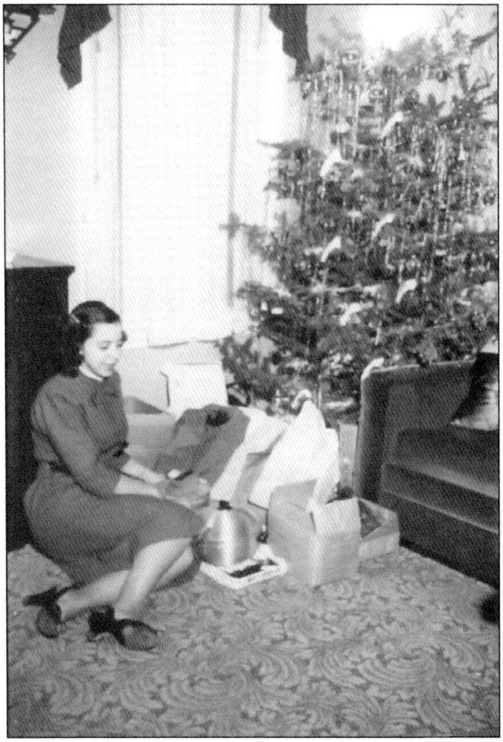

Hilda Bulah looked forward to her turn to sit under the Christmas tree. Here, she gazed at the beautifully wrapped boxes and admired the presents. (Hilda Bulah Morris.)

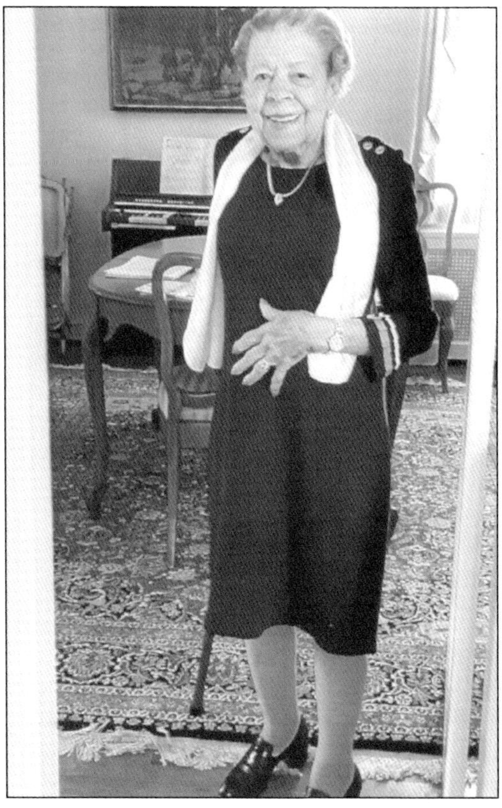

Grace and class are the two words that best describe Hilda Octavia Bulah Morris. Pictured here at the youthful age of 99, she is the oldest living member of the Hockessin Bulah family. She is also the oldest living former student of Hockessin Colored School #107C, which she attended from 1929 to 1935. (Lanette R. Edwards.)

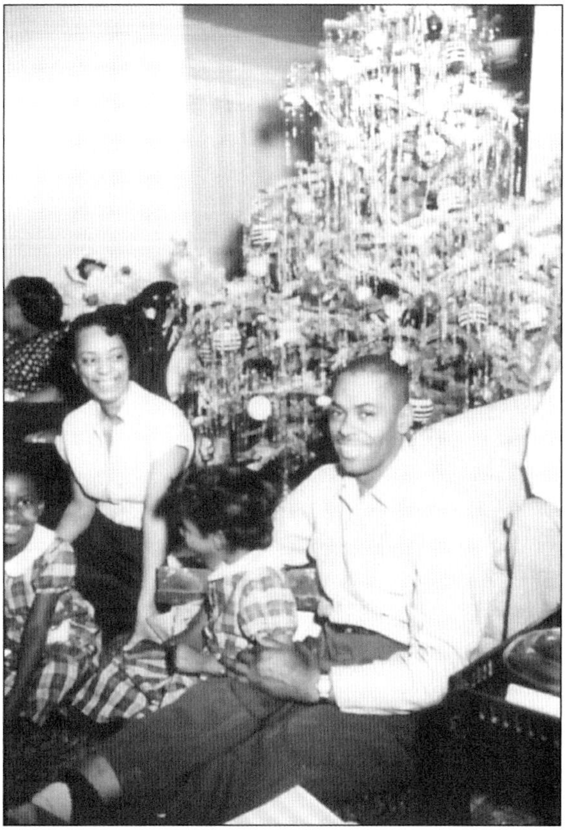

Posing for a picture while sitting still underneath a Christmas tree takes poise and patience. After everyone smiled for the camera, for the girls, it was back to the business of unwrapping presents. Below, the men of the Bulah family enjoyed a blissful holiday watching the smiling faces of the women and children. (Both, Hilda Bulah Morris.)

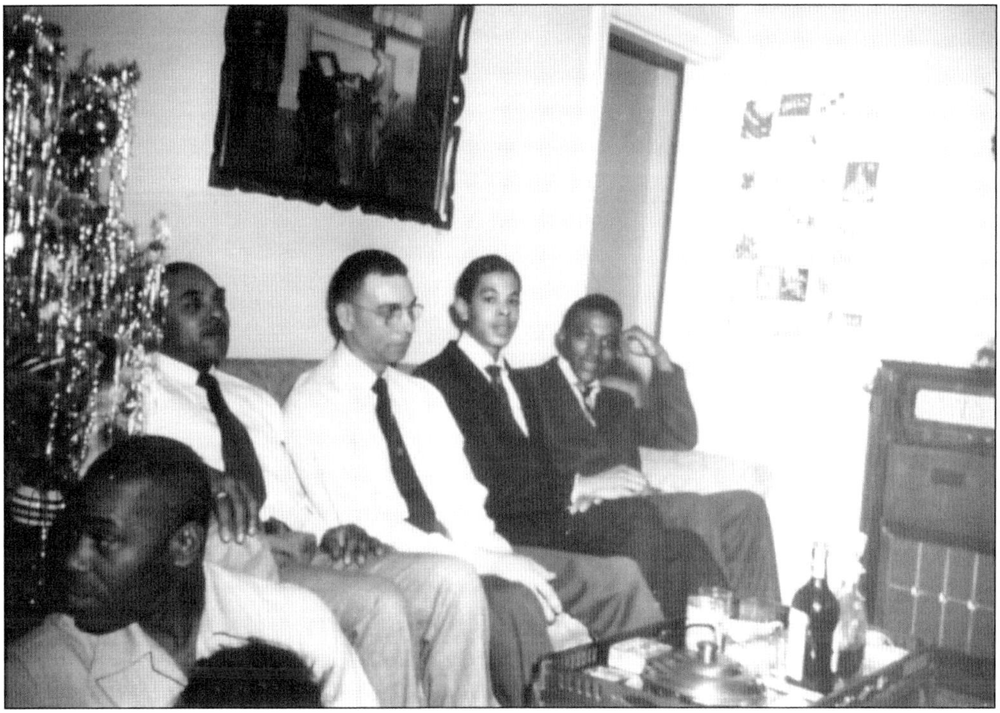

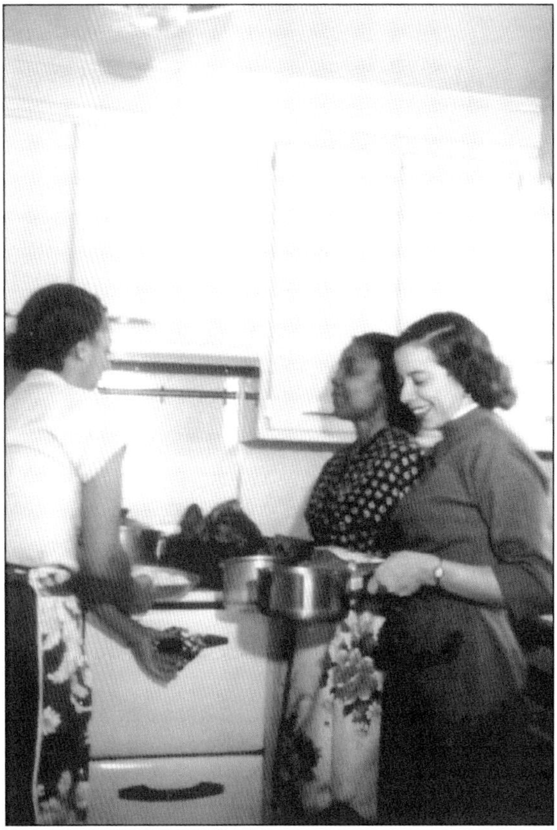

Mary Bulah (left), Ardella Bulah Marshall (center), and Hilda Bulah Morris laughed as they worked diligently in the kitchen to prepare the Christmas meal for hungry family members and guests. (Hilda Bulah Morris.)

This 1957 photograph (also featured on the cover of this book) shows members of the Stitch in Time Sewing Club with their families and friends. The club was founded in 1950 by Elsie Cornish. Pictured here are, in no particular order, Charles Boddy, Ardella Bulah, Fred Bulah, Hilda Bulah, Sarah Bulah, Shirley Bulah, Dorothy Copper, Richard Copper, Elsie Cornish, Louis Cornish, Ann Henderson, Nora Knott, Floyd Marshall, Lloyd Morris, Eliza Peterson, Martha Peterson, Edwina Poindexter, Madeline Williams, John Woolfolk, Mary Woolfolk, and Tom Woolfolk.

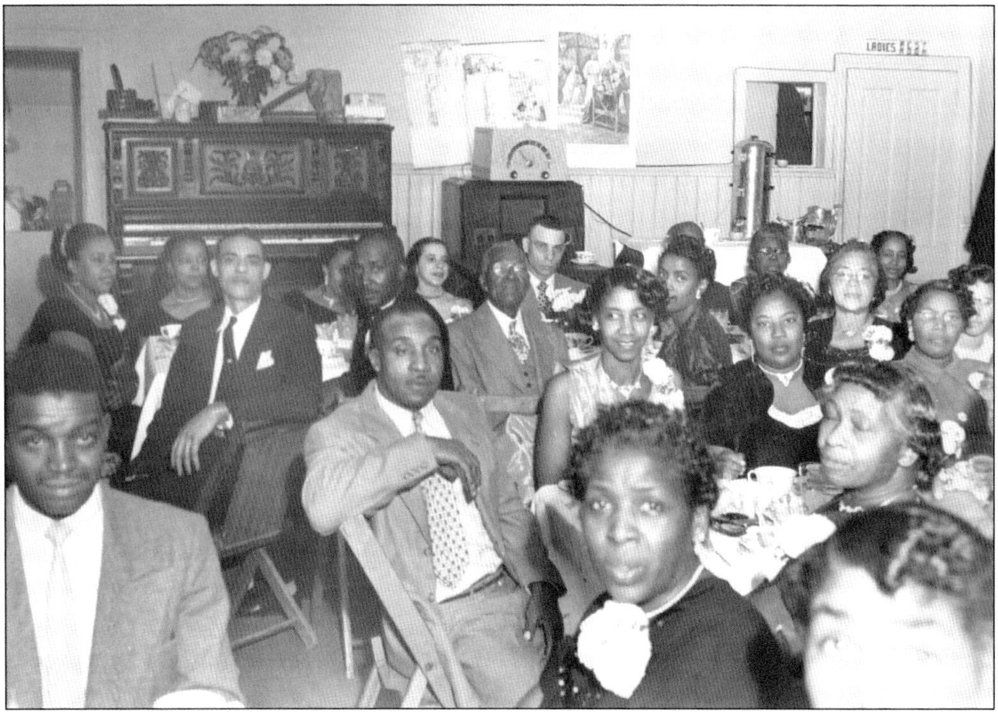

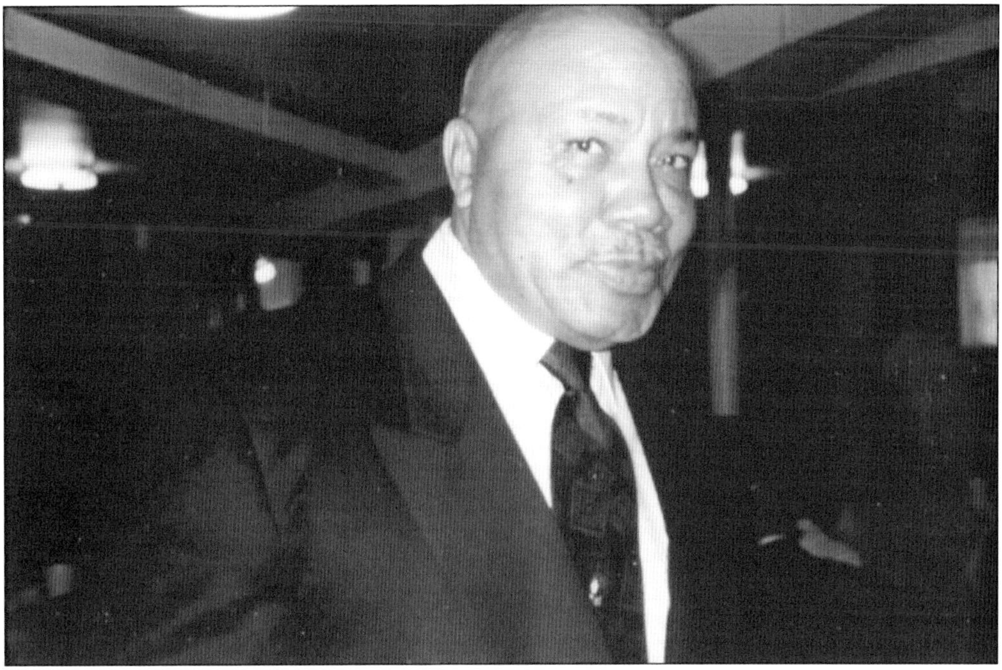

A former student of Hockessin Colored School #107C, Isaiah "Ike" Watters attended the school from 1937 to 1942. He was the classmate of Sonny Knott. He later married his grade school sweetheart, Gwendolyn Peterson. (Isaiah Watters.)

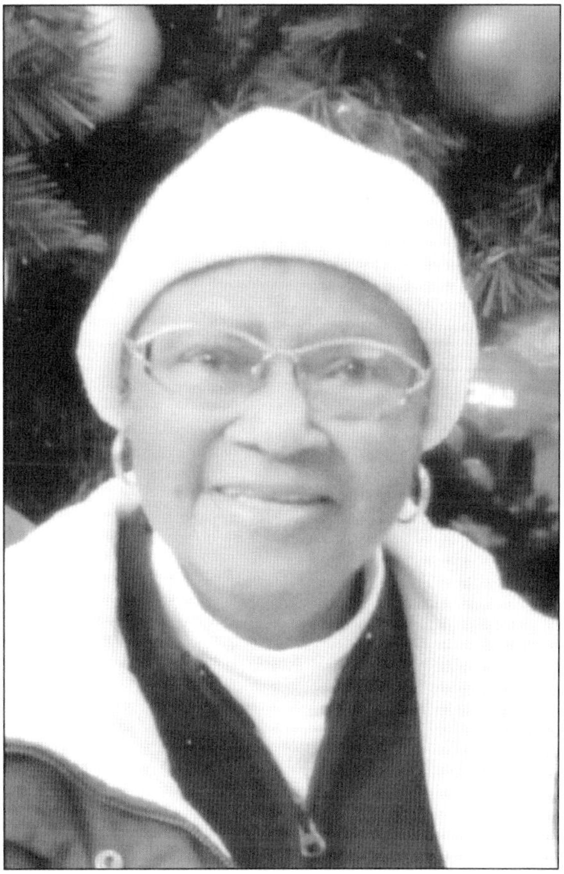

Pictured below is Ike Watters's sister, Beatrice "Bea" Watters, who attended #107C. Bea matriculated to Howard High School in the 7th grade, and she remained at the school until she completed 12th grade. (Isaiah Watters.)

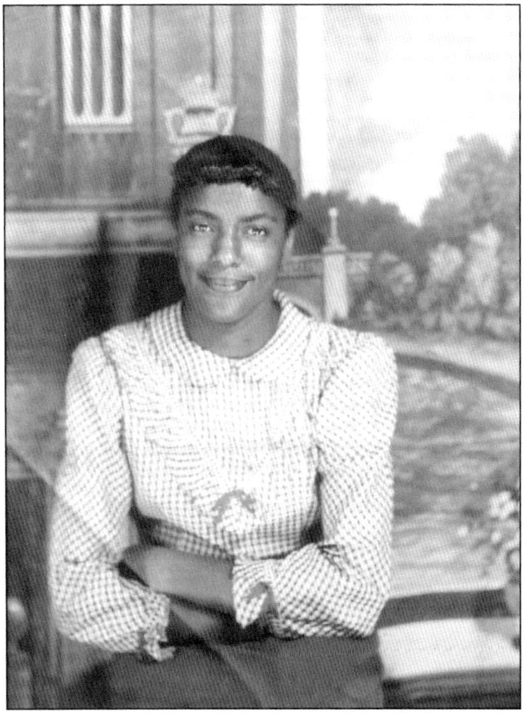

Edwina Poindexter was raised on the land of her parents and grandparents, which once served as the site of the original wooden framed schoolhouse of Hockessin Colored School #107C (formerly known as #3C). (Walter Macklin.)

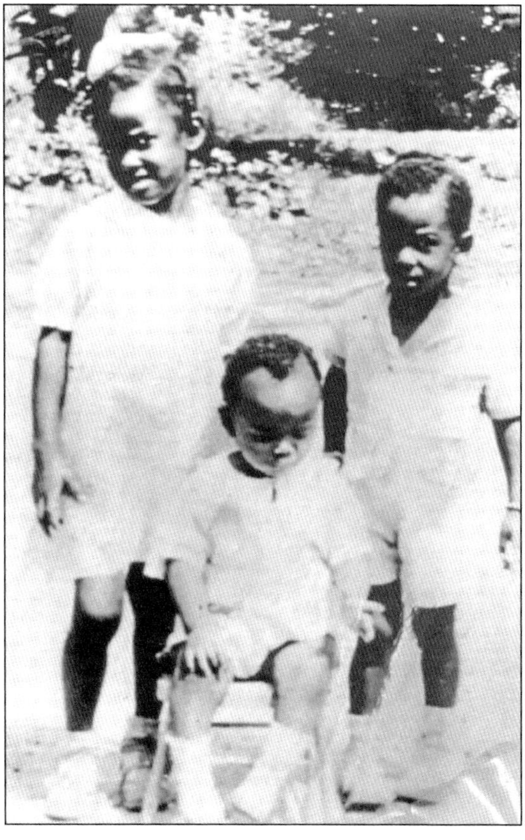

Edwina Poindexter (left) is pictured with her two younger brothers George (standing) and Clifford (sitting). Her fondest memories of #107C included participating in May Day celebrations with her classmates. (Walter Macklin.)

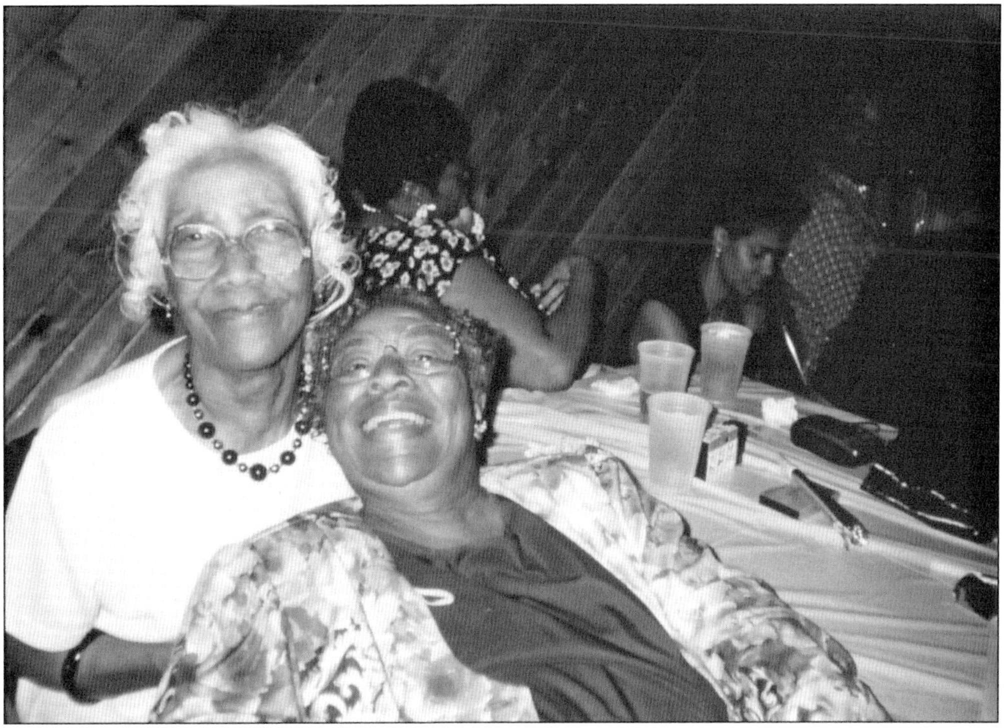

Lifelong learner Dorothy Copper enjoyed exploring new things and meeting new people. As a former student of Hockessin Colored School #107C, Dorothy took great pride in the beautification of the community. An avid artist, Dorothy began painting as a means to relieve stress. She encouraged residents to pursue the arts by hosting painting parties and providing lessons to mature and seasoned citizens. Dorothy is the creator of over 100 paintings, including watercolors, oils, and lithographs. Some of her works are featured in the Dorothy Copper Gallery housed at the First State Center for Diversity, Inclusion, and Social Equity at the Hockessin Colored School #107C. Copper (left) and Madeline Williams are pictured celebrating the joy of friendship and fellowship during a family and friends event at Hockessin Community Center in the 1980s. (Lois Johnson.)

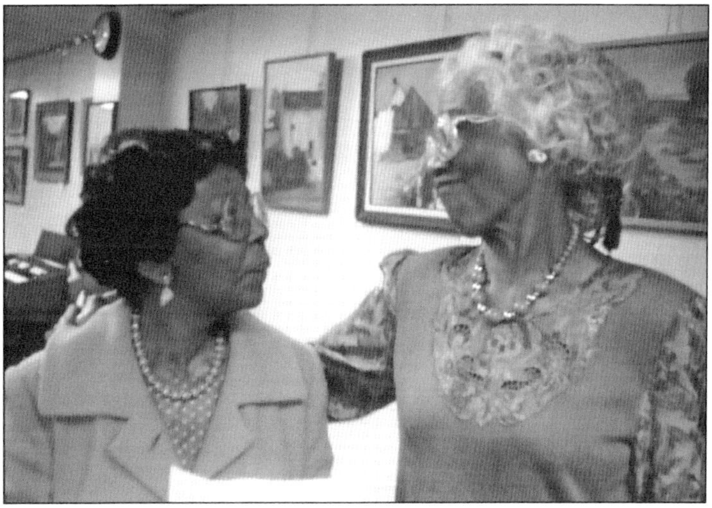

Shown sharing a moment in time and a stroll down memory lane, Dorothy Copper (right) and Ardella Bulah Marshall exchange pleasantries in this 1980s photograph. The two friends caught up during one of Copper's last art shows held at the Hockessin Community Center. This frame caught Copper actively engaged in comedic recruiting tactics. (Lois Johnson.)

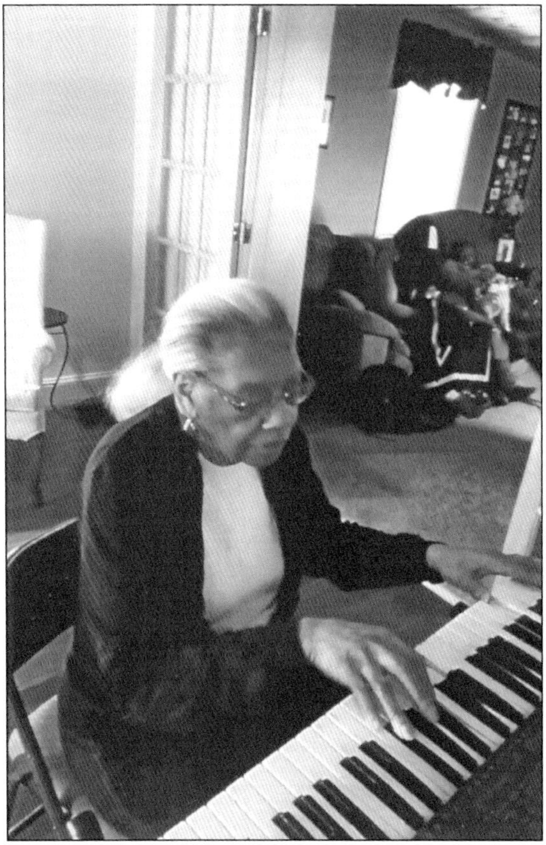

Mary Woolfolk was a teacher by profession. Originally educated and trained in the Commonwealth of Virginia, Woolfolk utilized her skills and talents to serve the community. Considered an advocate for colored children and families, She was forthcoming with ideas to support local colored children in pursuit of academic excellence. Pictured here playing the piano in her Hockessin home, Woolfolk never shied away from new adventures. At the age of 70, she taught herself how to play the piano. (John H. Woolfolk.)

On December 9, 1995, the Woolfolk family celebrated Mary Woolfolk's Pillar of the Community Award, which was presented during an honorarium program held at Chippey Chapel. (John H. Woolfolk.)

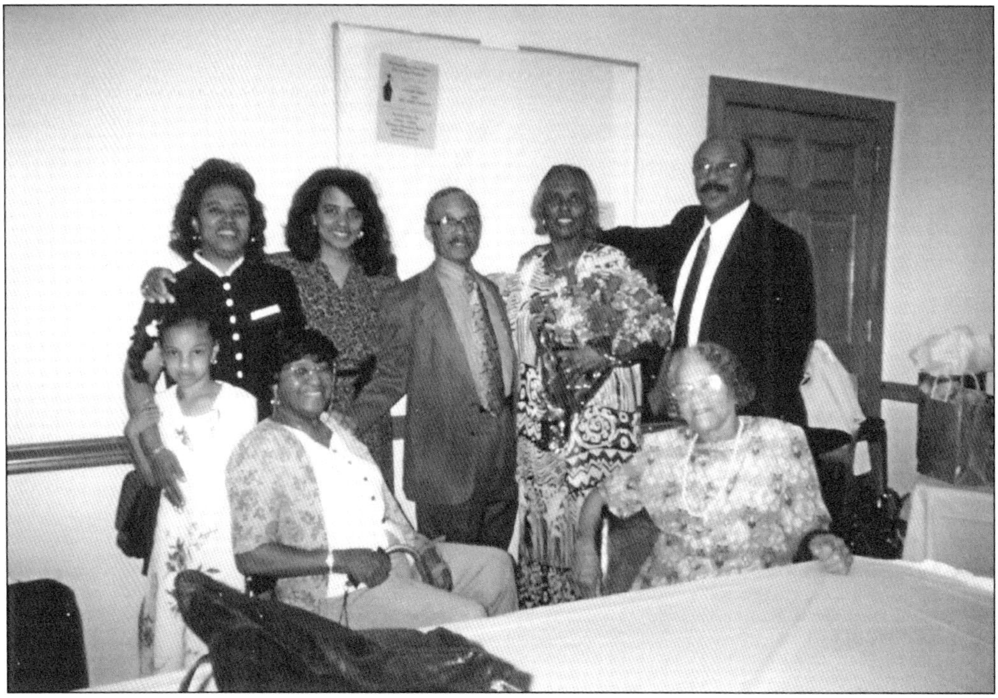

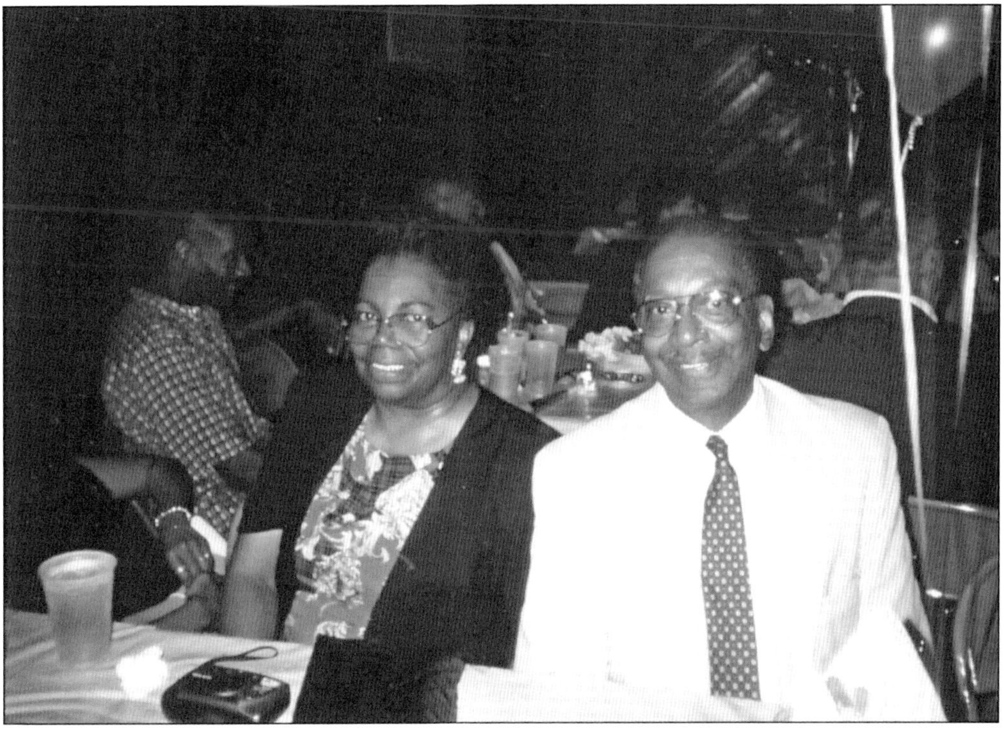

Jean Bolden Fleming attended Hockessin Colored School #107C. After attending Howard, she married Robert Fleming of Wilmington, Delaware, and they are shown in the above photograph. Pictured at right with their daughter Leslie, Jean was a longtime advocate and supporter of efforts to renovate Hockessin Colored School #107C. (Both, Byron Harvey.)

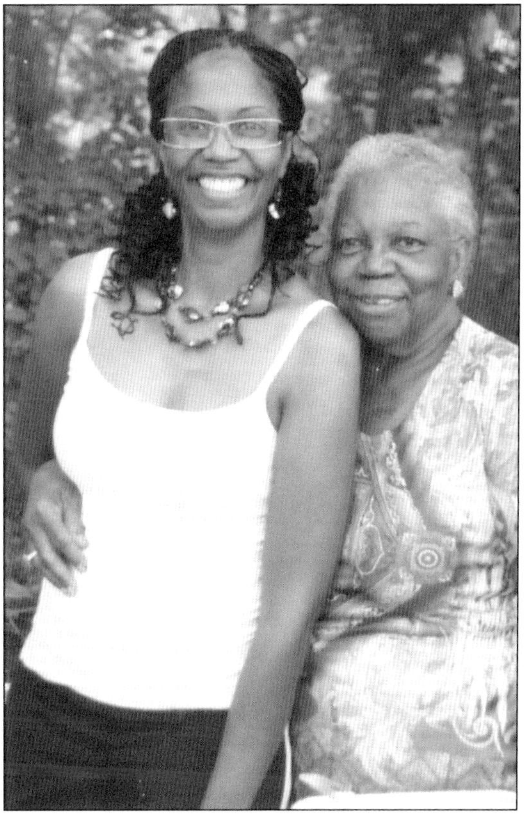

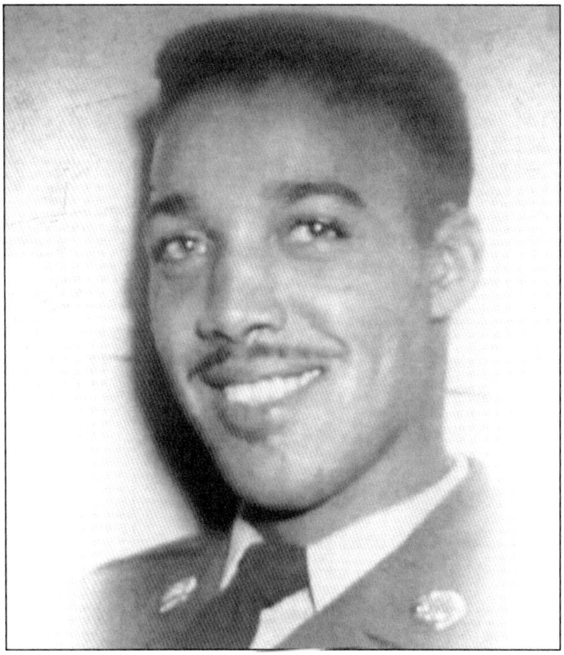

Many Hockessin Colored School #107C students honored their nation by pledging to defend the freedoms and rights of American citizens. Among those who enlisted in the Armed Services were Charles "Chickie" Miller (left), who attended #107C in the late 1930s, and Robert "Petey" Berry (below), who attended #107C in the late 1940s. Former Hockessin students recalled the day many Hockessin families drove to the Wilmington Train Station for a community send-off celebration as six of their native sons departed for military duties. Those six teenagers were Berry, Laurence Gasby, Andrew Harris, Ralph Johnson, James Henry Knott, and Bertwell Poindexter. Miller and Berry are pictured in their official military uniforms. (Both, Robert Berry.)

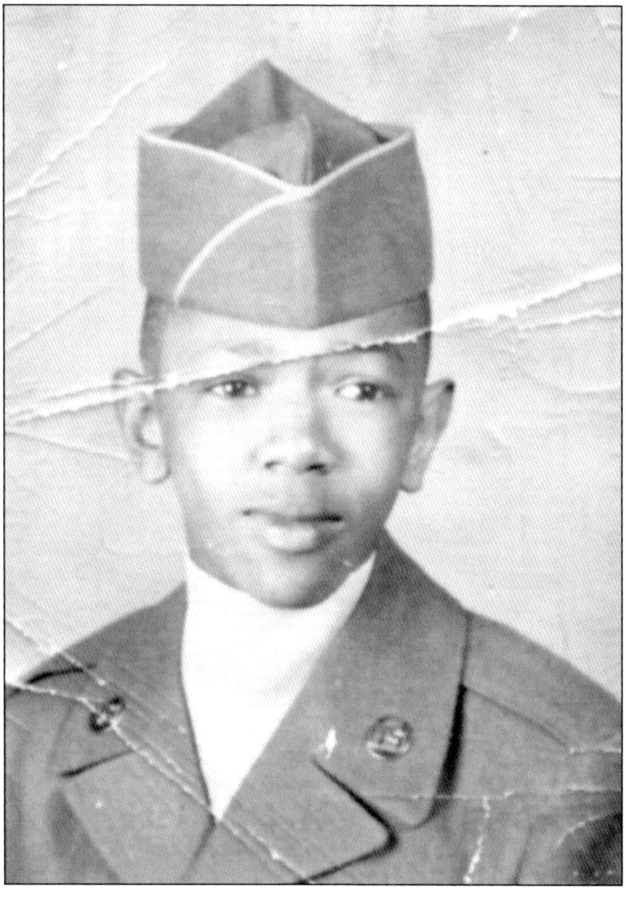

Herbert "Buncie" Carter (left) is pictured with the Coleman brothers (Charles and Ronald). All were former students of Hockessin Colored School #107C who attended for the duration of grades one through six. Buncie famously exclaimed, "Get a job, husk!" (Elizabeth Lester.)

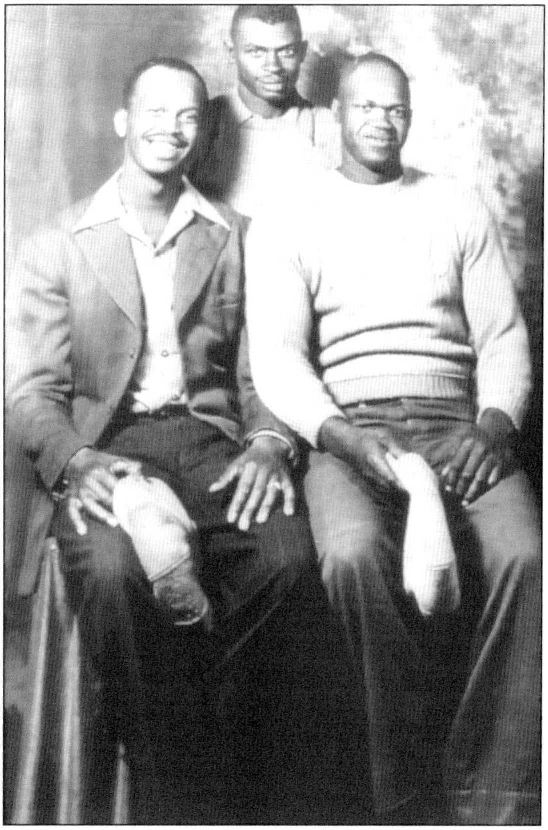

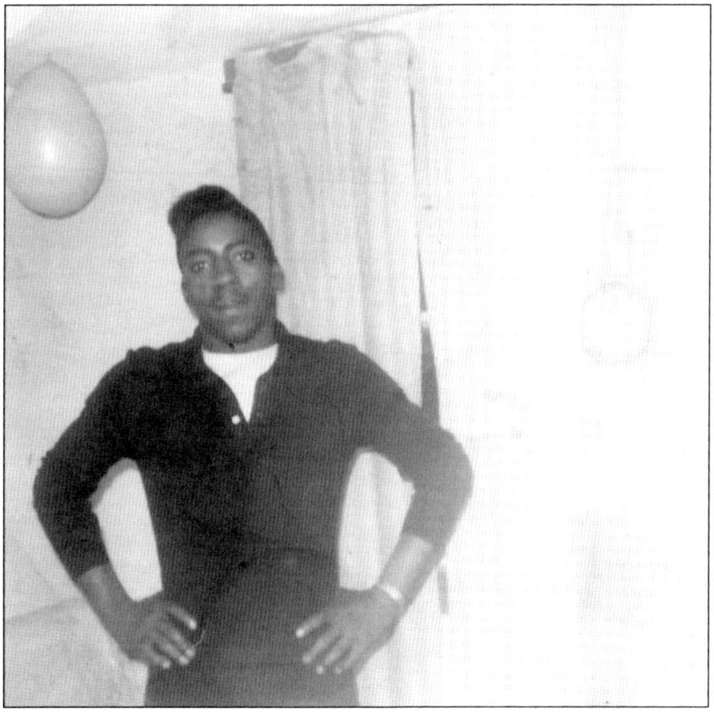

James Battin attended school at #107C. He was known as the protector of his younger sisters Ruth and Shirley. (James Battin.)

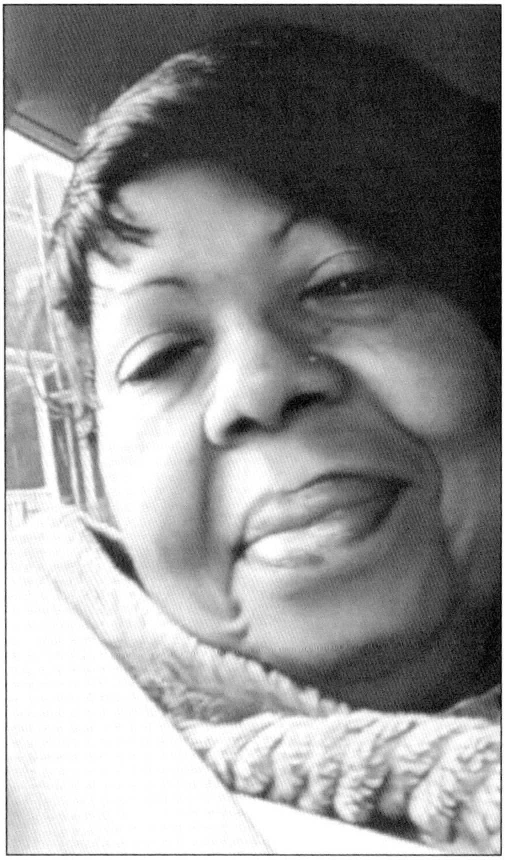

Shirley Battin (left) and her older sister Ruth Battin (below) enjoyed their days attending Hockessin #107C. Ruth attended #107C as early as 1947. School desks in the one-room schoolhouse were arranged in rows by grade level. Ruth sat in the same class row as Lois Williams. Shirley was a few years behind them. Both Battin sisters participated in school activities with their older brother, James. (Both, James Battin.)

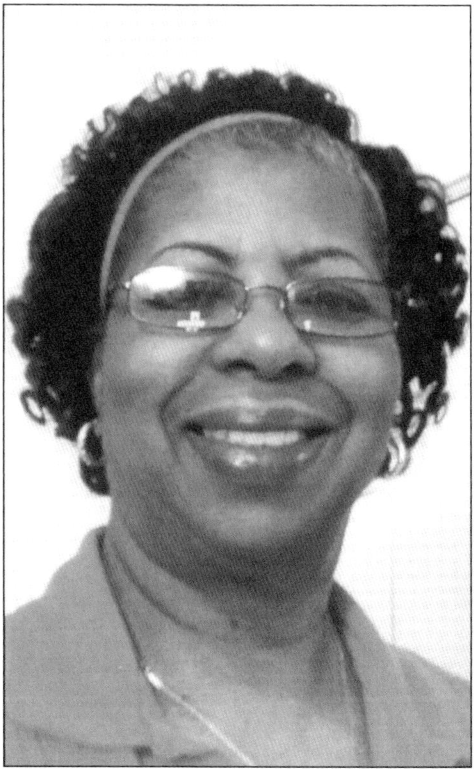

Samuel Peterson was one of the sons of Dorsey Peterson Sr. He and his siblings attended Hockessin #107C from first through sixth grades. Thereafter, Samuel attended the only high school for colored students in Delaware—Howard High School. After graduating from Howard High, he matriculated into Hampton Institute (now Hampton University). After graduating from Hampton Institute, Samuel returned to his alma mater and subsequently became a lifelong teacher at Howard High. (Elizabeth Lester.)

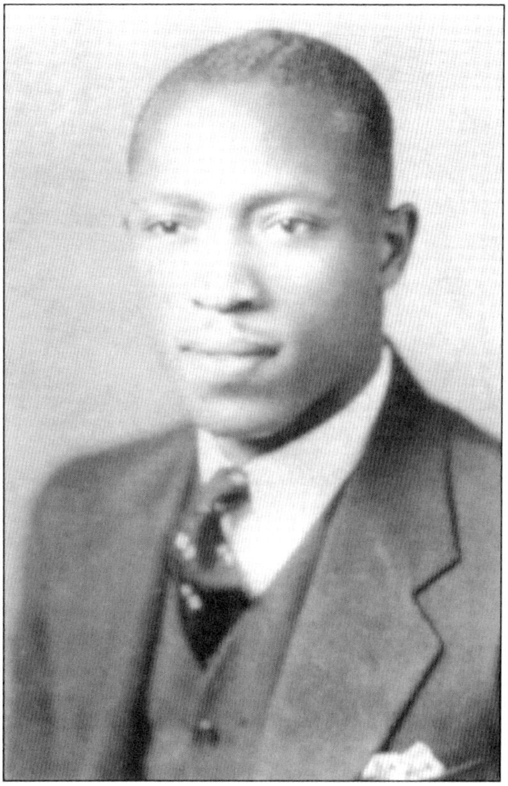

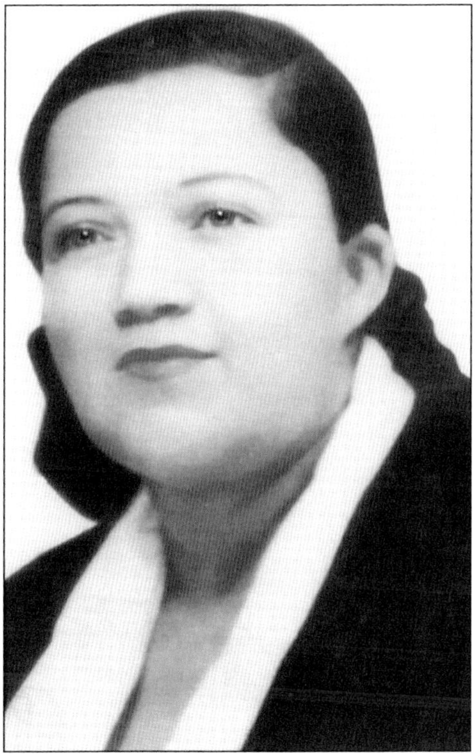

Orpha Peterson was the wife of Dorsey Peterson Jr. Orpha and Dorsey Jr. were major contributors and supporters of #107C. Dorsey Jr. served as a member of the board of trustees for several years and wore many hats within the community. He was affectionately known as "Pete" and served as the scout leader for Boy Scout troop No. 118, the boxing coach, and the bus driver for students attending Howard High School in Wilmington. Orpha and Dorsey Jr. became the parents of seven sons and one daughter. Their sons were members of the inaugural class of colored males that integrated the all-white school Hockessin #29. (Elizabeth Lester.)

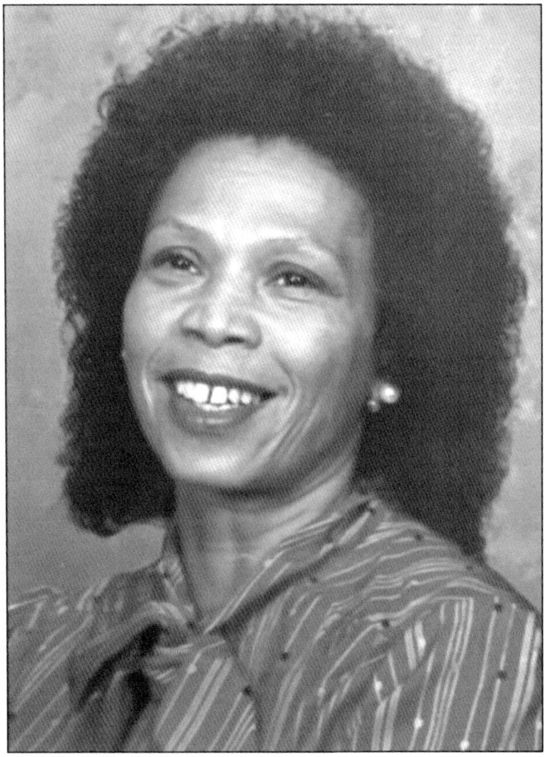

Gwendolyn Peterson is the oldest of nine children born to Dorsey Peterson Jr. and his wife, Orpha. She attended #107C in the early 1930s with classmates from the Carter and Johnson families. Gwendolyn married #107C classmate Isaiah "Ike" Watters. Pictured here as an adult, "Aunt Gwennie" has continued the tradition of sharing memories of her family and the colored school. (Montrell Peterson Ward.)

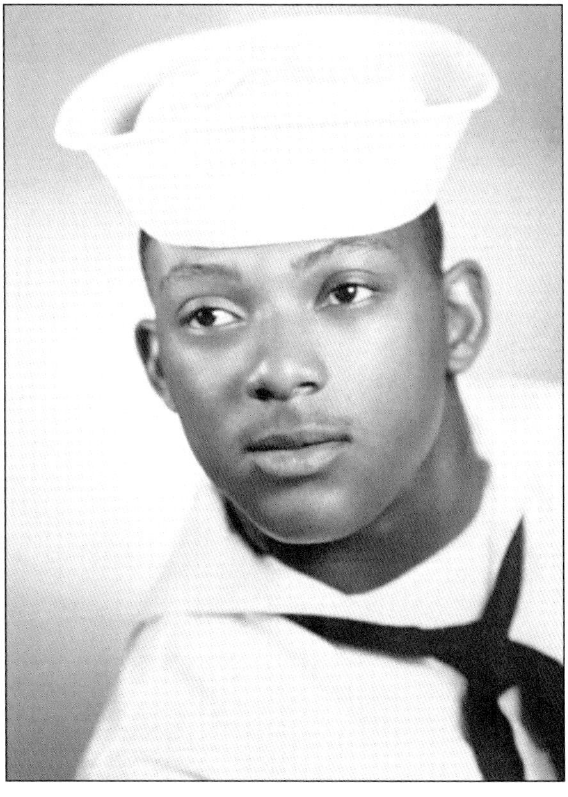

Luther Peterson attended Hockessin Colored School #107C with his older siblings Gwendolyn, Linwood, Lawrence, Louis, LeRoy, and Lester. He began attending #107C at the age of six. In 1954, he and his brother Lester were among the inaugural class of colored males who attended fifth grade at Hockessin #29. Luther is pictured wearing his official US Navy uniform that was issued when he enlisted during his late teens. (Elizabeth Lester.)

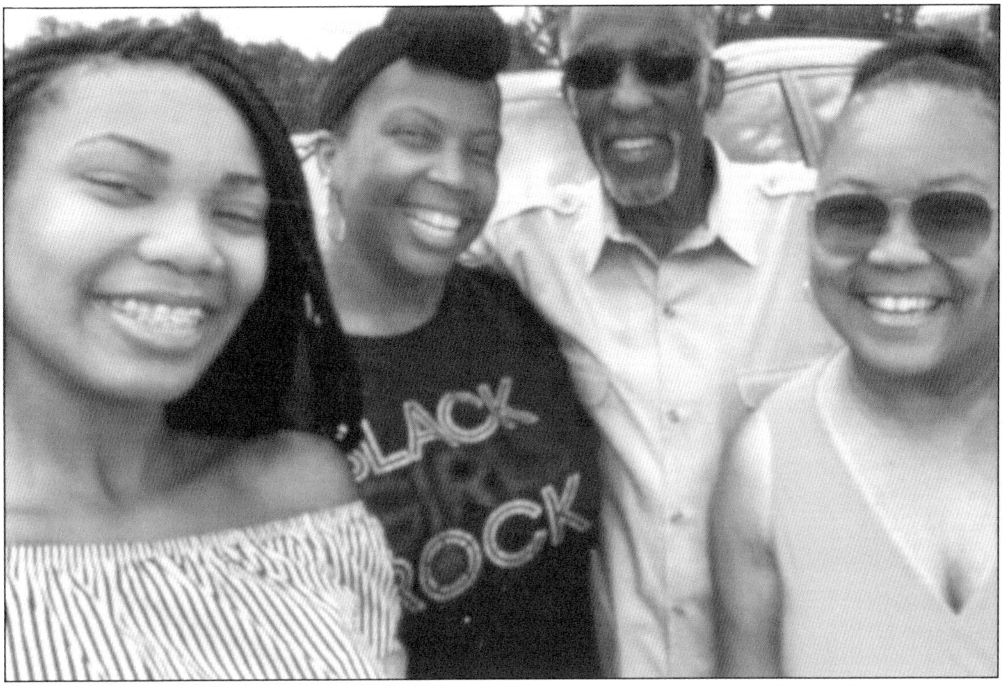

LeRoy Peterson is pictured with, from left to right, his granddaughter Jadan and his daughters Michelle and Montrell. Not pictured is his granddaughter Monica Peterson Taylor, PhD, a professor and program director in kinesiology at Temple University. Continuing the tradition of the Peterson family members serving as advocates for education, Taylor was elected to the Delaware County Council and as a member of the Pennsylvania State Board of Education in November 2019. (Montrell Peterson Ward.)

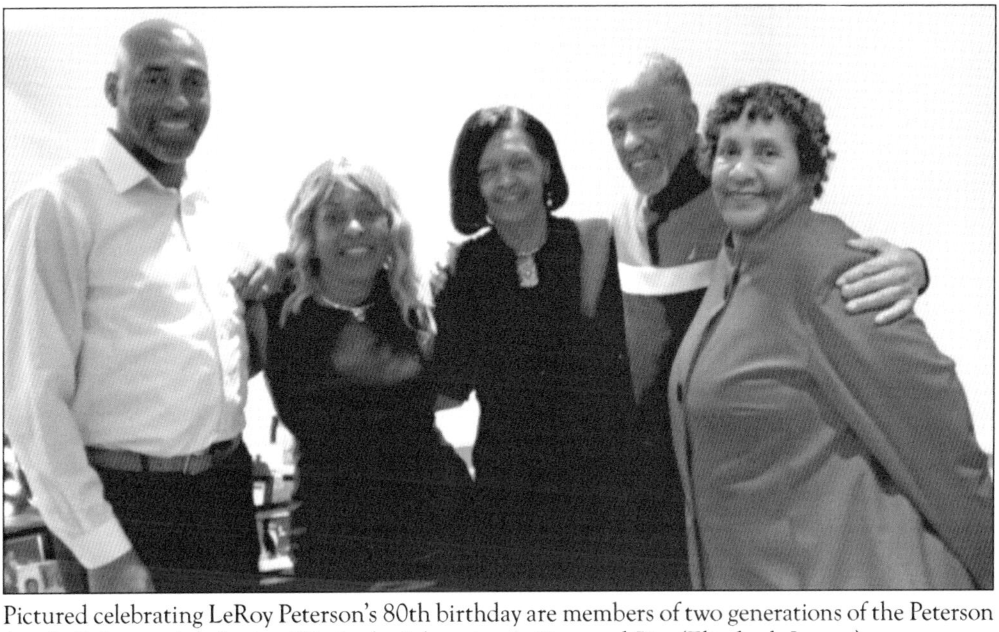

Pictured celebrating LeRoy Peterson's 80th birthday are members of two generations of the Peterson family (left to right): Lorin, Elizabeth, Adonnica, LeRoy, and Pia. (Elizabeth Lester.)

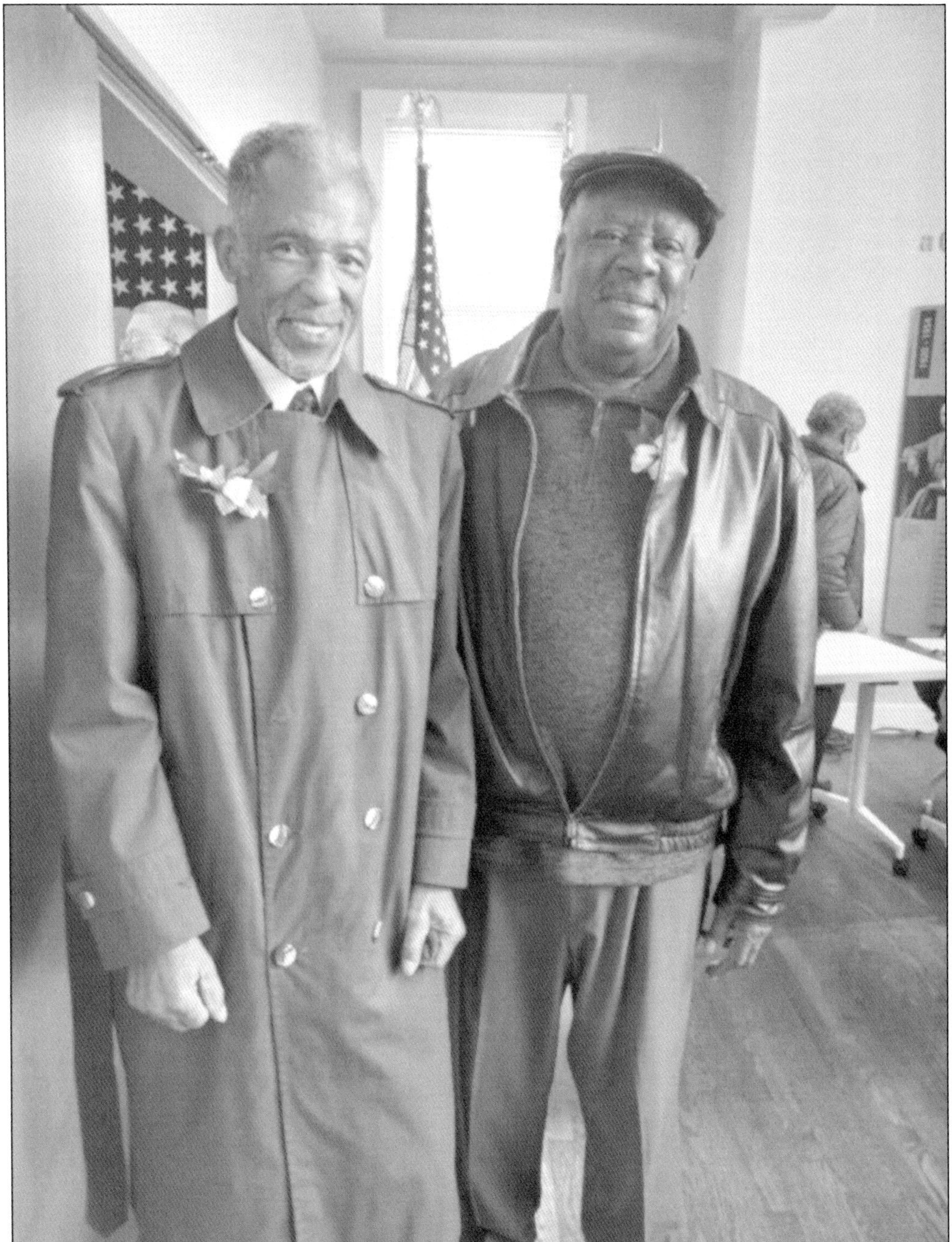

Dressed for a cold and sunny winter day, 83-year-old LeRoy Peterson (left) happily stood next to 92-year-old James Sonny Knott as they celebrated during the 2022 ribbon-cutting ceremony for the opening of the renovated Hockessin Colored School #107C Center for Diversity, Inclusion, and Social Equity. Peterson, a direct descendant of one of the oldest colored families in the Hockessin community, resides in the family's home on Mill Creek Road. He attended Hockessin Colored School #107C from 1947 to 1952. (Regina Smith.)

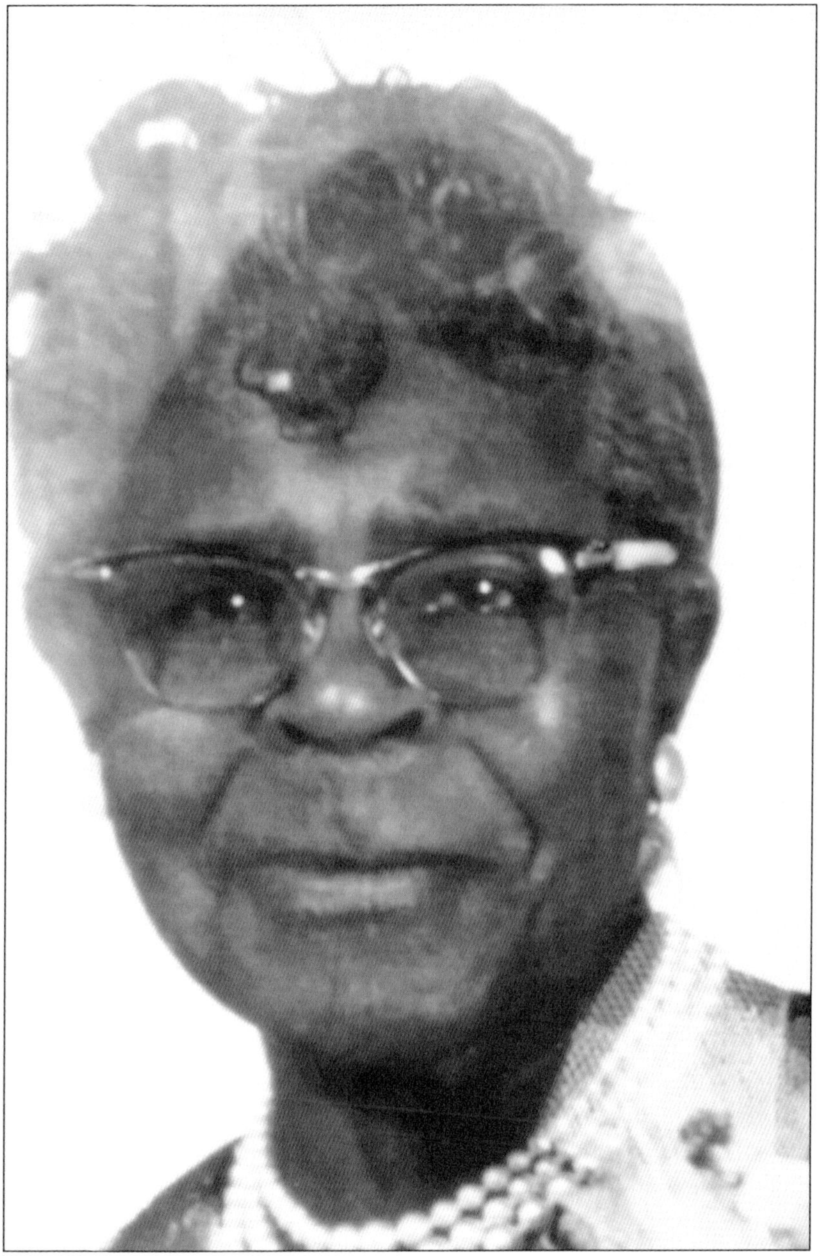

Louis and Elsie Cornish married in 1910. Their union lasted for 68 years. When Elsie became a centenarian, she maintained a healthy cognitive state through interpersonal interactions with those around her. She remembered the names of each visitor and the frequency of their visits. One of her favorite pastimes was tending to the cherry trees that lined her Hockessin property on Brackenville Road. All of her children attended Hockessin Colored School #107C. Pictured in her golden years, Elsie was the founder and sponsor of many clubs, including the prominent Stitch in Time Sewing Club in 1951. The club's mission was to sponsor projects to meet the needs of the community, which included donations to Governor Bacon Health Center and Lincoln University. Under the leadership of "Aunt Elsie," the club created beautiful original works. Their crafts were featured throughout the United States and in Quebec, Canada. (Elizabeth Lester.)

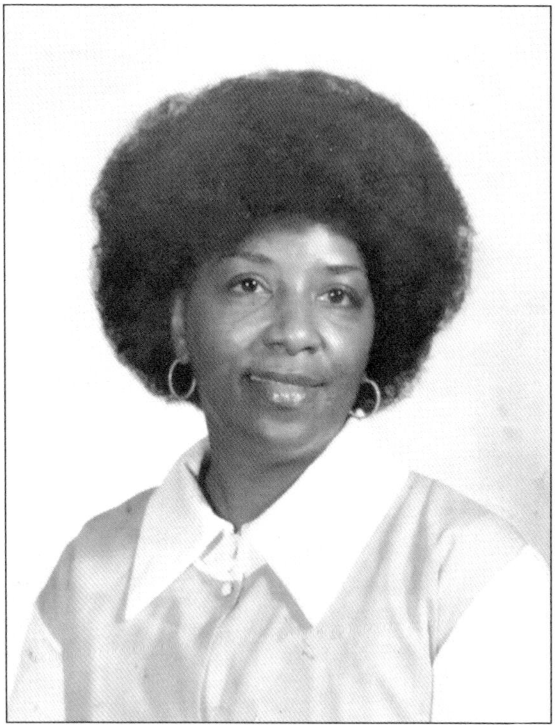

Lois (Williams) Johnson is a native of Hockessin and a former student of Hockessin Colored School #107C. Lois and her sister Lorraine were the second and third colored female students to integrate Hockessin School #29 after Shirley Bulah. Lois attended #107C for first through fourth grades. The 1977 image at left captures the true essence of Lois's character. Below, Lois Johnson is pictured standing with the assistance of her two-wheeled walker fondly known as her red Cadillac. At age 82, attending the ribbon-cutting ceremony with a warm and infectious smile, Lois welcomed everyone to the new Hockessin Colored School #107C Center for Diversity, Inclusion, and Social Equity. She shook her head in disbelief, and the long, arduous journey of this Hockessin butterfly faded away with tears of joy as she witnessed the rising of the phoenix—her precious #107C. (Both, Lois Johnson.)

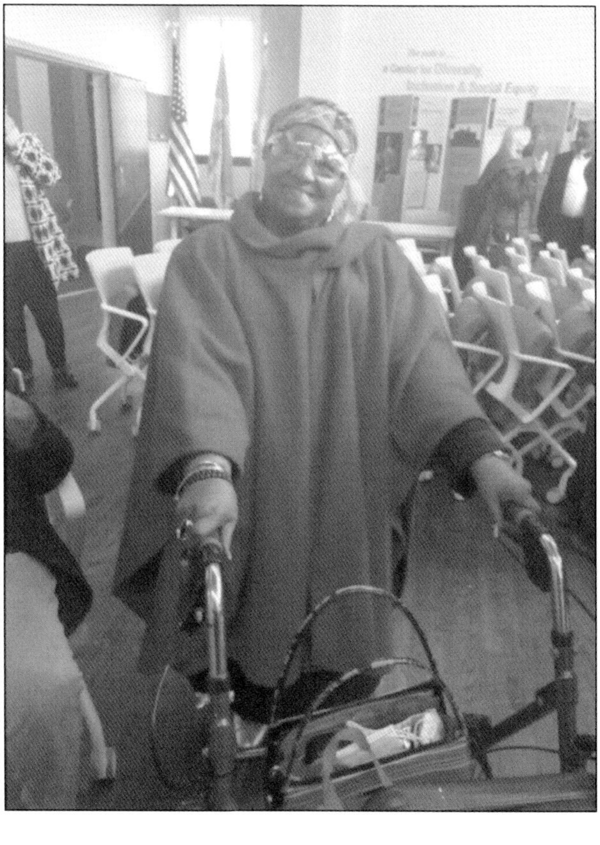

The children of Lois (Williams) Johnson carried the traditions of two Hockessin colored families: the Johnsons and the Williams. Pictured here are siblings (clockwise from left) Sarah, Kimberly, Dawn, and Ralph III. The Johnson family was actively engaged in programs and activities at Hockessin Colored School #107C. After the school closed in 1959, the Johnsons resumed their outings as the old school became the Hockessin Community Center. (Lois Johnson.)

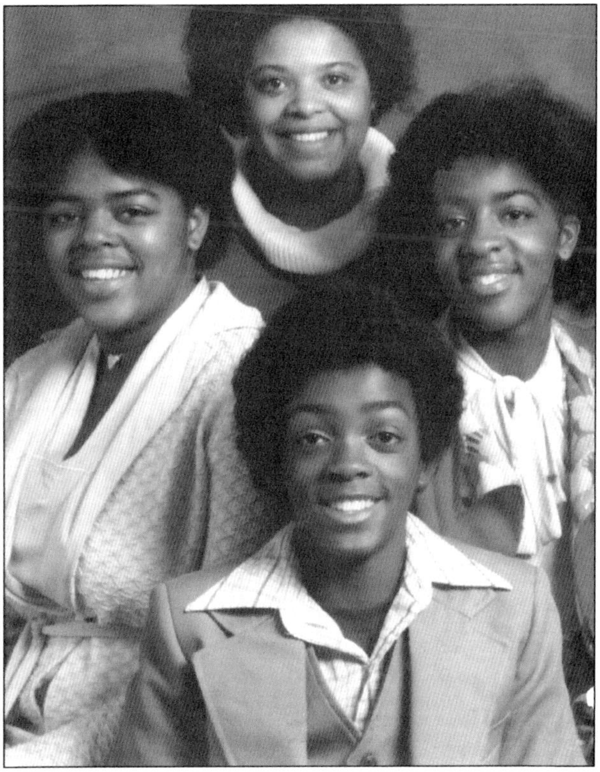

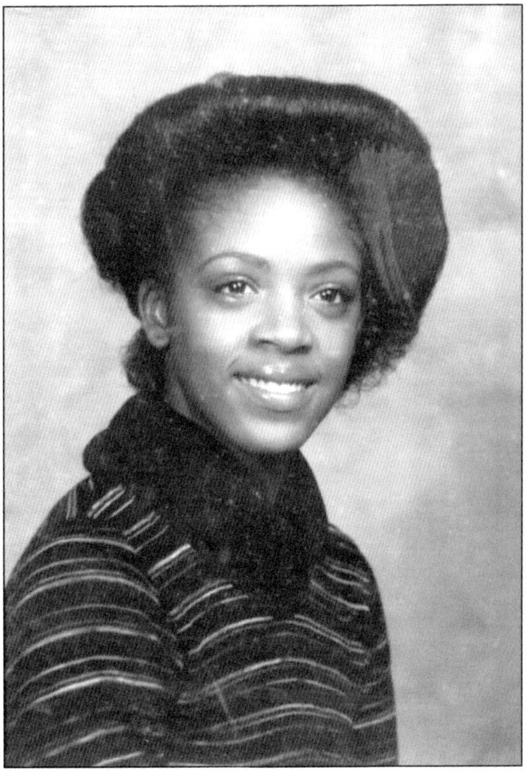

A graduate of Alexis I. duPont High School, Robin M. Johnson, the daughter of Lois and Ralph Johnson II, posed for this picture in the late 1970s after completing her program of study at Harcum Junior College. Robin credits her mother and the caring community of Hockessin Colored School #107C for her resilience. (Lois Johnson.)

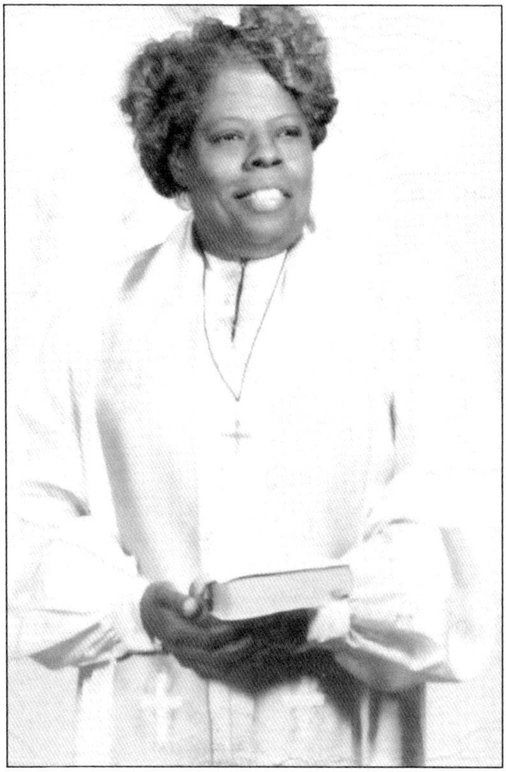

Rachel Johnson, a former student of Hockessin Colored School #107C, became an ordained minister with the African Methodist Episcopal church. (Charles Johnson.)

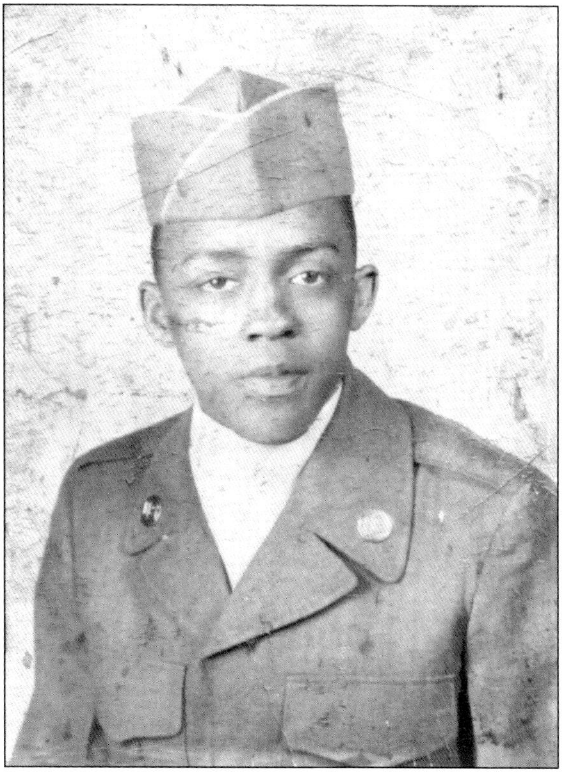

Ralph Johnson II attended Hockessin Colored School #107C. Ralph married Lois Williams, and they had several children. A picture of dedication, Ralph served the nation with pride and integrity. (Lois Johnson.)

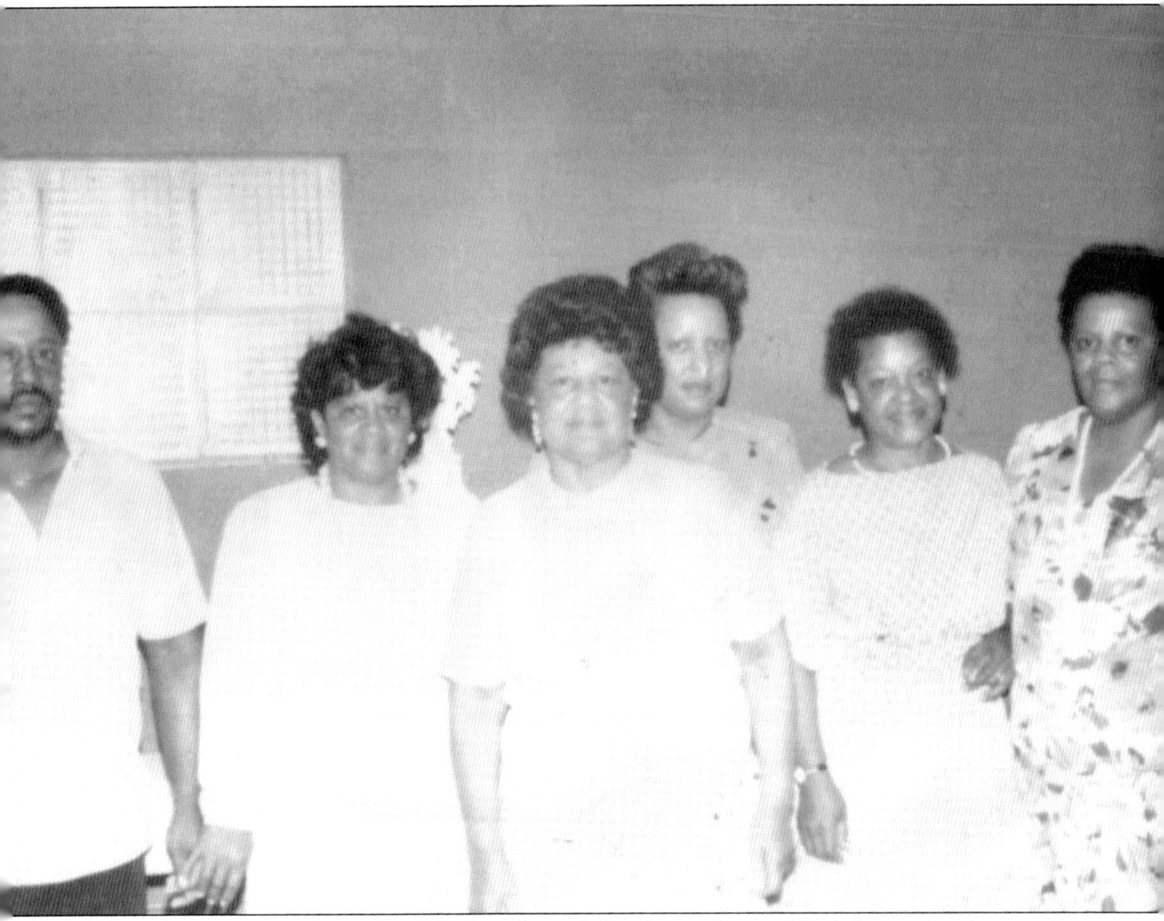

The New Castle County recorder of deeds indicated that descendants of the Johnson family owned vital parcels of land in Hockessin. Pictured from left to right are Charles, Ethel, Velma, Nancy, Mary, and Margaret Johnson. (Charles Johnson.)

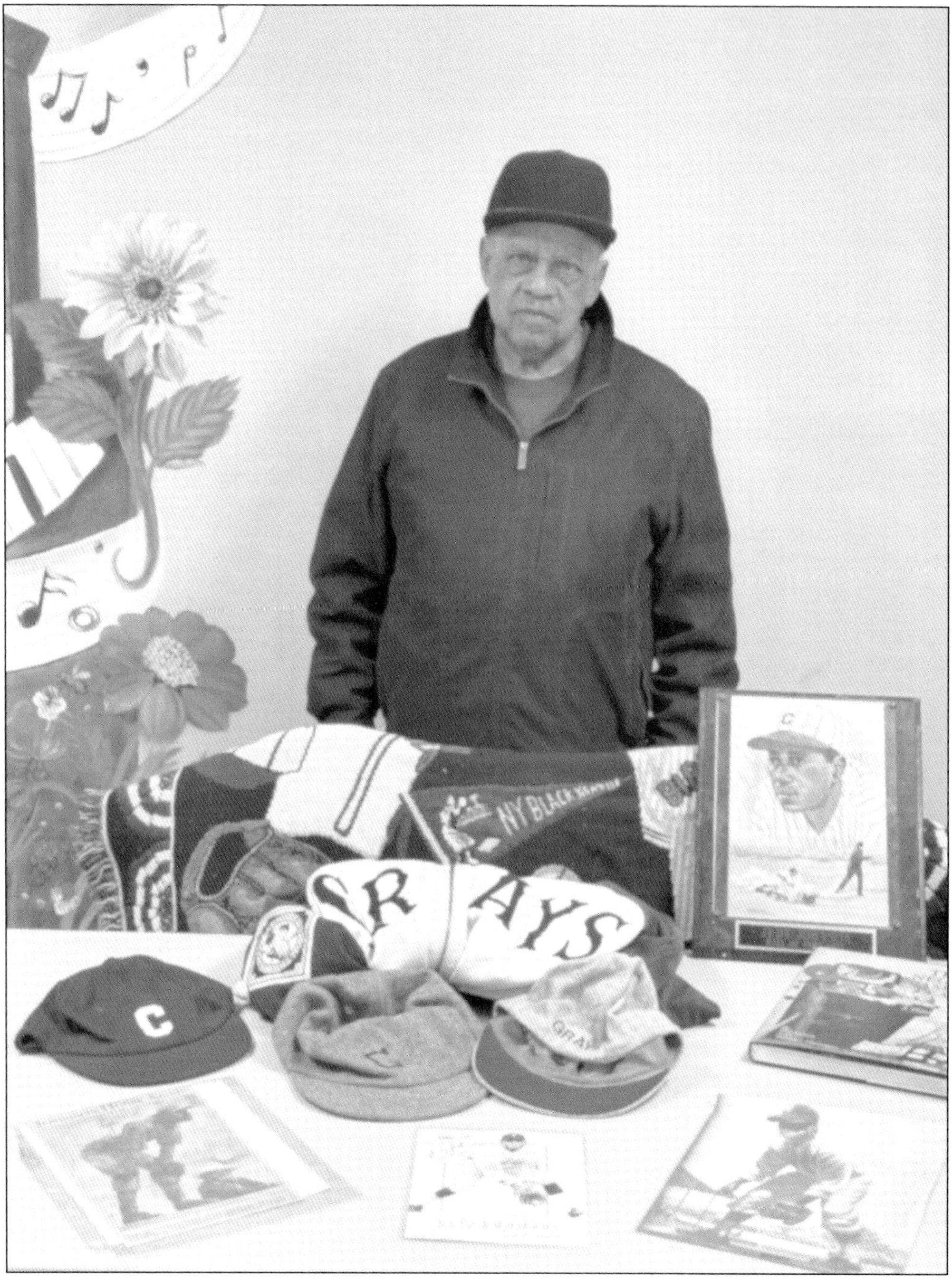

Charles "Charlie" Johnson is a former owner of a store that specialized in Negro League Baseball memorabilia. Johnson is pictured with a few of his prize possessions of hometown heroes and National Baseball Hall of Famers Judy Johnson and Nip Winters. Johnson reminisced about Hockessin baseball teams and their winning seasons. Among their rivals were the Buttonwood Tigers, Dover Connection, and Milford Yankees. At age 80, this former student of Hockessin Colored School #107C credits his love of baseball and strong work ethic to his grand-uncle Jacob Johnson, who was affectionately known as the "colored mayor" of Hockessin. (Lanette R. Edwards.)

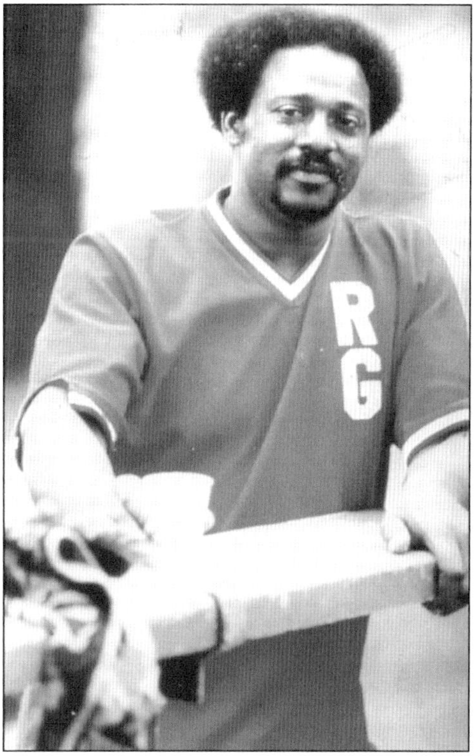

Charles Johnson, a player and coach, is pictured wearing a ruby-and-white Royal Gems uniform shirt. Known for his baseball-handling skills in center field, he showcased the raw talent of Hockessin's colored baseball players. (Joyce Thompson.)

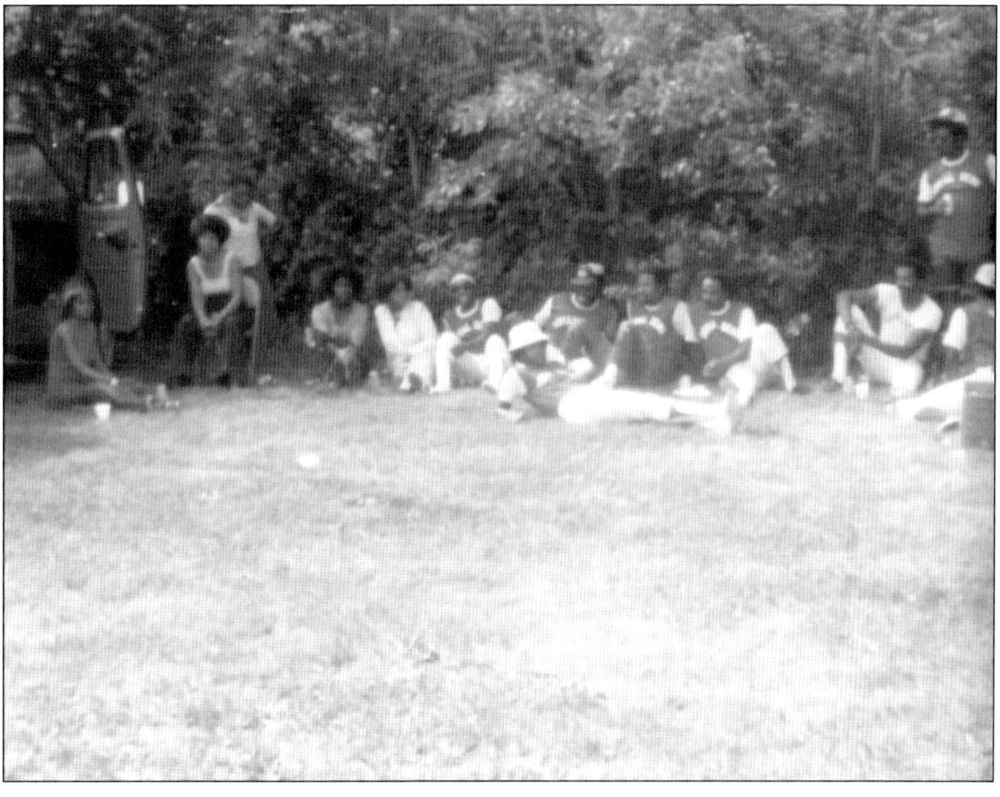

Archrivals from Newark, Newport (Belvedere), and Buttonwood colored schools played on the Hockessin field as early as the 1920s. The Royal Gems baseball team was known for speed and bag running. After the game, Royal Gems players relaxed in the cool shade of the home field trees. Among the players pictured here is Sammy "the Slugger" Johnson; often considered the redhead sensation, Johnson was a highly recruited third-baseman. (Charles Johnson.)

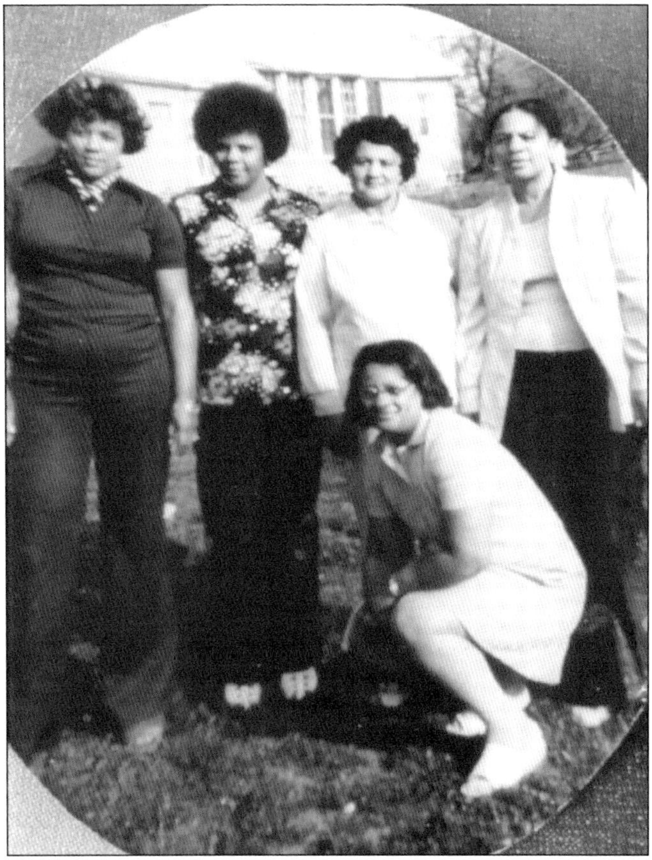

From left to right, Nancy, Margaret, Velma, Rosetta, and Ethel Johnson enjoyed an outing at the Sunday baseball games held on the fields in the rear of Hockessin Colored School #107C, which is visible in the background. The Johnson ladies were generational fans of Hockessin colored baseball teams, including the Hornets and the Royal Gems. (Joyce Thompson.)

In the Hockessin colored community, baseball was the celebrated sport of choice. Members of the Royal Gems and Hornets baseball teams included grandfathers, fathers, and sons from the same families. Below, baseball fans from the World War II era are enjoying the onset of a Sunday game as they relax on the grounds of Hockessin Colored School #107C. (Charles Johnson.)

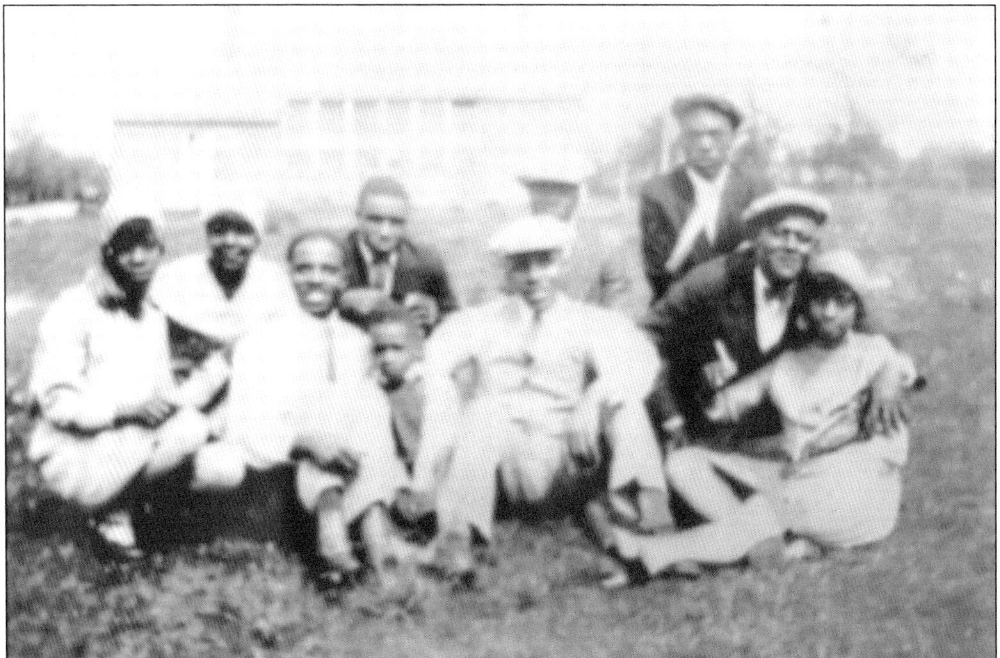

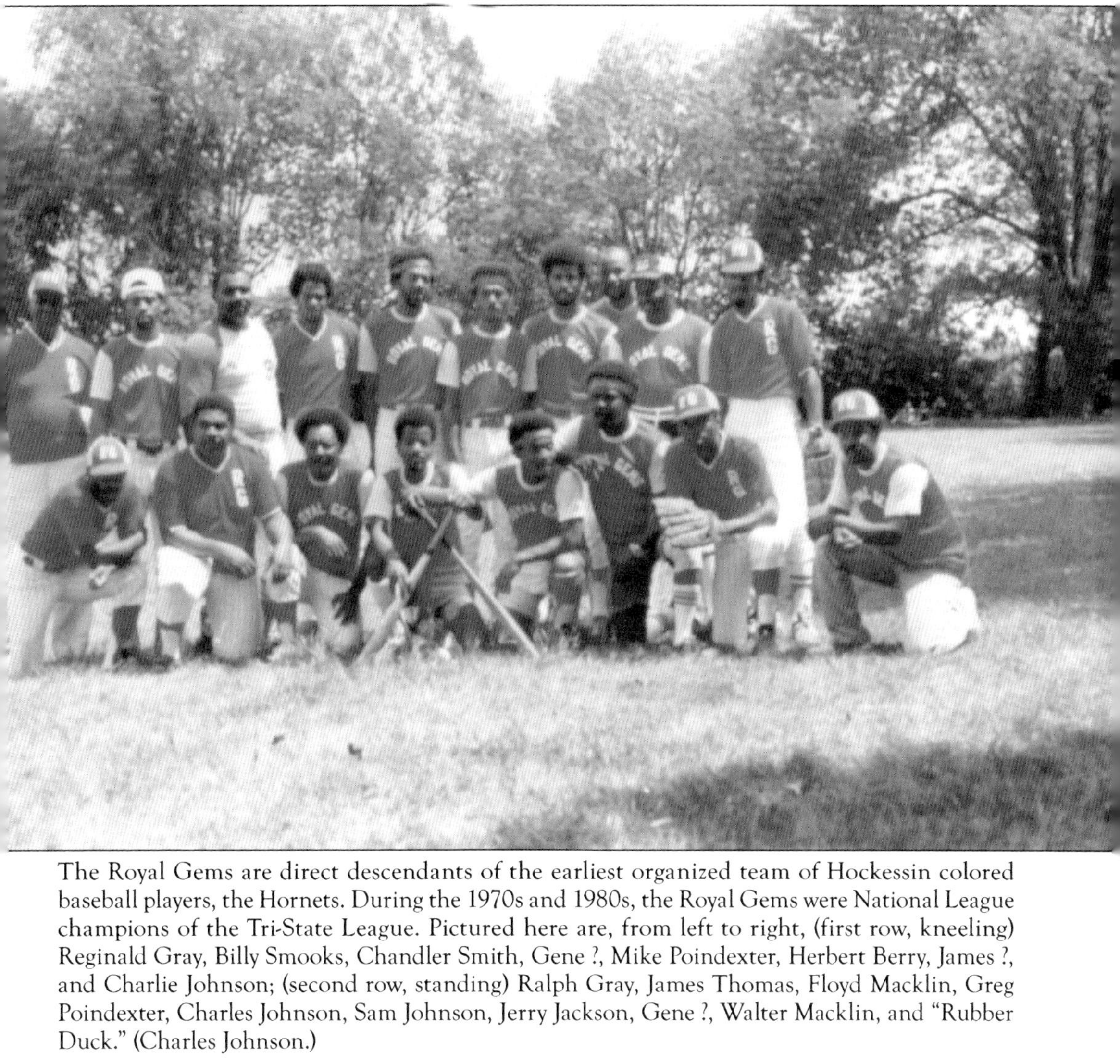

The Royal Gems are direct descendants of the earliest organized team of Hockessin colored baseball players, the Hornets. During the 1970s and 1980s, the Royal Gems were National League champions of the Tri-State League. Pictured here are, from left to right, (first row, kneeling) Reginald Gray, Billy Smooks, Chandler Smith, Gene ?, Mike Poindexter, Herbert Berry, James ?, and Charlie Johnson; (second row, standing) Ralph Gray, James Thomas, Floyd Macklin, Greg Poindexter, Charles Johnson, Sam Johnson, Jerry Jackson, Gene ?, Walter Macklin, and "Rubber Duck." (Charles Johnson.)

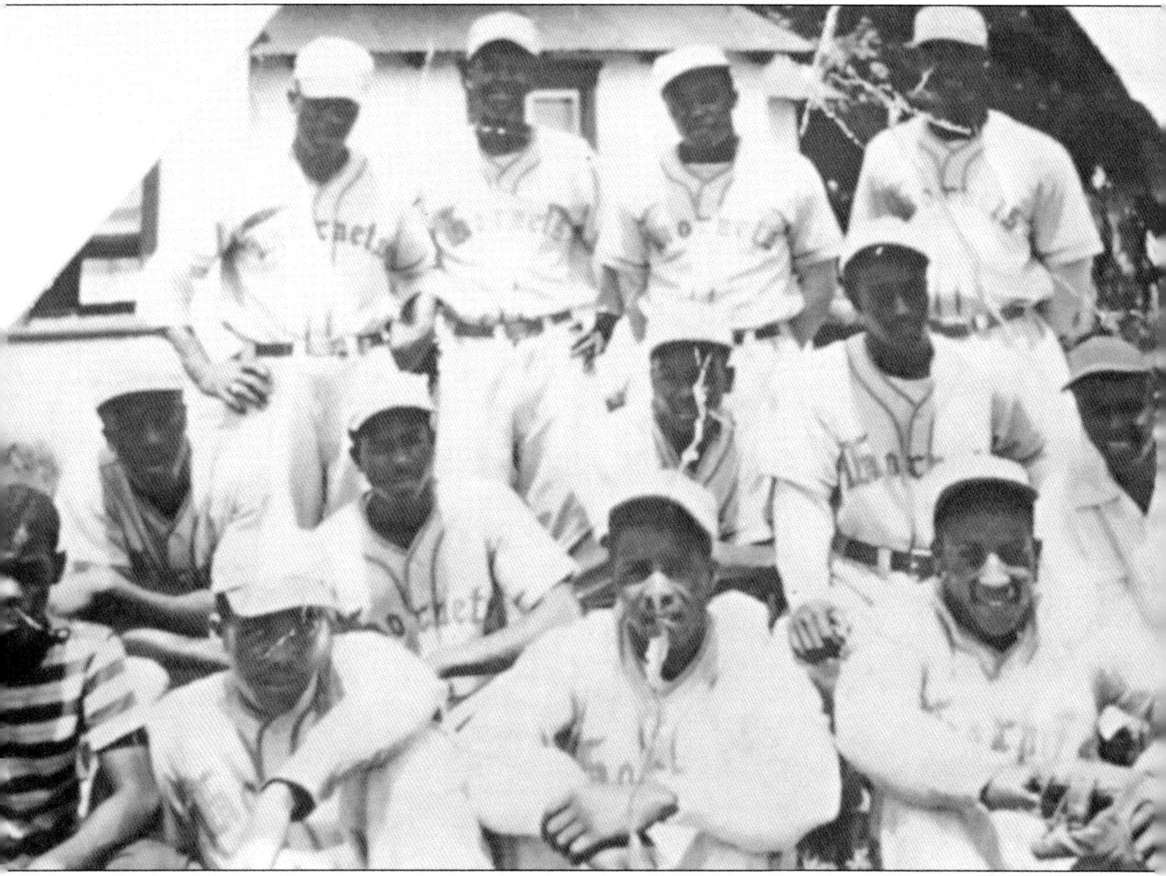

Meet some of the members of the 1940s Hornets baseball team from Hockessin, Delaware. Pictured here are, from left to right, (first row) Richard "Dickie" Miller (in the striped shirt), Charles "Chickie" Miller, Charles Bolden, and Leon Carter; (second row) Junie Davis, Billy Bolden, Clifford Poindexter, Junie Gasby, and Sherman Keys; (third row) Eve Coleman, Finney Coleman, John Gasby, and Ralph Gray. All of the players were former students of Hockessin Colored School #107C. (Charles Johnson.)

Five

The DuPont Experience
A Chosen Community

The Delaware Educational Commission of 1917 initiated a statewide study of schools and students that included students identified as "Colored," "Indian," "Moor," "Negro," and "White." John Rockefeller's General Education Board supported the studies with contributions from Pierre Samuel duPont and hired experts from Columbia University's Teachers College in New York to assess the circumstances surrounding the education of children in Delaware. In 1919, the Strayer report described the appalling conditions of Delaware's schools servicing both colored and white students. The state's educational commission recommended legislation to Delaware's general assembly based on their findings; this resulted in the passage of the 1919 Delaware School Code.

Concerned by the findings, duPont donated millions of dollars to the construction of new school buildings for all students. Hockessin Colored School #107C became a recipient of those efforts. The duPont family purchased the parcel of land at the school's present site. Pierre secured the land from Isabella duPont Sharp and Hugh Rodney Sharp. For nearly 20 years, Pierre engaged in a campaign to improve the condition of education in Delaware, particularly learning facilities for colored and white children. He enlisted the services of the New Jersey architecture firm Guilbert and Betelle. Ernest Foss Guilbert and James Oscar Betelle specialized in the construction of academic institutes.

On September 8, 1920, on behalf of the Delaware School Auxiliary Association, the wife of William K. duPont presented the deed for Hockessin Colored School #107C to the New Castle County Board of Education. The ceremony was well attended, with a large media presence. Hockessin Colored School #107C students transitioned from the wooden frame building on Grant Avenue to the newly constructed brick schoolhouse around the corner on Mill Creek Road, singing the duPont school song. Hockessin Colored School #107C was among the first "duPont Schools" built in the State of Delaware. For over 30 years, the grade school remained the sole center of education for colored people residing in Hockessin.

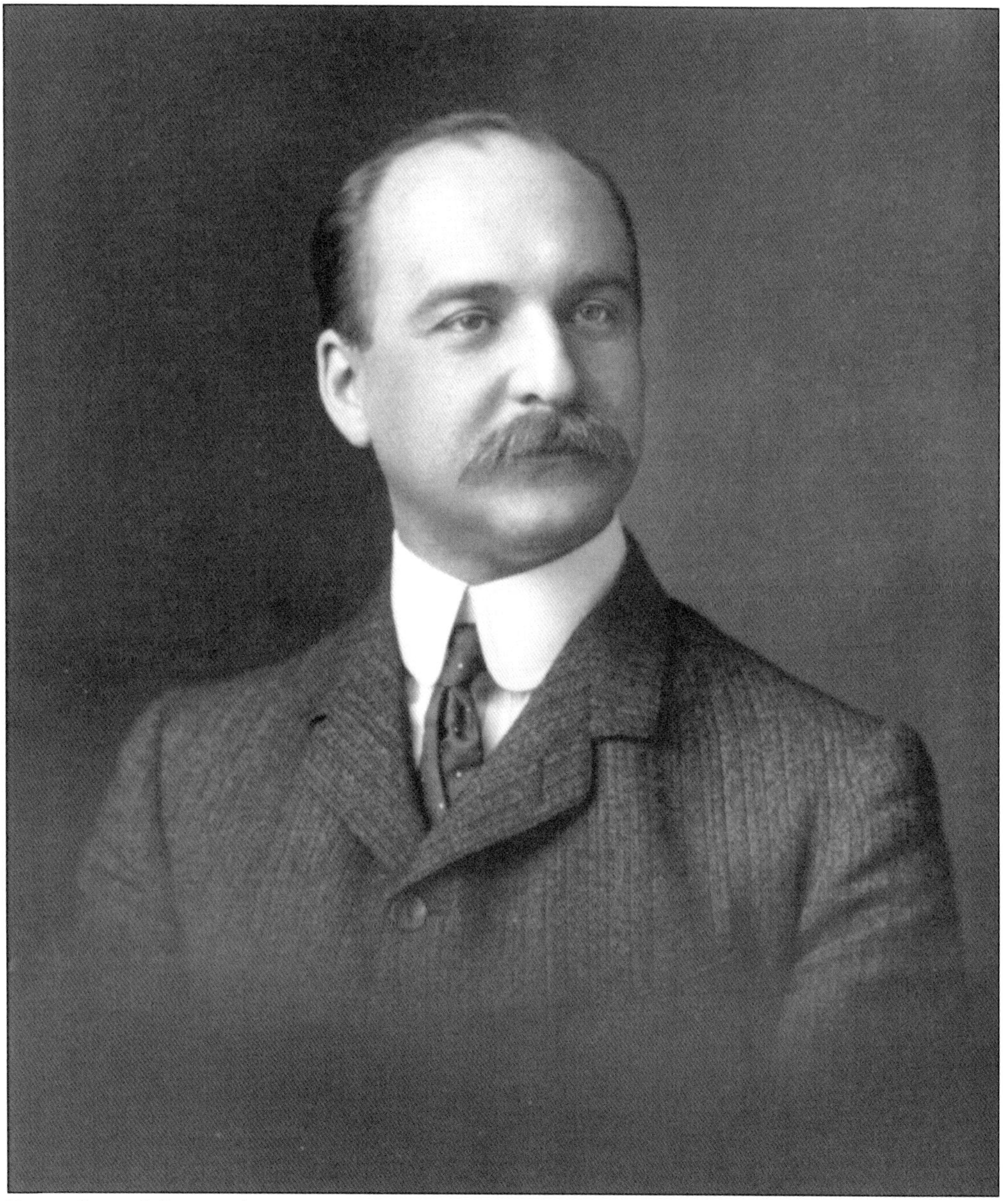

Pierre Samuel duPont, born January 15, 1870, was a businessman. He was the eldest of three sons and became the patriarch of the family after his father was killed in an industrial accident. In 1890, after graduating from the Massachusetts Institute of Technology (MIT), he assumed the role of superintendent with the family business. In 1919, duPont served as vice president of the state board of education. He commissioned a study on the condition of school buildings in Delaware. The information from the study was disseminated on October 15, 1919, and shared in the General Report on School Buildings and Grounds of Delaware by George Drayton Strayer. Strayer was a professor of educational administration at Columbia University's Teachers College. The Strayer report illustrated the appalling conditions of Delaware's schools. Spurred to action, Pierre built 86 schools for colored and white students, and Hockessin Colored School #107C was the third duPont School constructed. After enjoying a life committed to the greater good of society, Pierre S. duPont died on April 4, 1954.

Isabella Mathieu duPont Sharp, pictured here with her son Bayard Sharp, was the sister of Pierre S. duPont. A philanthropist in her own right, Isabella generously donated the land for the construction of the Hockessin Colored School #107C brick building. (Hagley Museum and Library.)

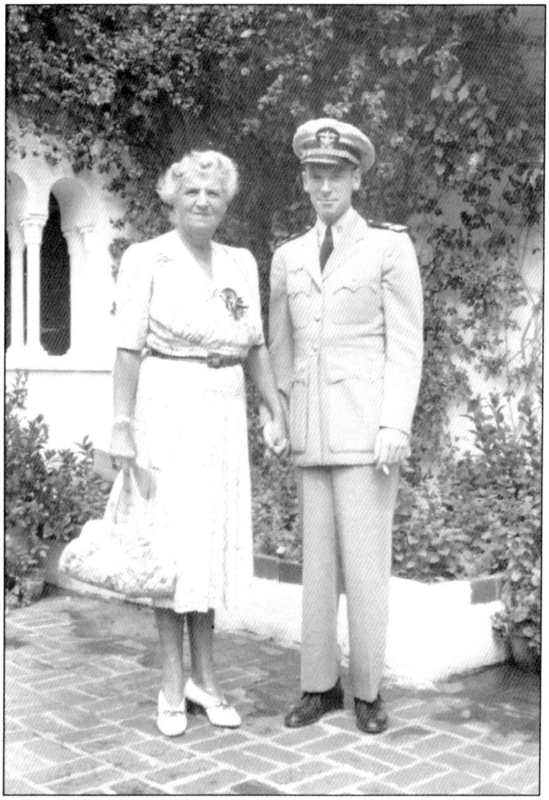

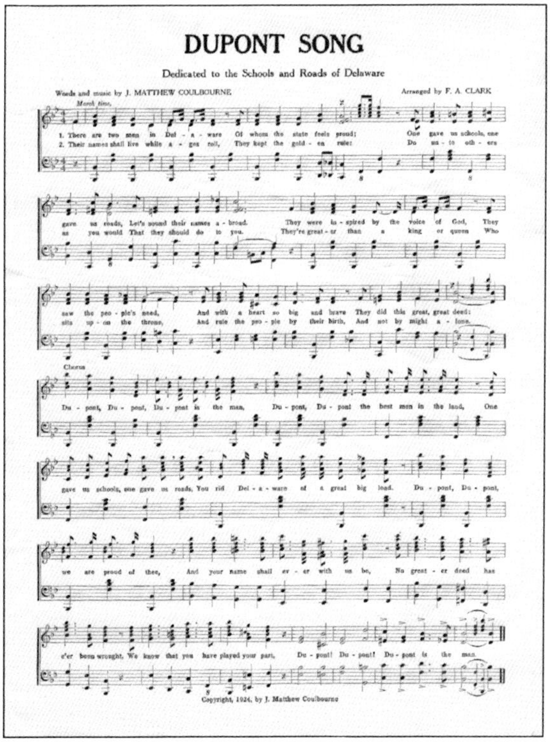

Written in 1924 by Jay Matthew Coulbourne, the "DUPONT SONG" was a tribute to T. Coleman duPont and Pierre S. duPont for their philanthropic contributions to education and the state's infrastructure. Coulbourne dedicated the song to the schools and roads in the state of Delaware. (Hagley Museum and Library.)

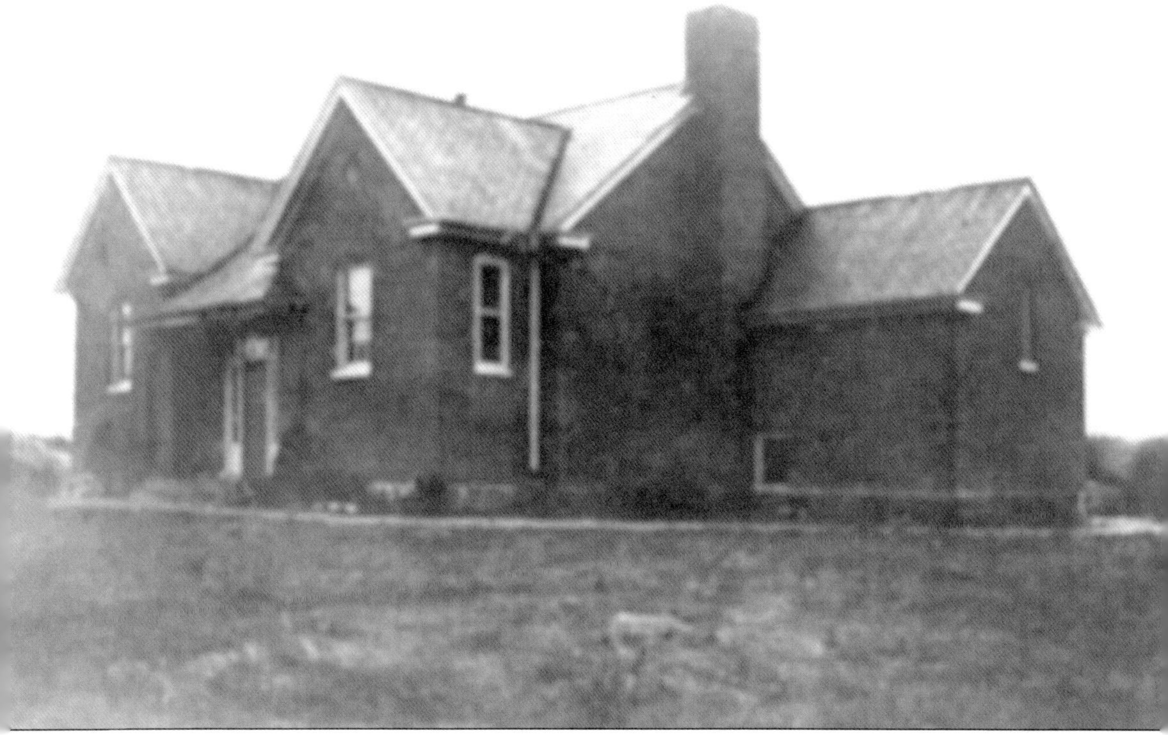

This 1920 picture features a frontal view of the Hockessin Colored School #107C brick schoolhouse. As a result of the 1919 Strayer report, a metric was used to measure five categories: location (site), building (structure), service systems (heating, ventilation, water, and plumbing), classroom (illumination, arrangement, and equipment), and special rooms (general use, official use, and special services). Although the old Hockessin Colored School #107C wooden framed building scored in the highest percentile among colored schools, in some categories, it ranked in the lowest percentile based on two glaring indicators, including that the school's geographical location along the local creek bed—and adjacent to an active railroad line—compromised the learning environment and the safety of its students.

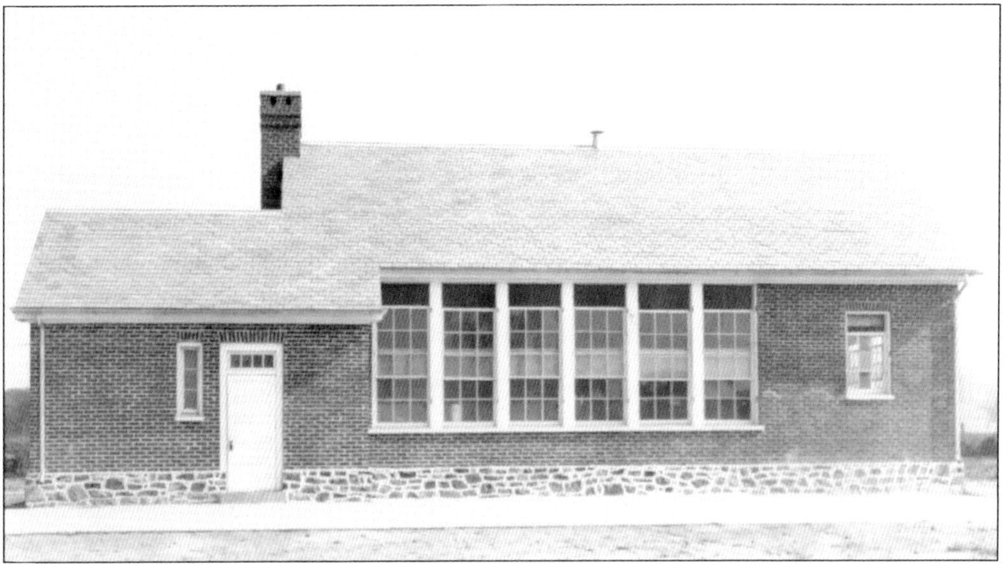

The brick Hockessin Colored School #107C was constructed to usher in a contemporary curriculum. The new school provided a state-of-the-art facility with modern amenities. Standard features included separate cloakrooms, indoor plumbing, bathrooms for boys and girls, a vestibule, and closets for school and janitorial supplies.

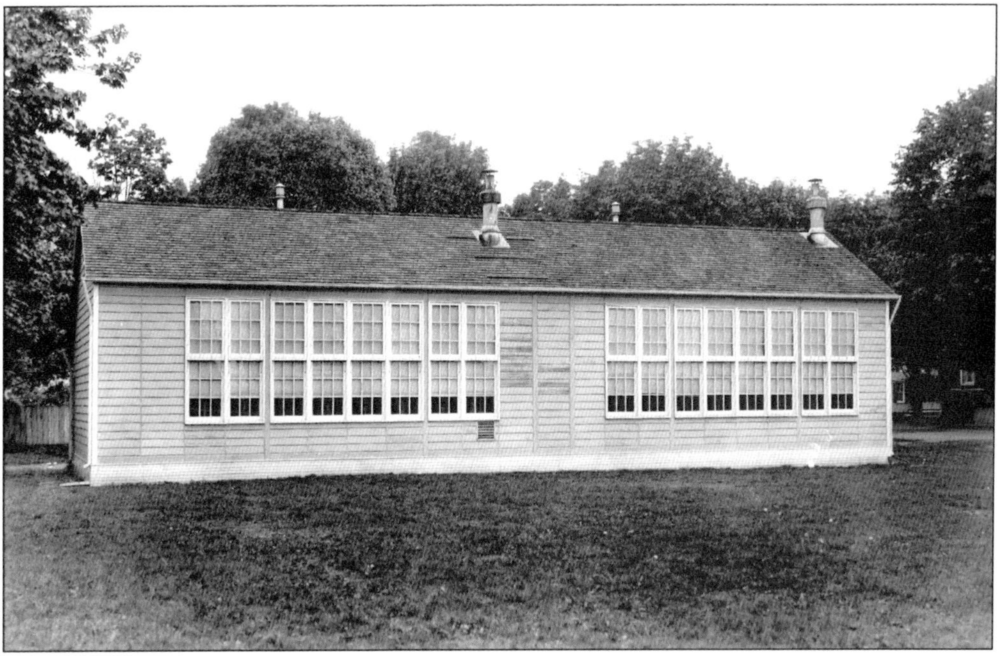

Smyrna #107 portable school was a two-room school building with wood siding and a central entrance. Each classroom had a large bank of eight windows on the rear wall. Construction started on this building on August 25, 1920, and was completed by September 13, 1920, at a cost of $16,550.29. This southern New Castle County duPont School was often confused with its numerical counterpart located in northern New Castle County. A resolution was reached by intentionally inserting the letter "C" to reflect the #107 colored school located in Hockessin. Smyrna #107, established for white students only, simply remained #107. (Hagley Museum and Library.)

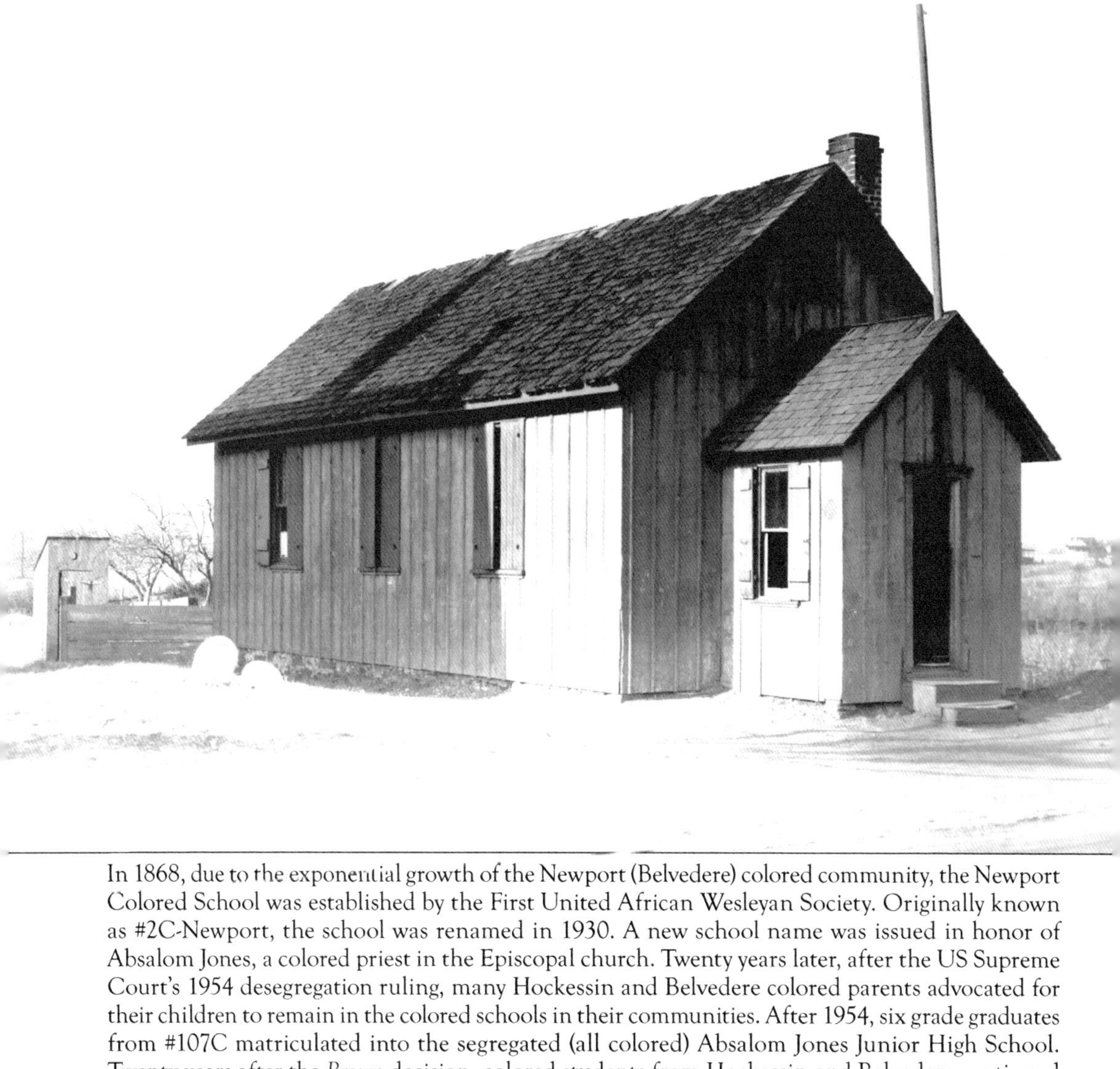

In 1868, due to the exponential growth of the Newport (Belvedere) colored community, the Newport Colored School was established by the First United African Wesleyan Society. Originally known as #2C-Newport, the school was renamed in 1930. A new school name was issued in honor of Absalom Jones, a colored priest in the Episcopal church. Twenty years later, after the US Supreme Court's 1954 desegregation ruling, many Hockessin and Belvedere colored parents advocated for their children to remain in the colored schools in their communities. After 1954, six grade graduates from #107C matriculated into the segregated (all colored) Absalom Jones Junior High School. Twenty years after the *Brown* decision, colored students from Hockessin and Belvedere continued to attend segregated schools. In 1976, the local board of education voted to close Absalom Jones, citing declining enrollment. In essence, Delaware's state-mandated school assignment and busing facilitated the decline in student enrollment at colored schools. This picture shows Newport Colored School, with the outhouse visible in the background at left. The photograph was taken around 1920, prior to the construction of the new duPont School erected in 1922. (Hagley Museum and Library.)

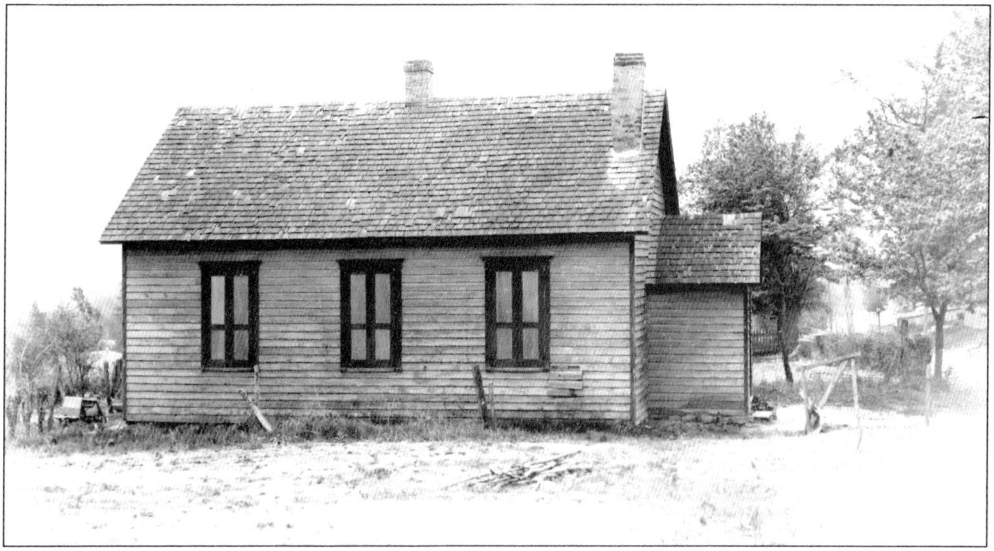

Unlike Hockessin Colored School #107C, the Christiana Colored School #111C was designed to resemble a cottage. This photograph was taken several months prior to the construction of the new school building that began on April 20, 1920. The new Christiana Colored School was a duPont School established on September 6, 1920. It was among the first schools in the state built by Pierre S. duPont. (Hagley Library and Museum.)

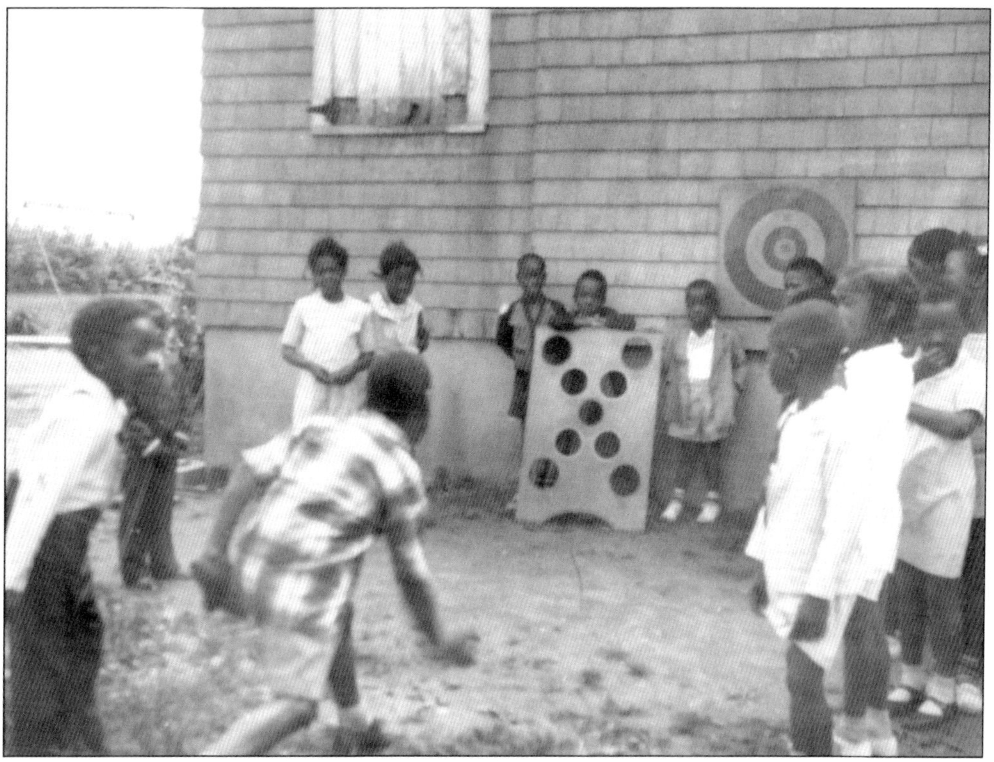

These children are enjoying an outdoor game of cornhole along the side of a duPont School building. This picture captures the anticipation of several of the youngsters who were eager to pitch a bag through the hole but waiting their turn to partake in the fun.

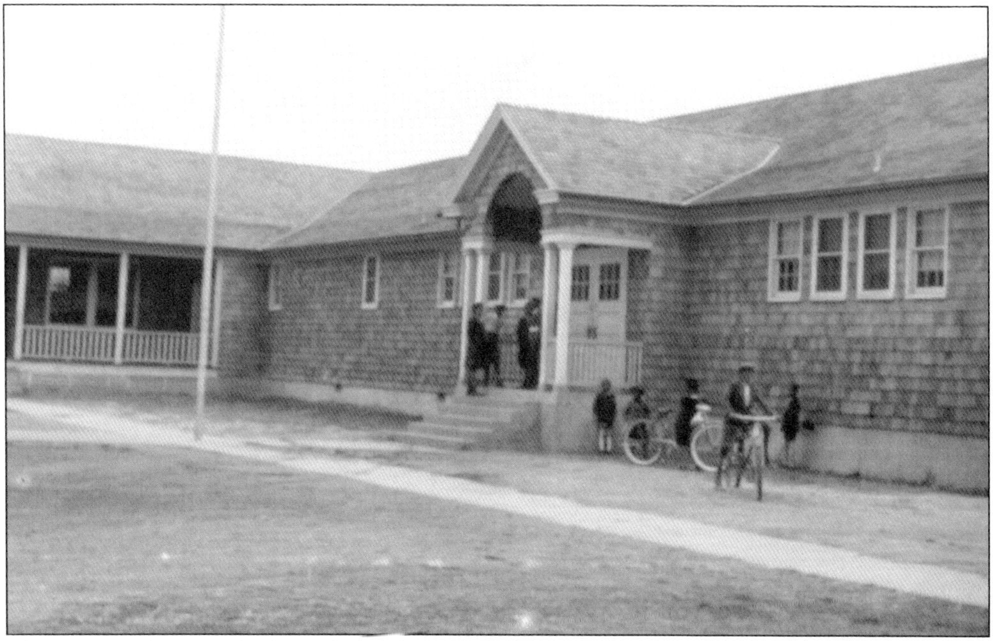

The c. 1920 photograph above shows the Newport Colored School campus. The original school, a one-room frame structure, was built in 1867 by citizens of the Newport colored community. In 1919, Pierre S. duPont selected the Newport (Belvedere) community for his statewide educational development and improvement plan. The new duPont School featured individual wood shingles for siding. The school was absorbed by the state for redistricting and renamed Newport Colored School #106. By the early 1920s, two additional buildings had been added to the campus. The tri-edifice pictured here consisted of multiple classrooms, an industrial shop, and a traditional auditorium. Below, young students are sitting with their teacher at a child-sized classroom table. These little ones appear to enjoy socialization time. (Above, Hagley Library and Museum.)

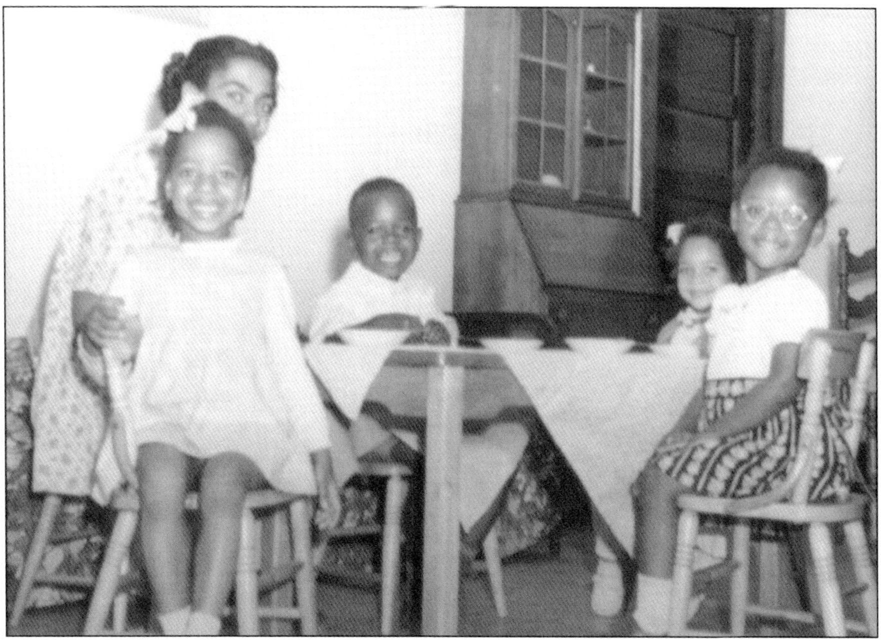

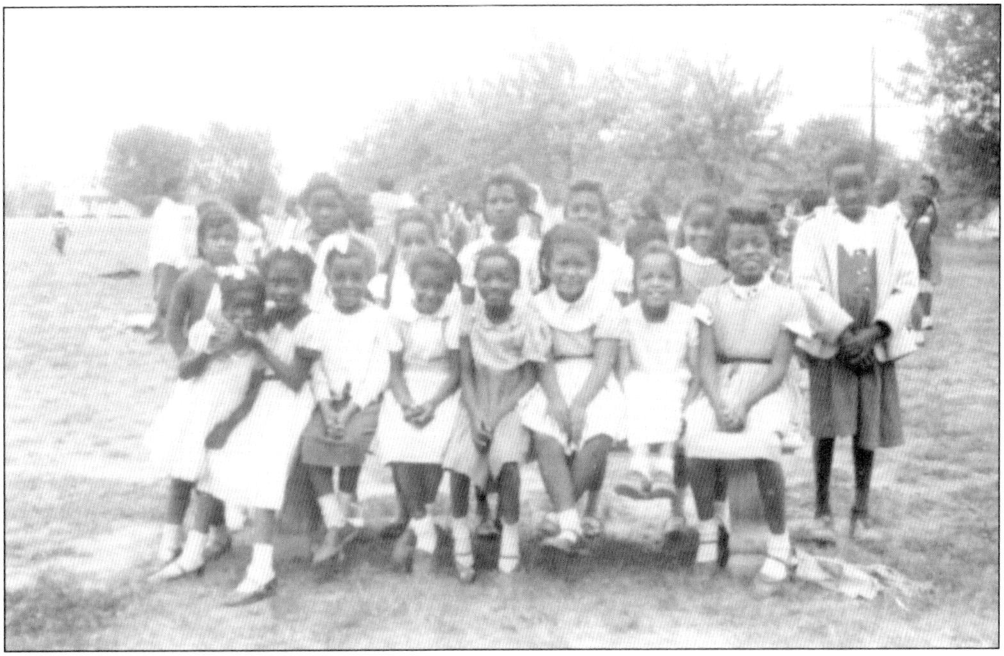

Cute as a button, primary school students sit for a group photograph. These young girls are all smiles in their nicely pressed dresses and Mary Jane shoes.

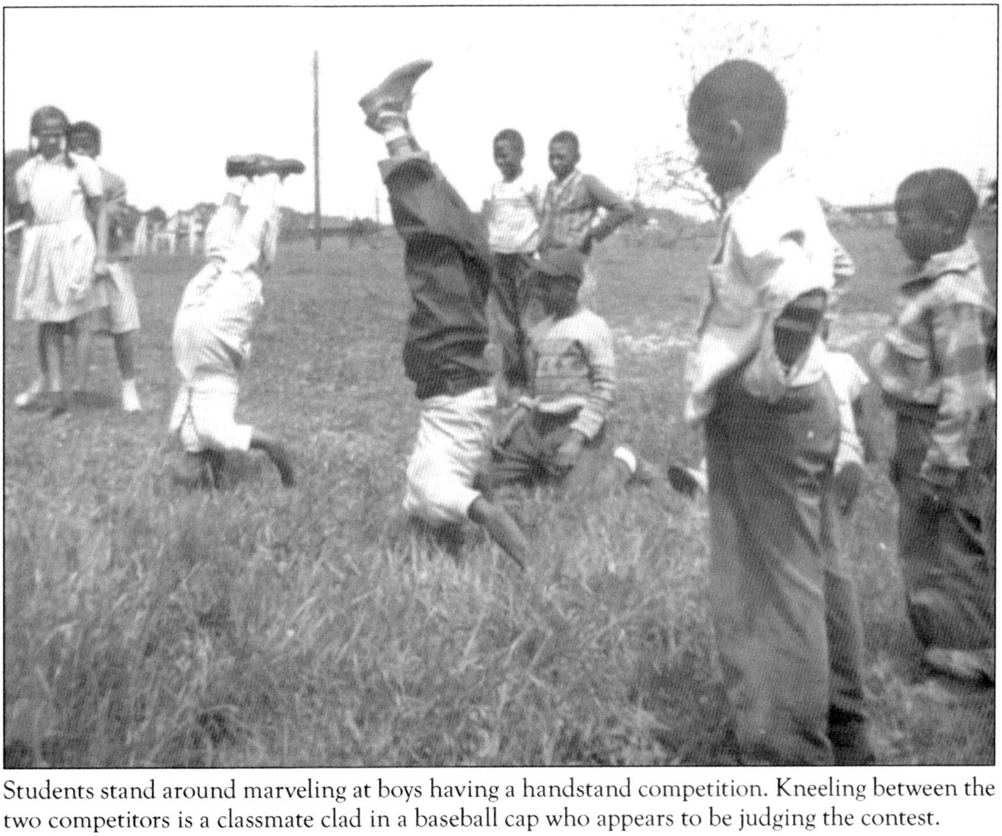

Students stand around marveling at boys having a handstand competition. Kneeling between the two competitors is a classmate clad in a baseball cap who appears to be judging the contest.

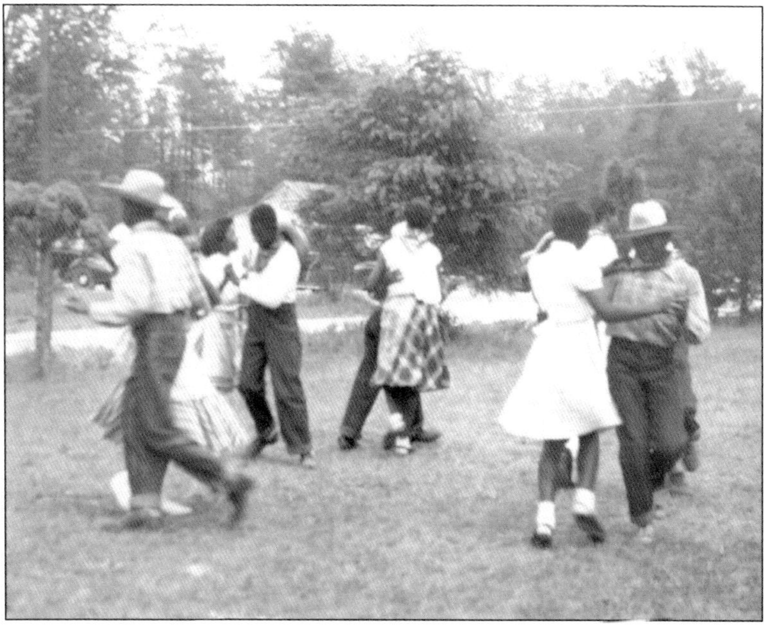

Do-si-do, and around they go! Dressed in traditional square dance Western attire, these talented youngsters indulged in schoolyard square dancing.

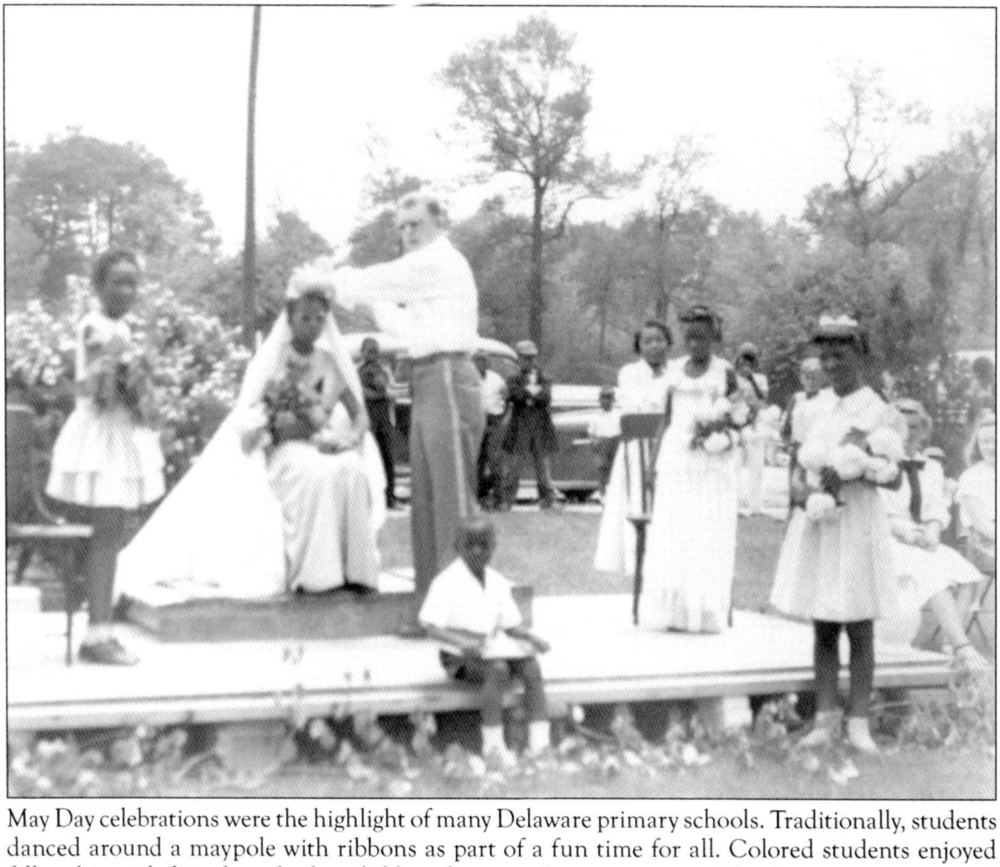

May Day celebrations were the highlight of many Delaware primary schools. Traditionally, students danced around a maypole with ribbons as part of a fun time for all. Colored students enjoyed fellowship with friends and other children from nearby communities. The festivities were capped off with the coronation of a May queen. Pictured are members of the May Day student court.

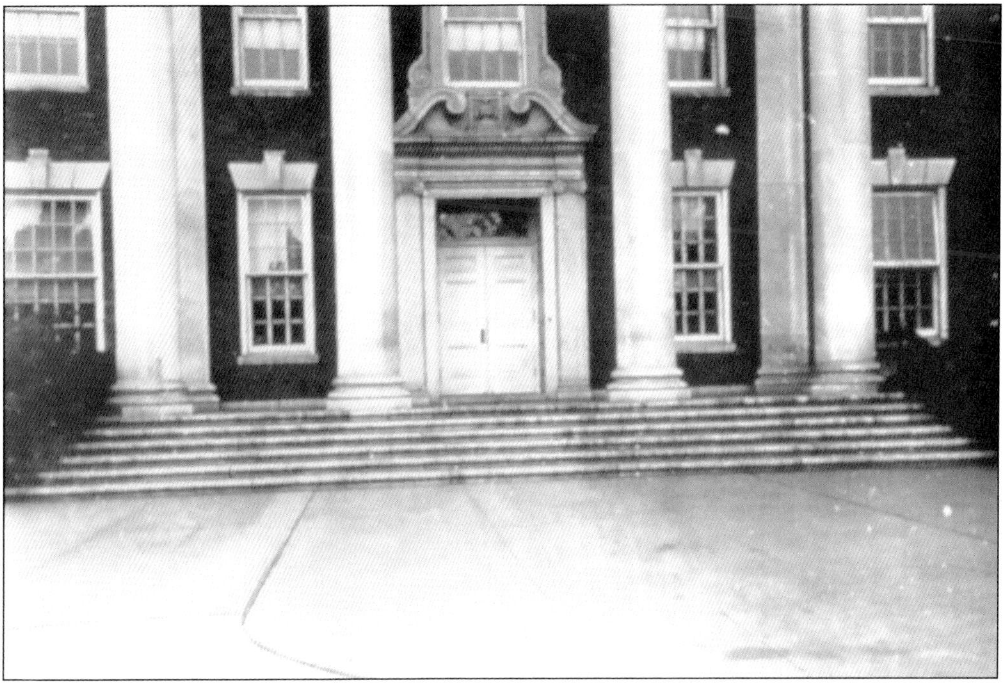

Howard High School was founded in 1867 as the only high school that admitted colored students in the entire state of Delaware; it held that title for more than 75 years. After attending Hockessin Colored School #107C for first through sixth grade, students attended Howard High School in Wilmington, Delaware, for grades 7 through 12. (Hilda Bulah Morris.)

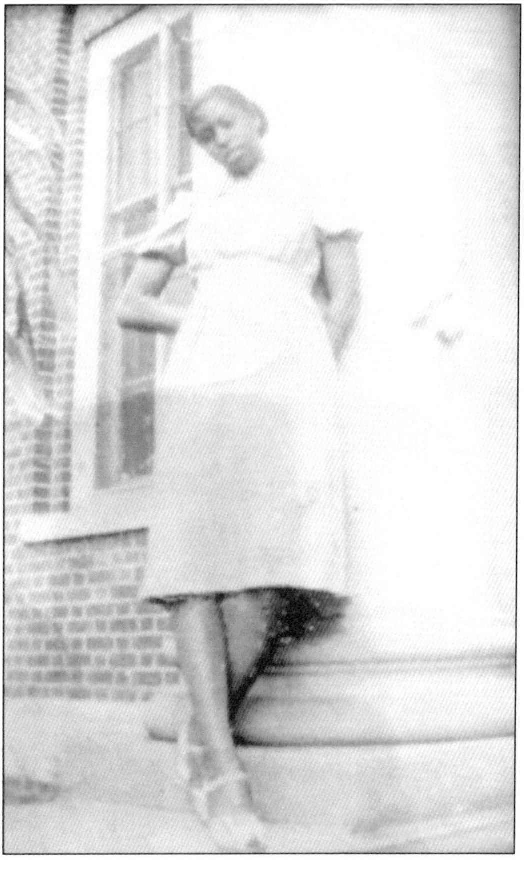

Bettye Peterson is pictured leaning against the stately columns of Howard High, a favorite venue for photographs. Ranking among the top students in her class, Peterson matriculated through West Virginia State University. Aside from her academic achievements, Peterson accomplished her ultimate goal of being a wife and mother. In addition to nurturing her family, one of her proudest efforts was being a nanny for Beau, Hunter, and Naomi—the children of Joseph Biden. (Elizabeth Lester.)

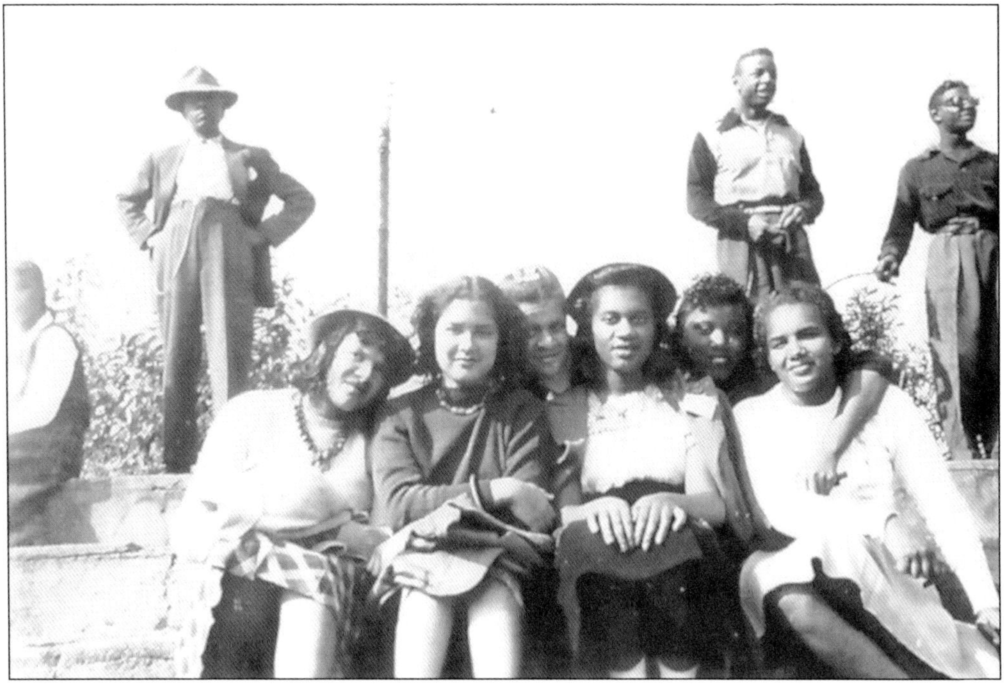

In 1942, a group of Howard High School ladies posed for this picture while attending the school football game. Meanwhile, male onlookers gazed in admiration. (Hilda Bulah Morris.)

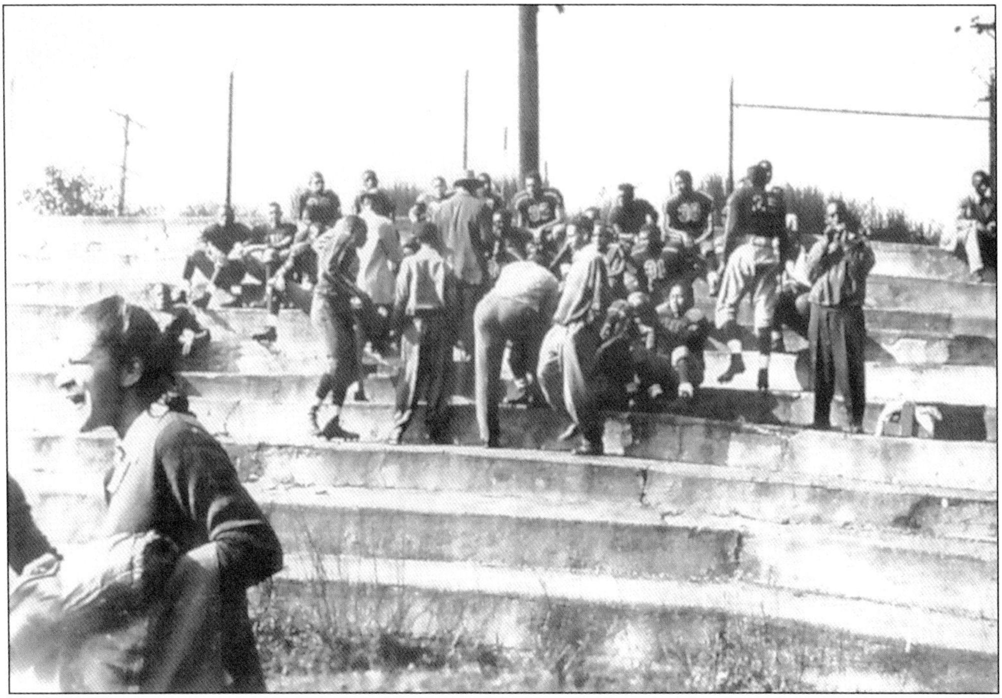

Enjoying an afternoon out, Howard High School students clustered on the stadium bleachers as they cheered for their beloved Howard Wildcats football team. (Hilda Bulah Morris.)

The Redcoats were a social club formed by a group of young ladies at Howard High School during the mid-1930s. As a sister-group to their male counterparts, the Falcons, they represented finer young womanhood and embodied school spirit. Pictured here are Frances Cornish of the Redcoats and Joseph Sims of the Falcons. (Hilda Bulah Morris.)

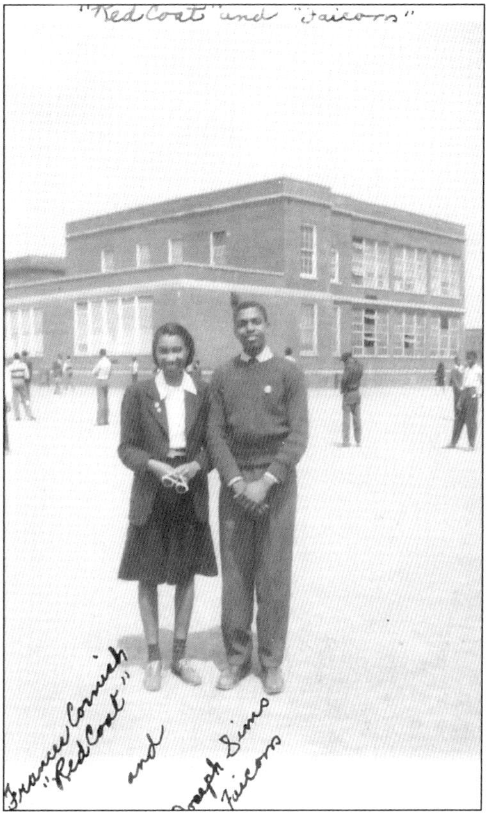

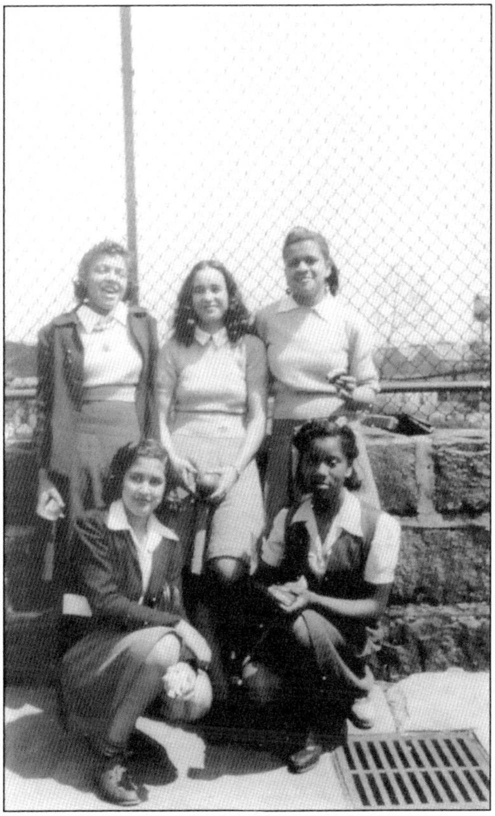

This photograph of the Redcoats was taken in 1942 at Howard High School. Two of the members are wearing their signature look—a red blazer. Pictured here are, from left to right, (first row, kneeling) Geraldine Hudson and Francis Cornish; (second row, standing) Loretta Kent and two unidentified underclass recruits. This photograph was taken by Redcoat upperclassman Hilda Bulah. (Hilda Bulah Morris.)

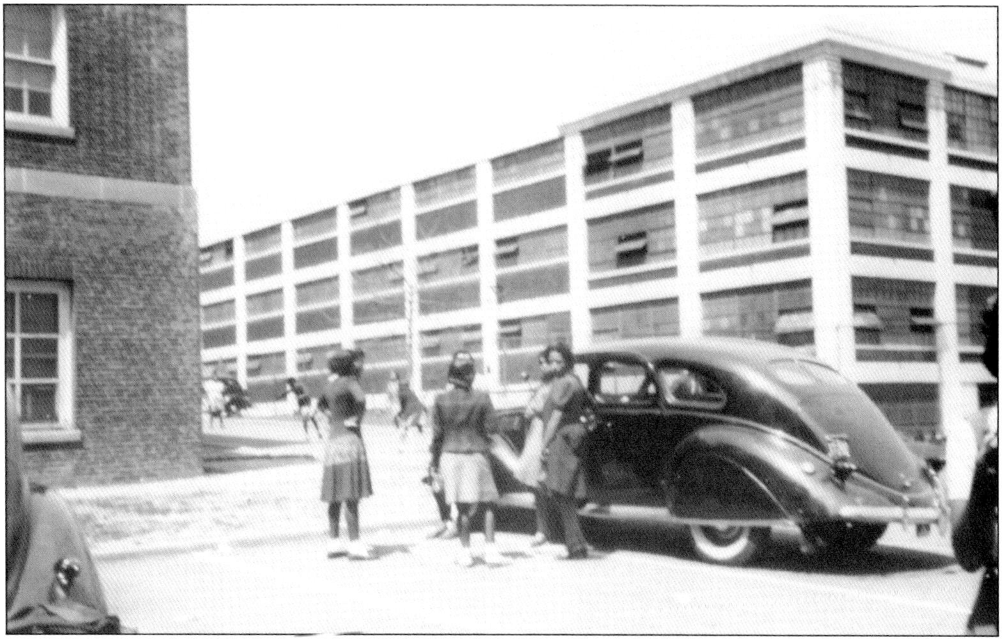

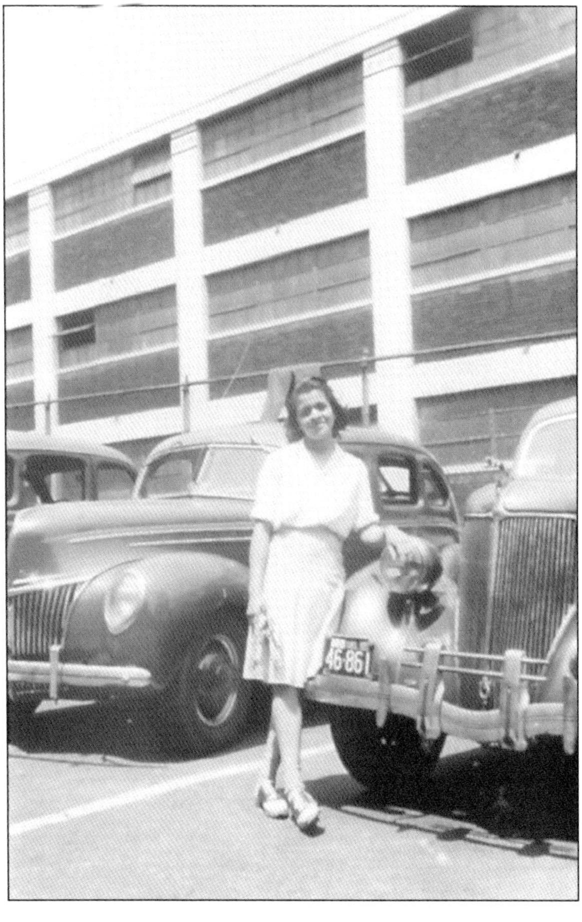

During midday lunch breaks, Howard High School students often gathered in the student parking lot to listen and dance to the latest tunes. Upcoming school activities were the focal points of conversation. The privilege of driving an automobile to school was one of the perks of being an upperclassman. (Hilda Bulah Morris.)

One of Hilda Bulah's closest friends, Geraldine "Teeny" Hudson, was the daughter of the head custodian at Howard High. Teeny is pictured standing next to her father's automobile. (Hilda Bulah Morris.)

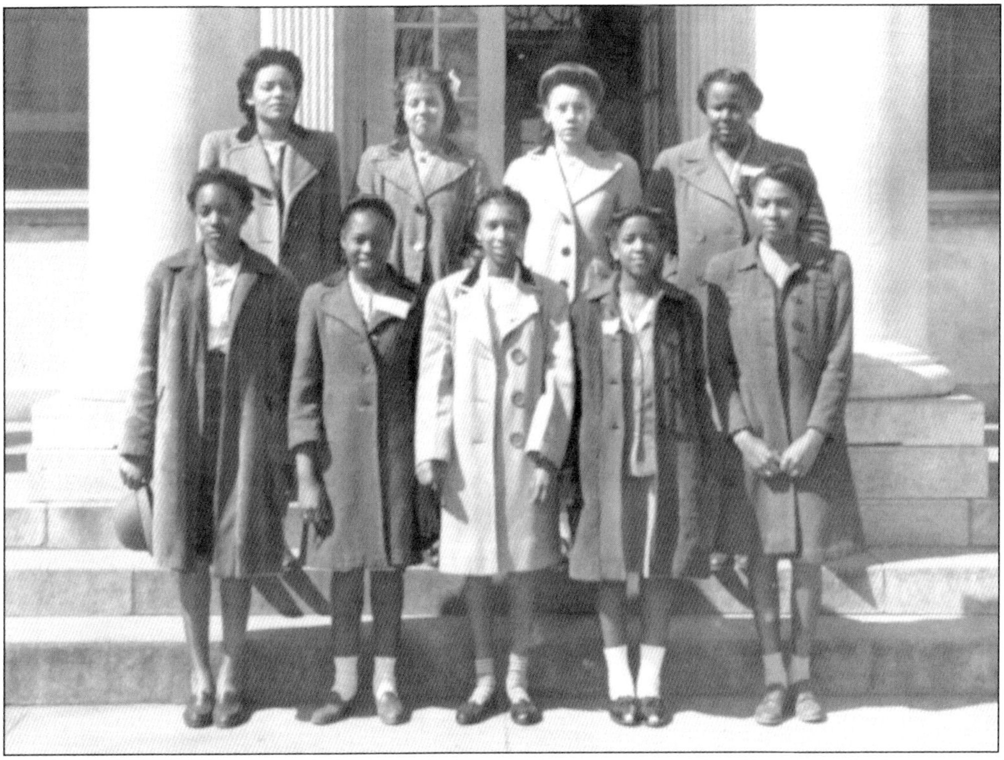

This collegiate female body of future teachers stood proudly before the doors of Conrad Hall at State College for Colored Students (now Delaware State University). For nearly six decades, this academic hub was the only facility available to colored students pursuing higher education in Delaware.

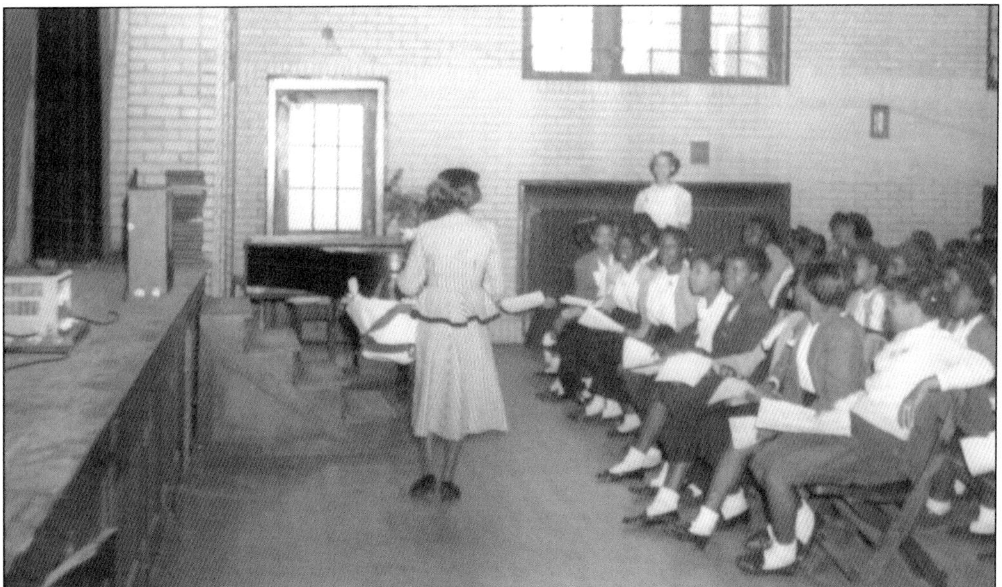

Donning business attire, two colored teachers assembled students for the dissemination of information. Collectively, they strategized methodologies to enrich the educational experiences of these young collegiate women.

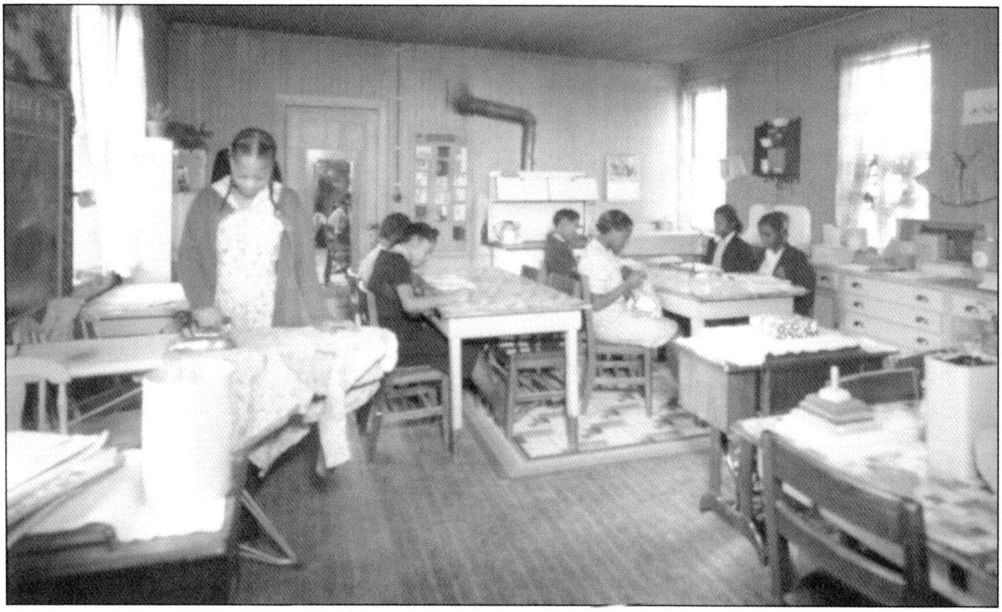

Students in home economics class studiously attended to their tasks, which including ironing, sewing, and needlepoint. Learning and mastering home maintenance was a generational tradition for girls in the colored community. The New Homemakers of America (NHA), founded in 1945 for colored girls, paralleled Future Homemakers of America for white girls. Originally established as segregated entities, the two merged in 1965 but retained the Future Homemakers of America name.

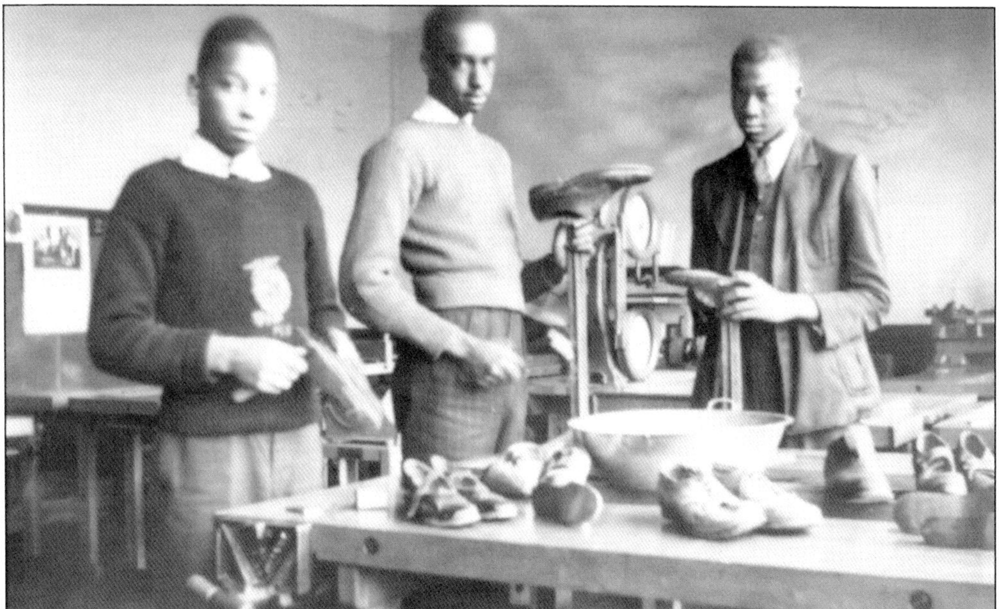

Three unidentified students are pictured honing their cobbler and shoe-repair skills as they utilize the shoe-lasting equipment. Shop class offered students an opportunity to acquire technical skills that provided the hands-on experience necessary for certifications and employment. In addition to completing traditional academic coursework, students becoming proficient in a trade was an essential part of the high school curriculum.

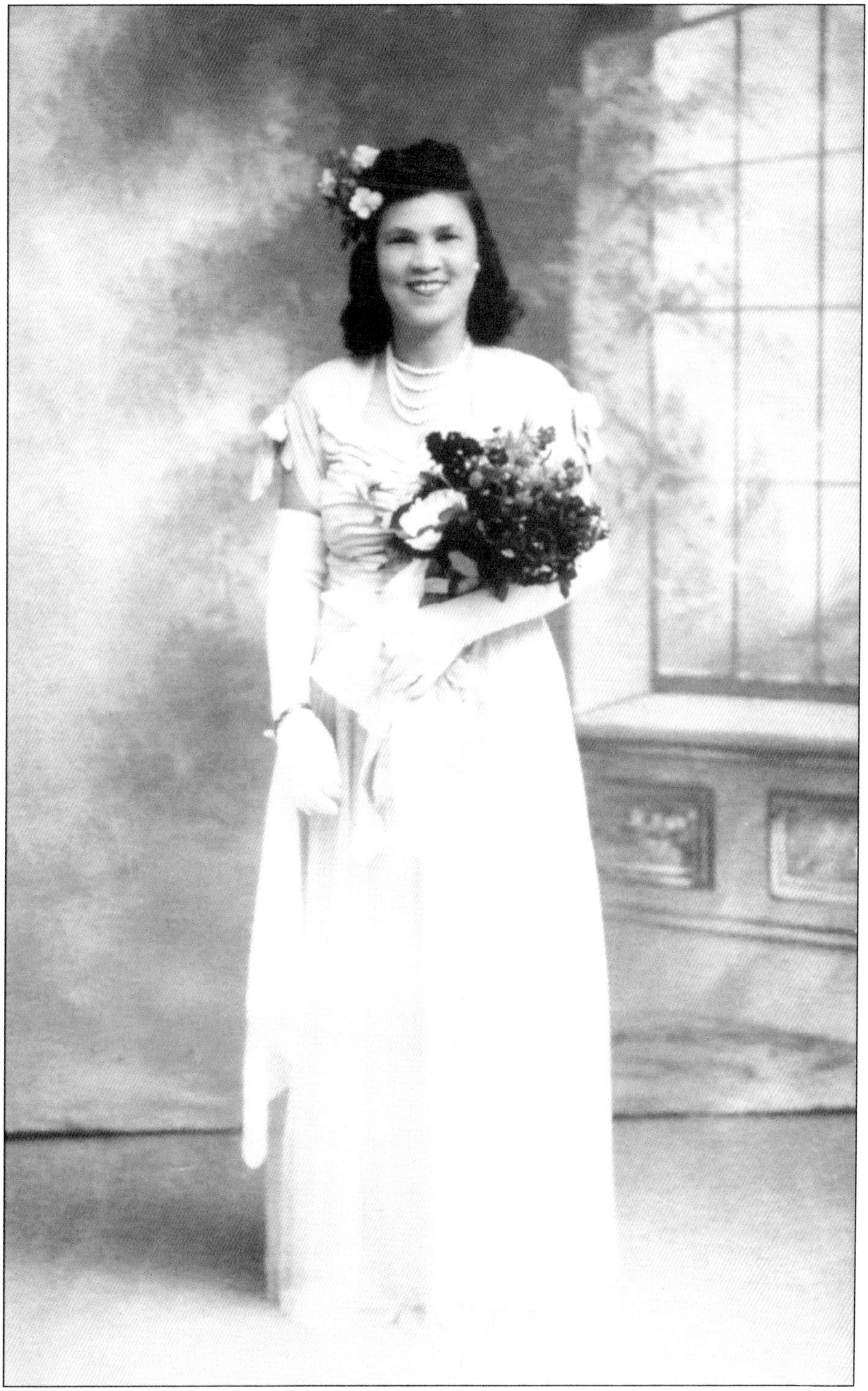

Lucille Fleming was a vision of loveliness in her white formal gown and gloves. Howard High School classmates raved about her ability to root any seed. She was the "green hand" of the horticulture society. She eventually married Elwood Fleming. (Hilda Bulah Morris.)

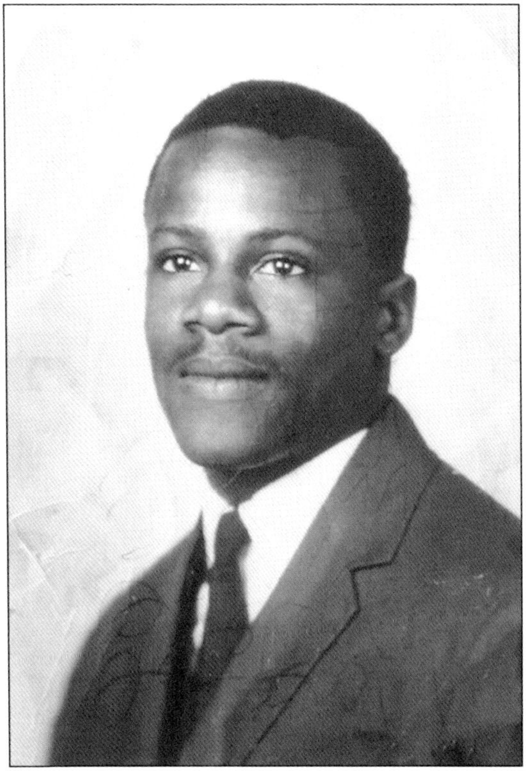

The Gray brothers attended Hockessin Colored School #107C from first through sixth grades. The eldest brother, Wilmer, entered #107C with classmates Lois Williams and LeRoy Peterson. After completing primary school, the Gray brothers attended Howard High School. Pictured are Reginald (left) and Stanley Gray (below), the younger brothers of Wilmer. These photographs were taken during their upperclassmen years at Howard High. Wilmer, Reginald, and Stanley are third-generation #107C attendees. Their grandfather was Herbert Carter, the father of Ethel Carter Gray. (Both, Charlotte Knott.)

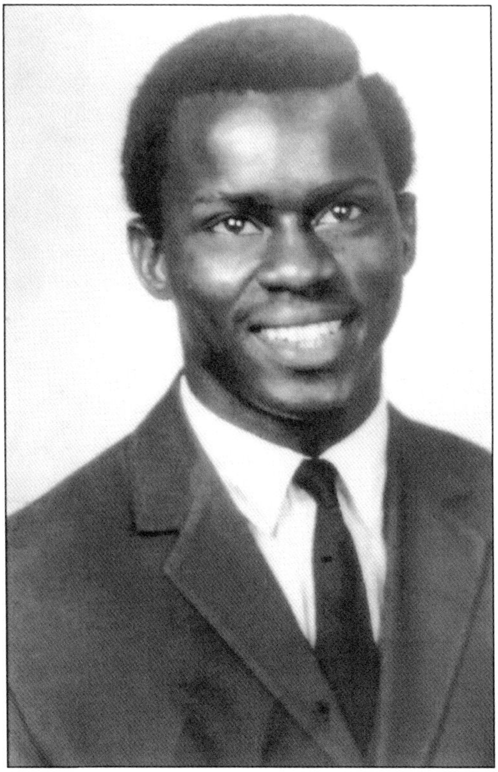

Romaine Harris and her brother Andrew "Mikey" Harris attended Hockessin #107C from first through sixth grades. They participated in school and community activities with their childhood friends and neighbors. Romaine and Charlotte Knott attended elementary, junior high, and high school together. Both ladies enrolled in the cosmetology program at Howard High School. Romaine is pictured during her underclassman years. Romaine and Charlotte remain the embodiment of "best friends forever." (Charlotte Knott.)

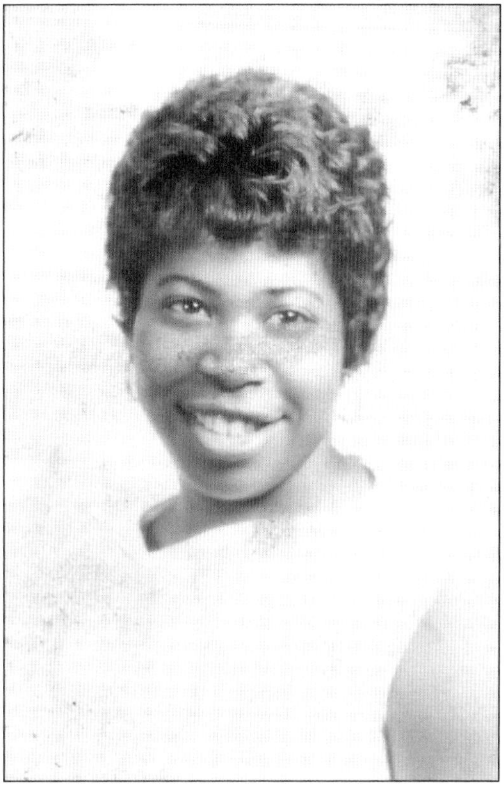

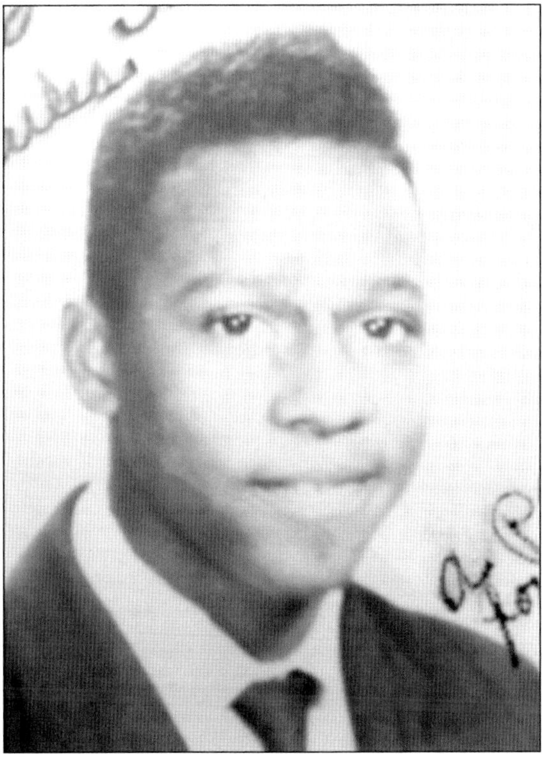

Charles "Charlie" Johnson is the Hockessin colored community's "Mister Baseball." A member of the largest Hockessin colored family, with over 25 members who attended #107C, Charlie and his siblings carry the mantel of their forefathers. Charlie attended first through sixth grade at #107C from 1949 to 1954. He was known to have the most important student responsibilities at the school—heating the furnace at the beginning of each school day, raising the flag, and hanging the chains for the swings. As a member of the school's Boy Scout troop No. 118, Charlie's attentive nature afforded him opportunities to learn by doing. After leaving #107C, Charlie attended Absalom Jones for junior high. He was among the first colored students from Hockessin to integrate Alexis I. duPont High School. This photograph shows Charlie Johnson as an underclassman attending Alexis I. duPont High School in the late 1950s. (Romaine Harris.)

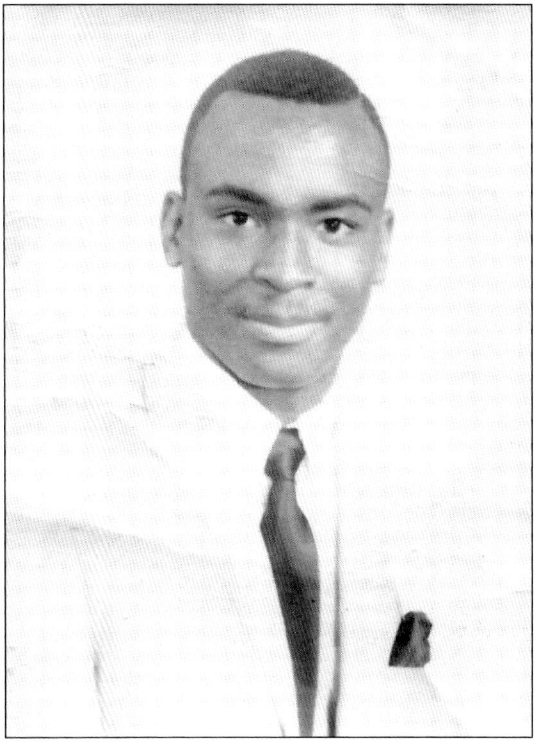

Walter "Mack" Macklin attended Hockessin Colored School #107C and Alexis I. duPont Junior and Senior High School with classmates Stanley Gray and Pia Peterson. This photograph shows Mack as an upperclassman in the late 1960s at Alexis I. duPont High School. After graduating high school, Mack attended Delaware State College, where he played baseball for four years. He graduated from Delaware State University in the class of 1975. (Walter Macklin.)

Charlotte Knott is the female personification of a colored student's educational journey before and after the school desegregation court cases at the state and federal levels. When Charlotte entered first grade at #107C, she sat in student desks that held memories of three generations of her family members. One of her classmates was Shirley Bulah. Charlotte and Shirley were among the fourth and final decade of students who attended Hockessin Colored School #107C. However, the duo would travel two significantly different school paths. After completing six years at #107C, Charlotte, with the support of her parents and family members, chose to attend Absalom Jones Junior High under the watchful eye of principal John Taliaferro. Charlotte continued the legacy of the Knott family and transitioned to Howard High School with classmates Margaret Johnson and Nancy Johnson. Charlotte graduated with the class of 1960, maintaining the Knott family tradition of being proud Howard wildcats. (Charlotte Knott.)

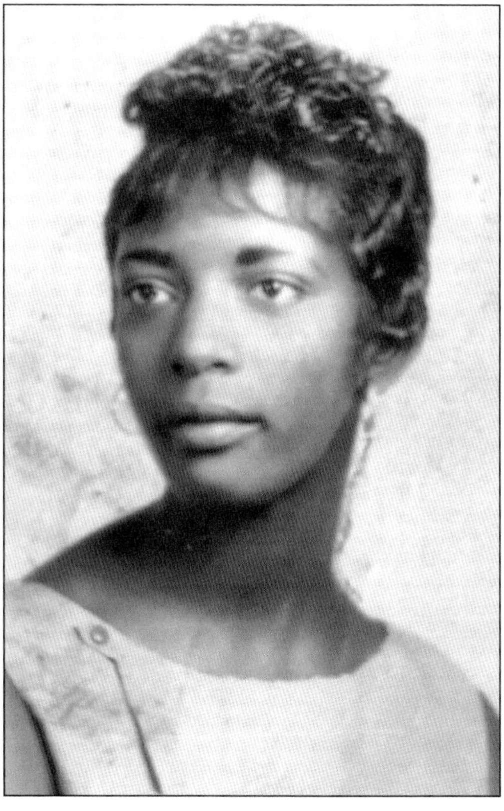

Six

The Bulahs of Hockessin

A Family of Advocates

Frederick Bewley was born on February 26, 1883, to Thomas Frederick Beuley and Emiline Beuley. He was welcomed by his older siblings Martha, Charlotte, Harriet, and David and followed in birth by Harry, Mary, Frank, and Ellen Hanna. By the end of the decade, the Bewley family had transitioned from Maryland to Delaware under variations of spellings of their surname, including Buly, Beuley, Beulah, and—ultimately—Bulah.

The family worked on several farms owned by Mitchell family members residing in Mill Creek Hundred. The patriarch of the Mitchell family, Thomas Mitchell, established roots in Hockessin in 1796. The Mitchells were owners of several tracts of land consisting of hundreds of acres. They secured operations of farms with the assistance of hired laborers, and among the laborers were members of the Bulah family. Collectively, the Bulahs benefited from the fruits of their labors, resulting in land acquisition and property ownership. Thomas Bulah and his wife, Emilee, and their children worked for J Howard Mitchell, Henry C. Mitchell, and Joseph Mitchell IV. The Bulahs' primary residence was located off Brackenville Road near Limestone Road.

At age 21, Fred Bulah married Ida Dorsey on June 18, 1906. Together, they parented several children—Addie, Thomas, Emily, Ardella, Delma, Johnny, and Freddie; they also raised one granddaughter named Hilda. On January 12, 1925, Fred purchased property on Limestone Road. He owned, farmed, and rented his land. He also worked as a laborer at National Vulcanized Fiber Mill in Yorklyn, Delaware. The Bulah children walked two miles to and from Hockessin Colored School #107C. This later became the impetus for the ground-breaking case *Bulah v. Gebhart* (1952). The State of Delaware became the catalyst, and Hockessin provided the alternative path.

Spurred by the wheel of time, the Bulahs of Hockessin embraced a standard of decency. The evolution of their surname became their testament of fortitude. For the Bulahs, sickness, death, marriage, adoption, racism, and even war meant one thing beyond the natural optics of life: change was inevitable.

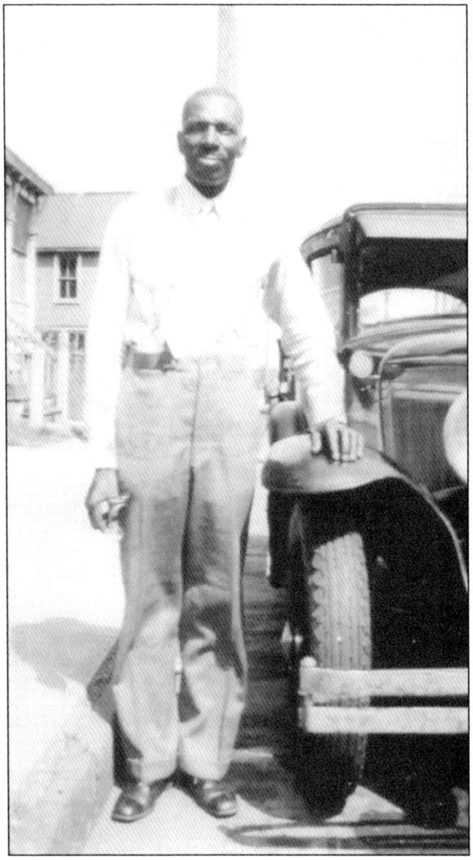

A man of few words, Fred Bulah maintained his family tradition of an honest day's work for an honest day's pay. Fred was a serious and sincere man. He taught himself to read and write and learned the trade of business through the admiration and trust of his employers. This photograph was taken around 1935 during a trip Fred took to Pennsylvania to visit with his brother Frank. Although he never attended Hockessin Colored School #107C, he and his sister Hattie Bulah Murry were financial contributors to the upkeep of the framed school for many years. Hattie occupied the old school building as her primary residence before purchasing a two-story house located across the field from the school. As history would have it, the Gebharts were the owners of the house purchased by Hattie and her husband, Virgil. The two families—Bulah and Gebhart—would become intertwined, as they were destined to meet again under different circumstances. (Hilda Bulah Morris.)

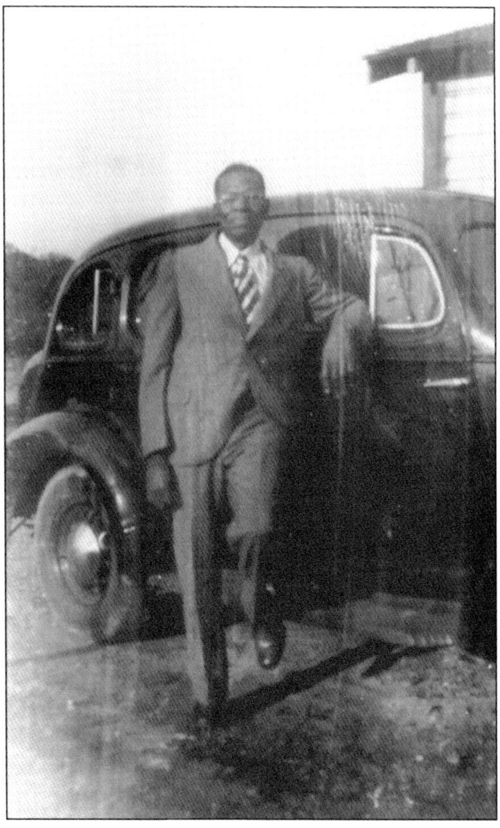

Fred Bulah became a property owner on January 23, 1925. He is pictured standing next to one of his automobiles parked in his driveway on the side of his home around 1935. (Hilda Bulah Morris.)

Ida Bulah, a domestic worker for the McVaugh family, was known for her kind and gentle demeanor. Fred and Ida (pictured standing next to Fred's car) parented several children. Here, the Bulahs are dressed in their Sunday best. Ida's sheer dress is adorned with a kitchen apron. This photograph was taken on the Bulah property as Ida paused her housekeeping activities to greet her husband. (Hilda Bulah Morris.)

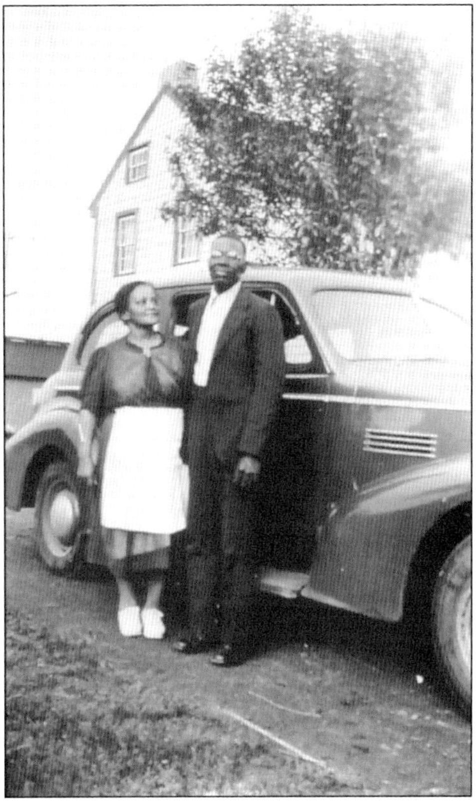

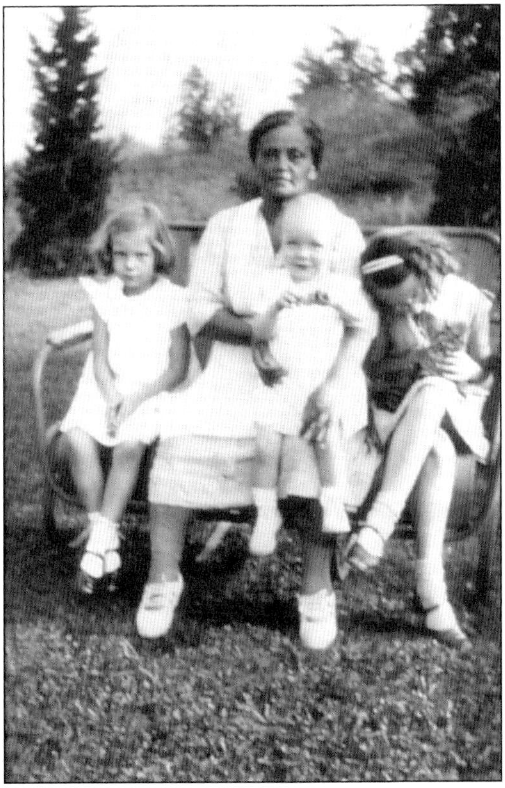

Ida Dorsey was born in November 1888 in Chester County, Pennsylvania. Raised by her parents, Ida attended elementary school in Kennett Square. She met Fred Bulah, who was a frequent visitor to the area. After marrying Fred, she moved to Hockessin, where she secured a position as a housekeeper and nanny for the McVaugh family. This picture was taken around 1930. (Hilda Bulah Morris.)

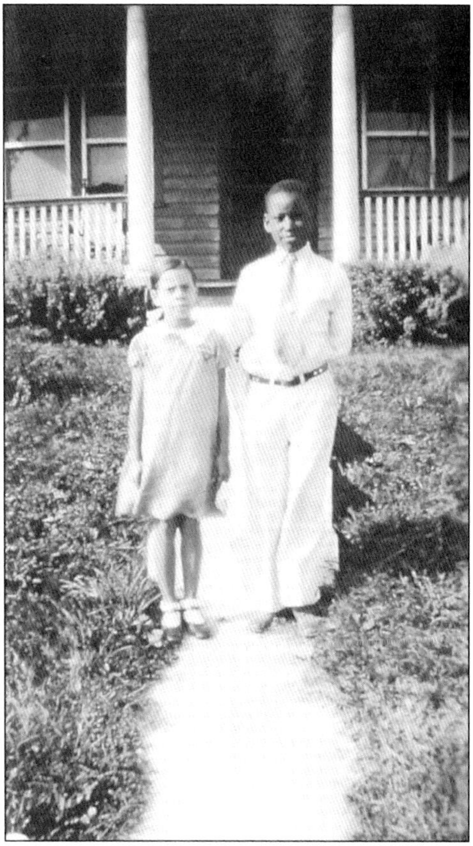

Hilda Bulah was four years younger than her uncle Freddie Bulah Jr. They were the best of buddies and great seekers of fun, frolic, and mischief. Pictured standing in front of their Hockessin home are Hilda (left), age 9, and Freddie, age 12. (Hilda Bulah Morris.)

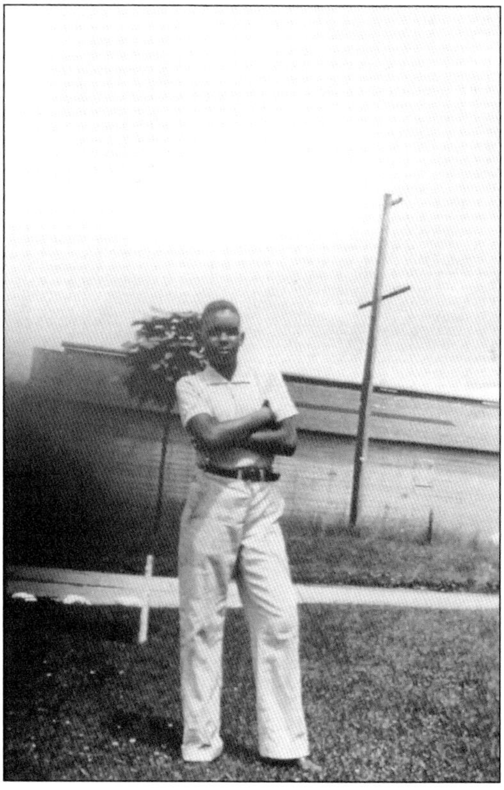

Many relatives visited the Bulah family. Some remained and provided extra support during the planting and harvest seasons. Among those who made Hockessin their home was Ida Bulah's nephew Johnny Dorsey. Of the Bulah children, Dorsey was closest in age to Freddie. He attended several years of schooling at Hockessin #107C, where he befriended classmate James Sonny Knott. Dorsey is pictured standing in the yard near the main house on the Bulah farm. (Hilda Bulah Morris.)

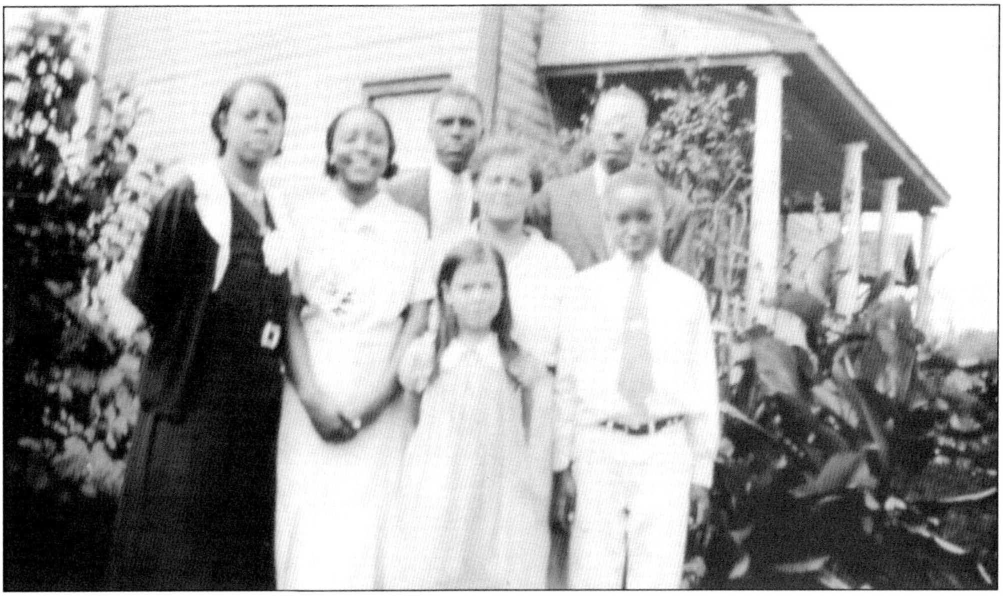

The Bulah family included children Addie, Tom, Ardella, Emily, Delma, Freddie, and the oldest grandchild, Hilda, daughter of Addie. All of the Bulah children attended Hockessin Colored Schools. Delma passed away within the first year of her life. Emily passed away shortly after completing her primary studies at #107C. Pictured here are, from left to right, (first row) Hilda and Freddie; (second row) Mary, Ardella, and Ida; (third row) Tom and Fred. (Hilda Bulah Morris.)

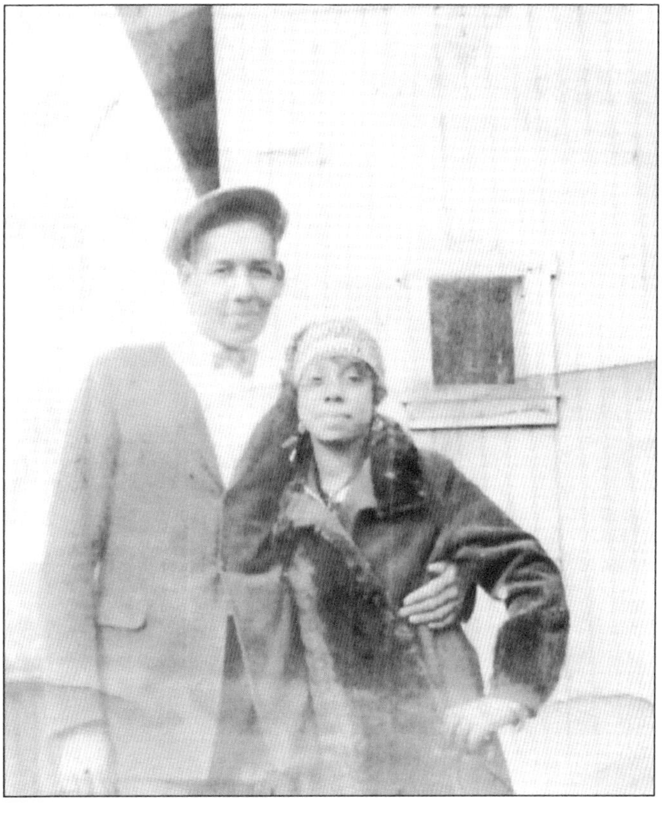

Pictured is the oldest of the Bulah children, Addie Bulah, and her husband, Horace Bostic Sr. Addie attended the wooden frame Hockessin #107C and later became a talented seamstress in Philadelphia, where she worked in the tailor shop owned by her aunt Anna. (Hilda Bulah Morris.)

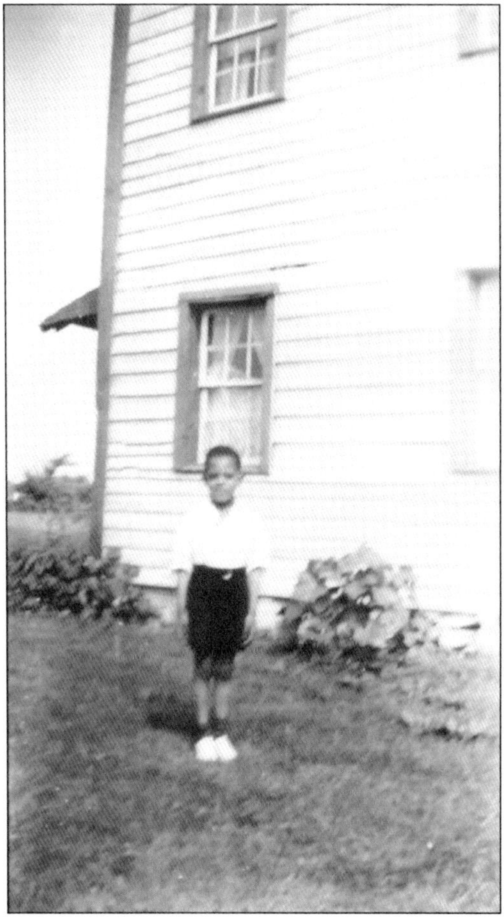

Horace Bostic Jr. spent most of his days with his parents and fraternal grandparents. Both resided in Philadelphia, Pennsylvania. Excited to visit his older sibling Hilda, young Horace enjoyed the hustle and bustle of life on the family farm with chickens, two pigs, a milking cow, two plow steers, and two horses. (Hilda Bulah Morris.)

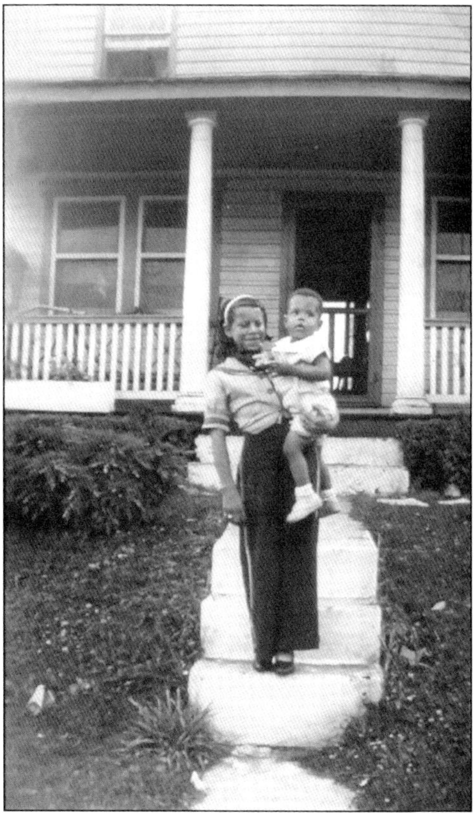

Pictured here with baby Horace Bostic Jr., Hilda Bulah posed for the camera in front of the Bulah home on Limestone Road in Hockessin. (Hilda Bulah Morris.)

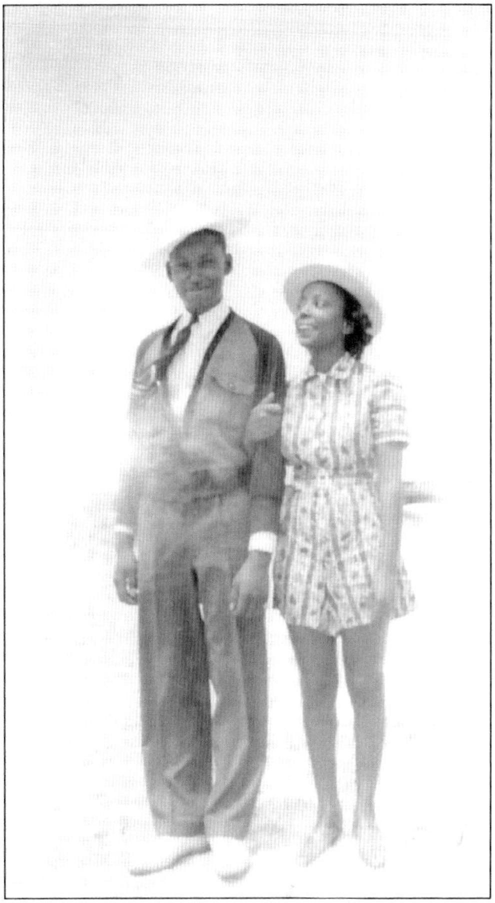

Hockessin colored families found summer employment as domestic workers for white families traveling to local beaches. It was common for entire colored families to work for hire during summer vacation months. In the below photograph, Ida Bulah (center) posed with her daughters Addie (left) and Ardella as they admired the freedom of relaxation at the New Jersey shore. In the image at right, Ardella joined her younger brother Freddie to take in the sights of ocean waves and games along the boardwalk in Wildwood, New Jersey. Not pictured is Hilda Bulah, who was the designated photographer for this outing. (Hilda Bulah Morris.)

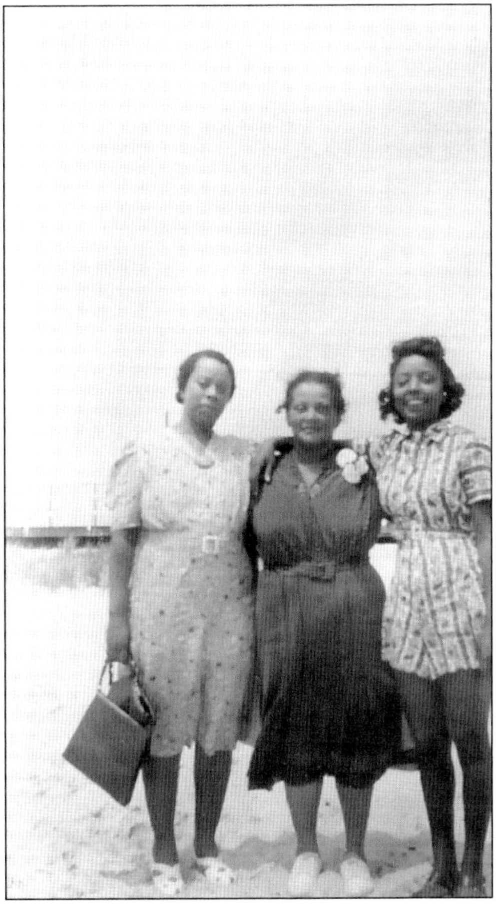

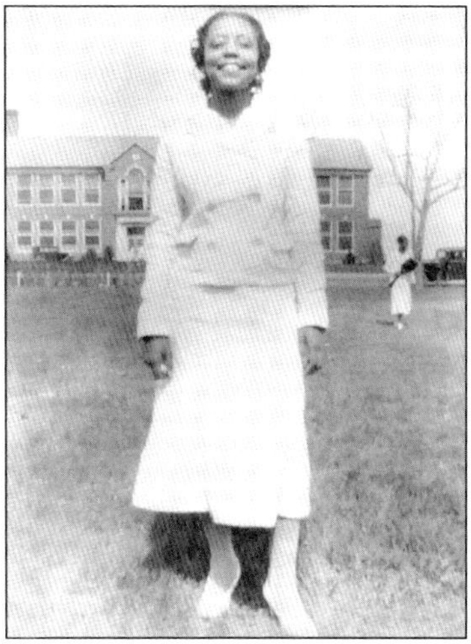

Ardella Bulah was a proud graduate of the Howard High School class of 1932. She attended the State College for Colored Students (now Delaware State University), where she earned a degree in education. (Hilda Bulah Morris.)

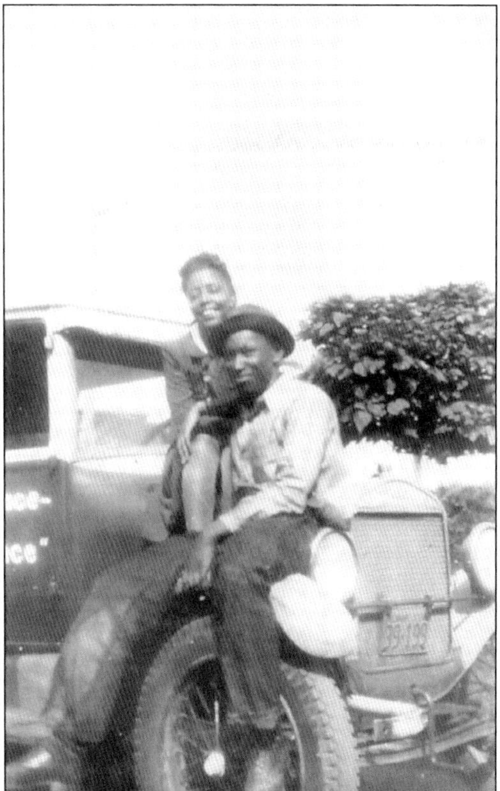

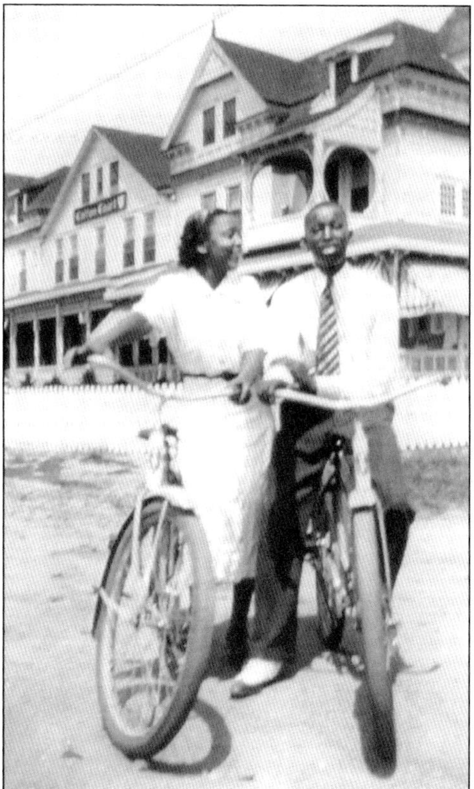

In the image at left, siblings Ardella and Freddie Bulah enjoy a happy moment while sitting on Freddie's automobile, "Leaping Lena." Freddie purchased the Model T from his aunt Hattie Bulah Murry. Although riding bikes was an enjoyable experience for Ardella and Freddie, the automobile was the preferred method of travel for fun outings to places like the movie theater and the roller-skating rink in Kennett Square, Pennsylvania. The owners of the skating rink allowed colored people to skate at their establishment only on Sundays. At right, Ardella and Freddie are riding bicycles together during their downtime. Ardella was a summer attendant for the children of the Schneider family, who resided on Broom Street in Wilmington, Delaware. (Both, Hilda Bulah Morris.)

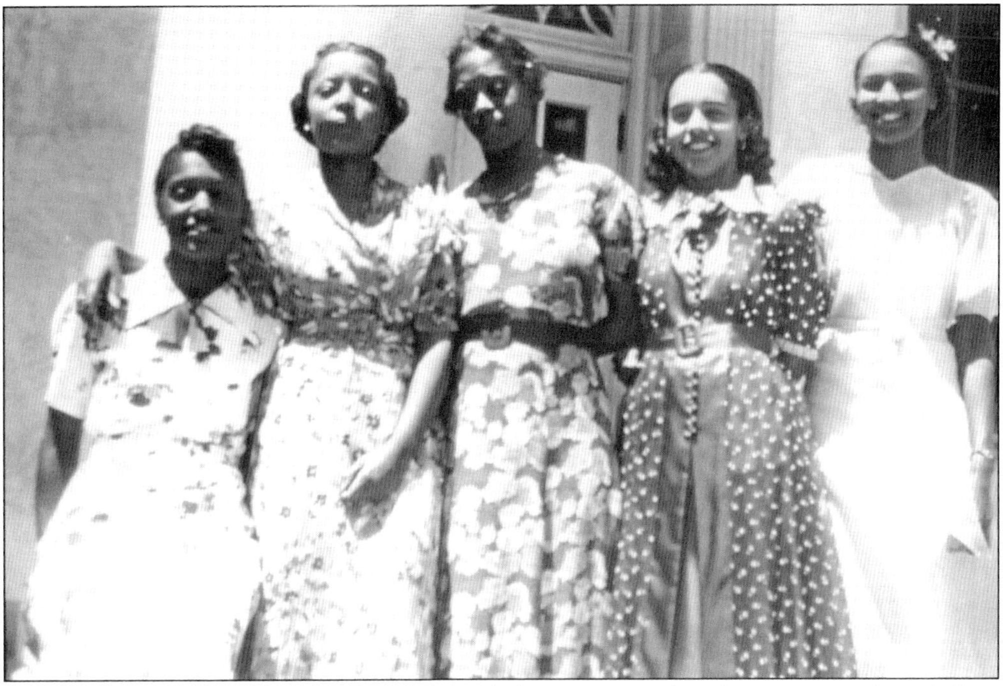

Above, Ardella Bulah (second from left) poses with dormitory friends and roommates at State College for Colored Students (now Delaware State University). Below, Ardella (visible near the bottom of the image in the center foreground) and her classmates celebrate their wonderful achievements as the class of 1936. (Both, Hilda Bulah Morris.)

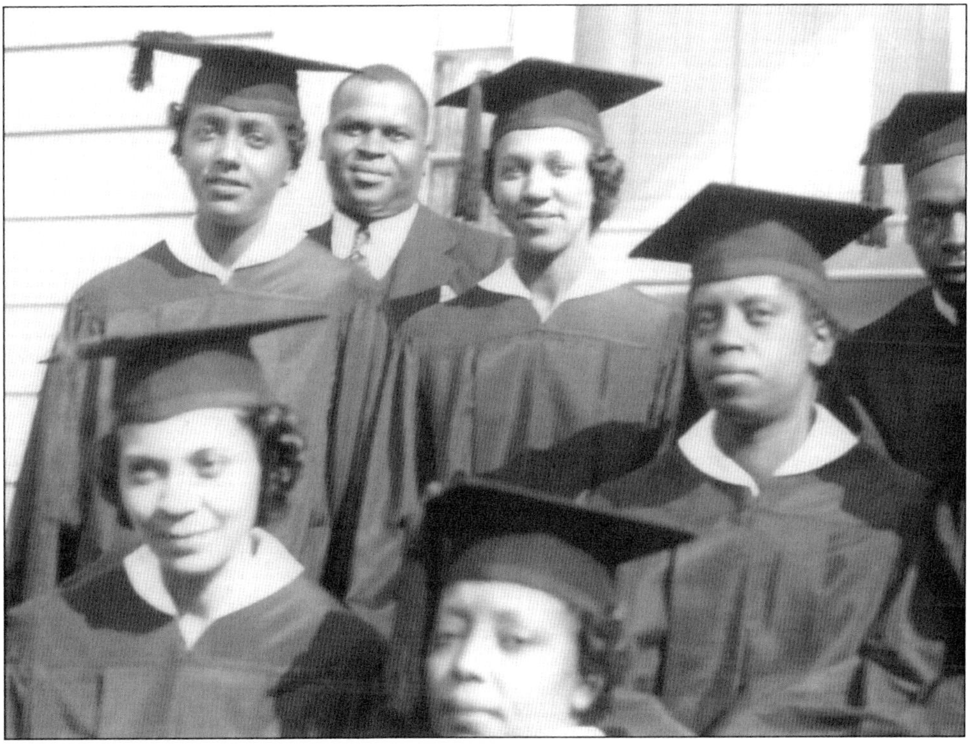

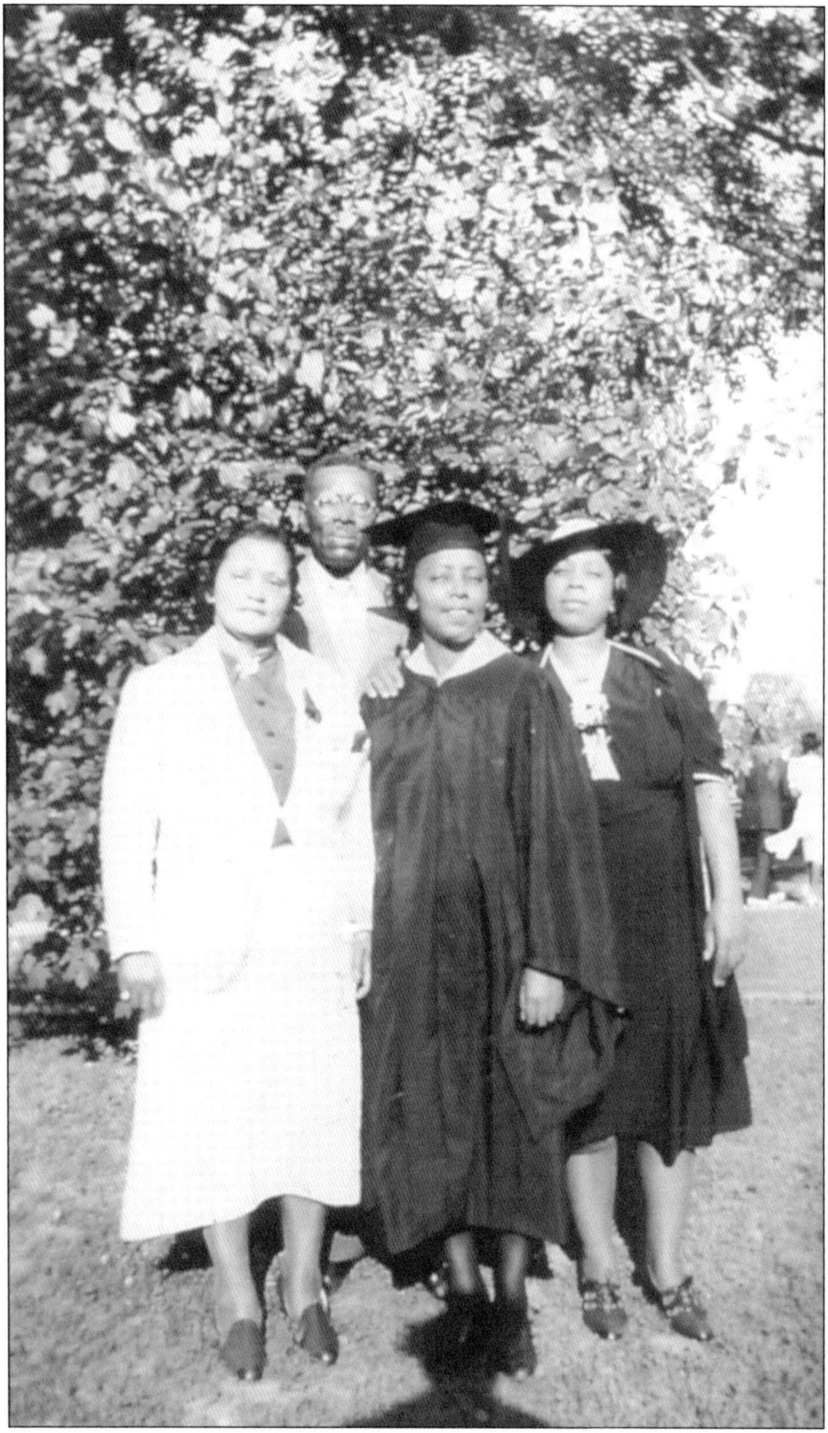

Pictured at Ardella Bulah's college graduation ceremony are, from left to right, Ida, Fred, Ardella, and Addie Bulah. After graduating, Ardella became a teacher in lower Delaware (Sussex County), where she briefly lived before returning to Hockessin to become a caretaker for her ailing mother, Ida. (Hilda Bulah Morris.)

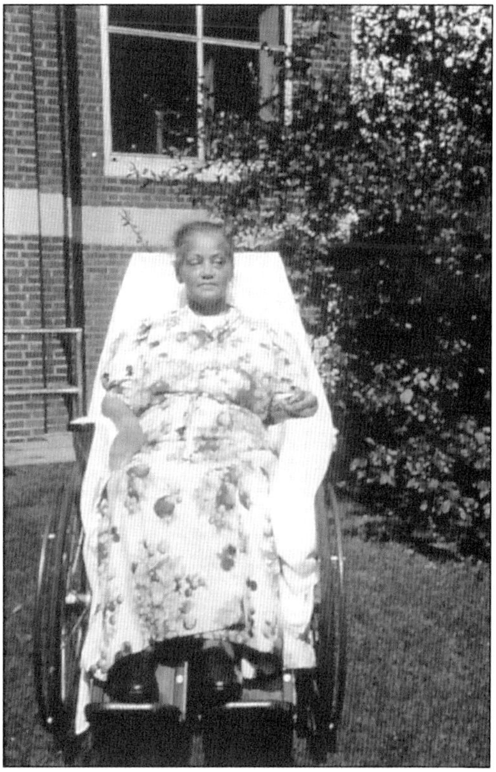

After Ida Bulah was diagnosed with a terminal illness, her health began to deteriorate. However, according to Hockessin residents, Ida's kind eyes, warm heart, and gentle spirit remained intact. Below, Ida is receiving well wishes from her children Ardella and Freddie during a family weekend visitation at Wilmington Memorial Hospital. Ida succumbed to her illness in November 1941. (Both, Hilda Bulah Morris.)

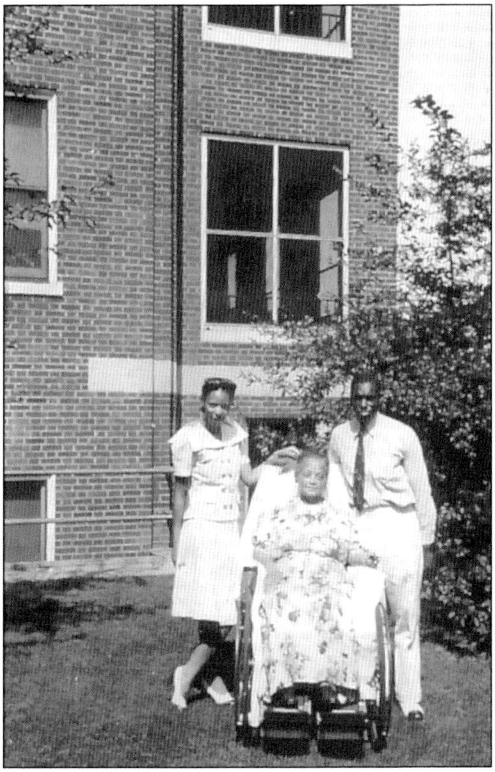

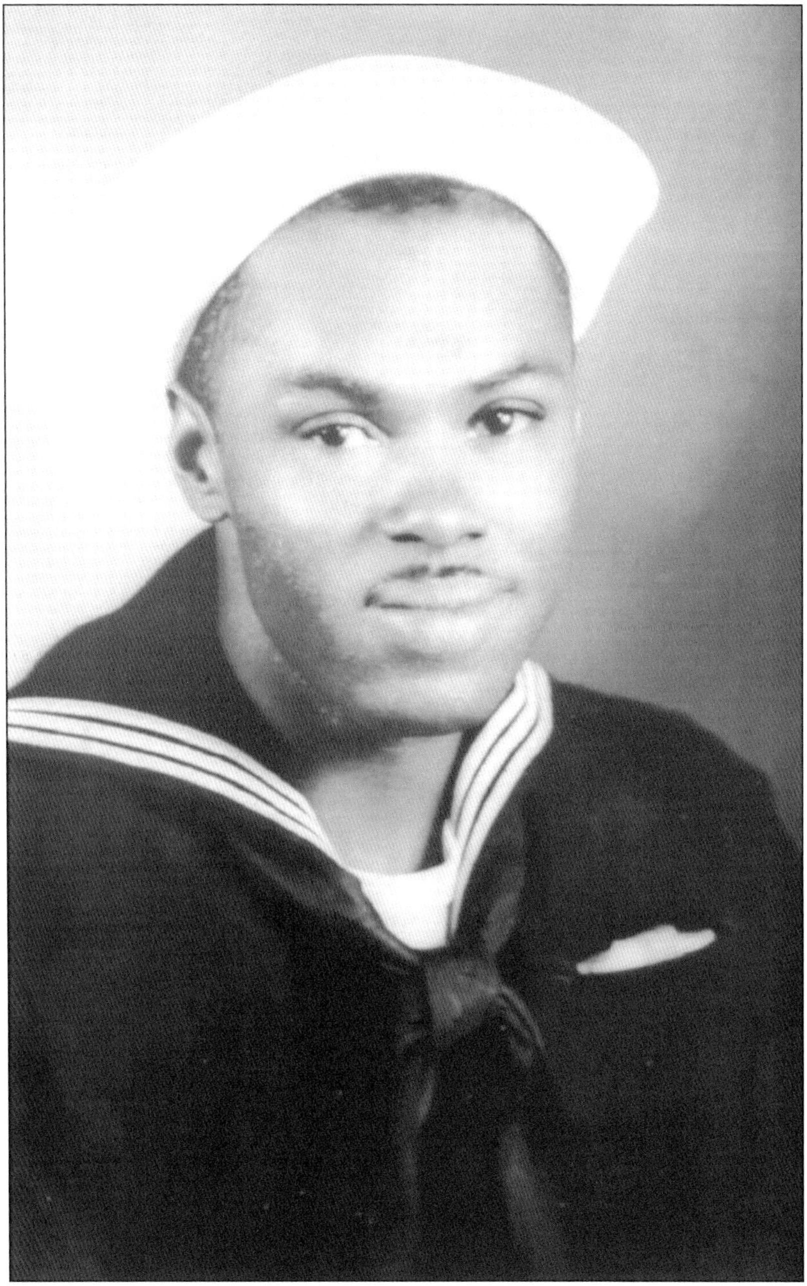

Thomas "Tom" Bulah was the eldest male child of Fred and Ida Bulah. Named after his grandfather, Tom was born and raised in Hockessin. He attended Hockessin #107C in the wooden framed school building. Tom began working with his father at the mills in Yorklyn until an unfortunate mill accident resulted in him being severely injured. After healing from a broken leg and other injuries, Tom departed Vulcanized Fiber Mill and secured employment with Arctic Roofing in Edgemore, Delaware. After graduating from Howard High School, he enlisted in the US Armed Services in March 1944. Tom's rank was steward's mate first class. He was assigned to the Carrier Aircraft Service Unit 64 in Fleet Port in San Francisco, California. After receiving an honorable discharge, Tom returned and worked at Arctic Roofing until his retirement. (Hilda Bulah Morris.)

After the war, Tom Bulah utilized his skills to assist his fellow neighbors by organizing and chartering the first—and only—all-colored fire department in the State of Delaware. He dedicated many years of service to the Belvedere Volunteer Fire Company, which serviced surrounding colored communities. In March 1951, Tom was appointed chief of the Belvedere Fire Company. Tom Bulah's automobile was equipped with a standard fire alarm siren and flashing lights. (Hilda Bulah Morris.)

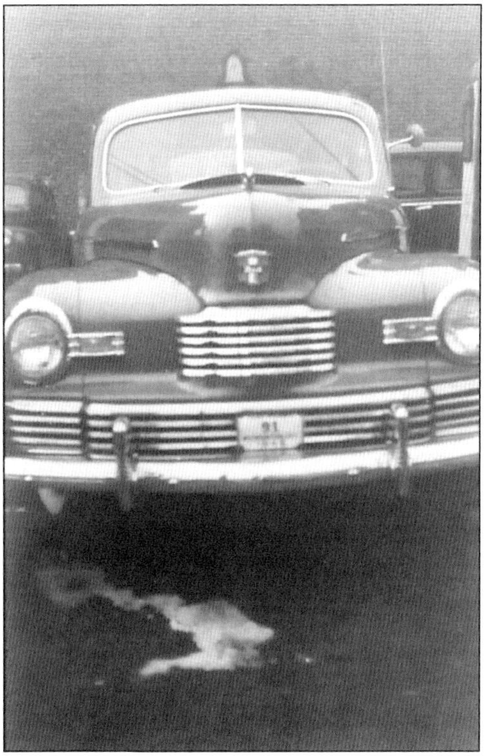

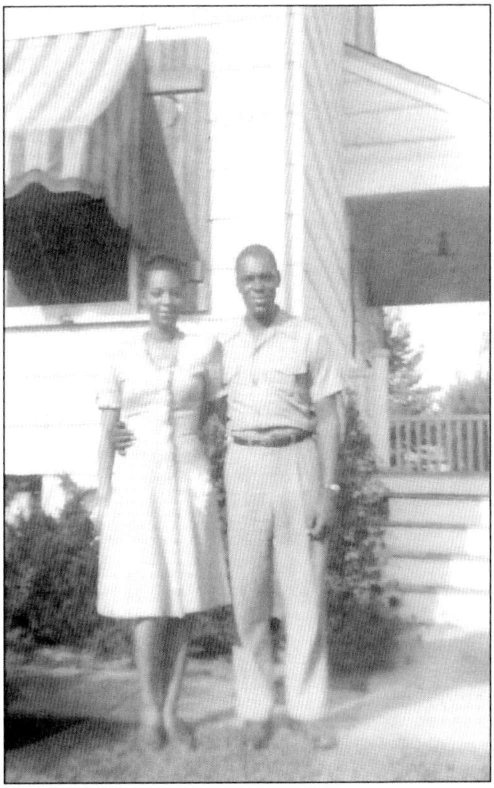

Tom Bulah is pictured here with his wife, Marie. This photograph was taken at their home in Belvedere in the summer of 1951. (Hilda Bulah Morris.)

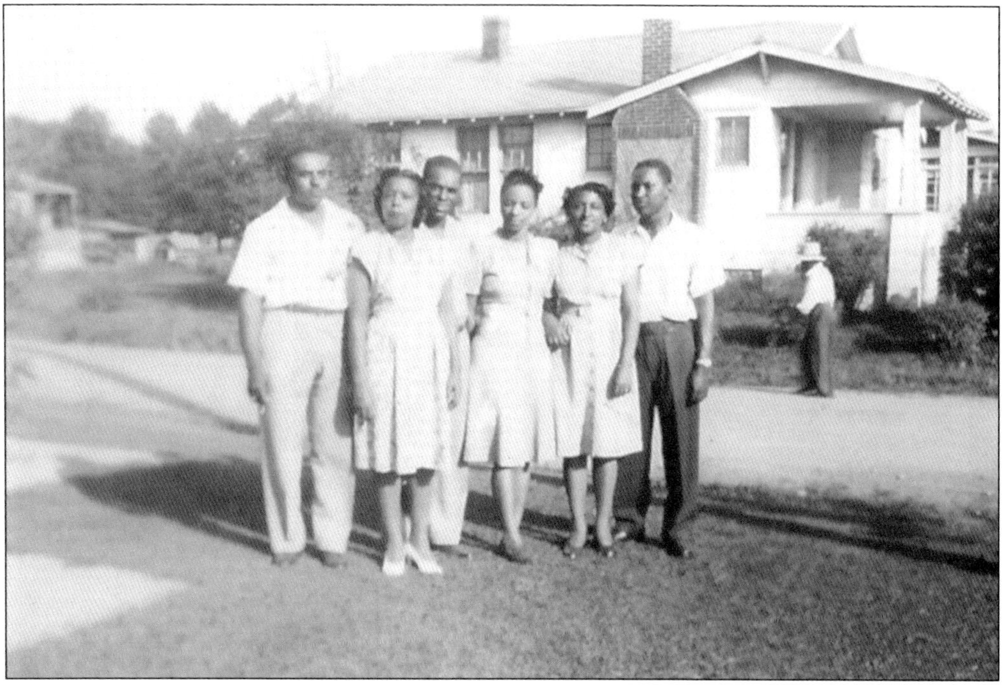

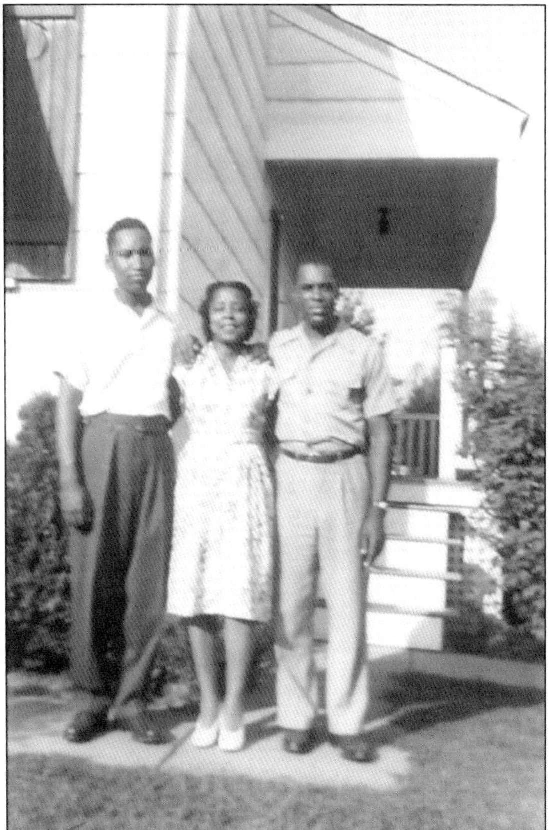

Spring was especially fun for the Bulah family. The Bulah siblings are pictured above at Tom Bulah's home with their spouses. From left to right are Floyd and Ardella Marshall, Tom and Marie Bulah, and Ruth and Freddie Bulah. This picture was taken in Belvedere, Delaware, in the spring of 1952. (Hilda Bulah Morris.)

Posing for the camera is a trio of Bulah siblings—Freddie (left), Ardella (center), and Tom. (Hilda Bulah Morris.)

An avid outdoorsman, Freddie is pictured with his wife, Ruth, as they enjoyed one of their favorite pastimes—fishing. (Hilda Bulah Morris.)

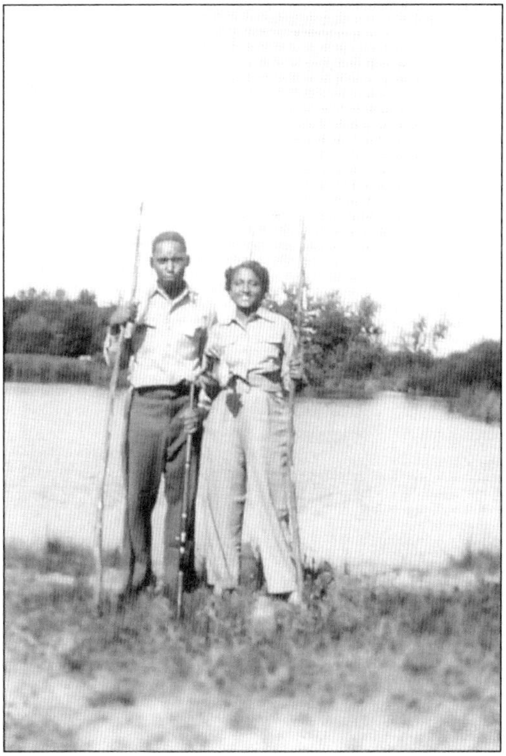

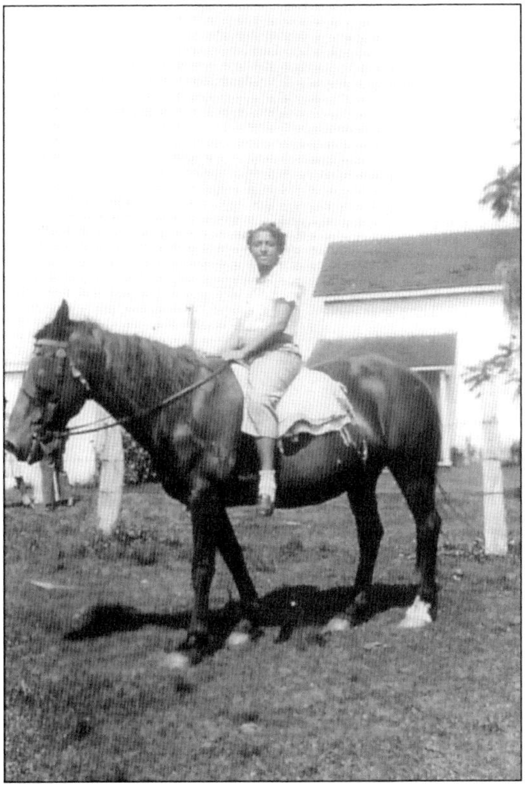

Freddie Bulah met his match in Ruth, who was known to have a fondness for animals. Here, Ruth is sitting atop Mabel, one of the Bulah farm mares. (Hilda Bulah Morris.)

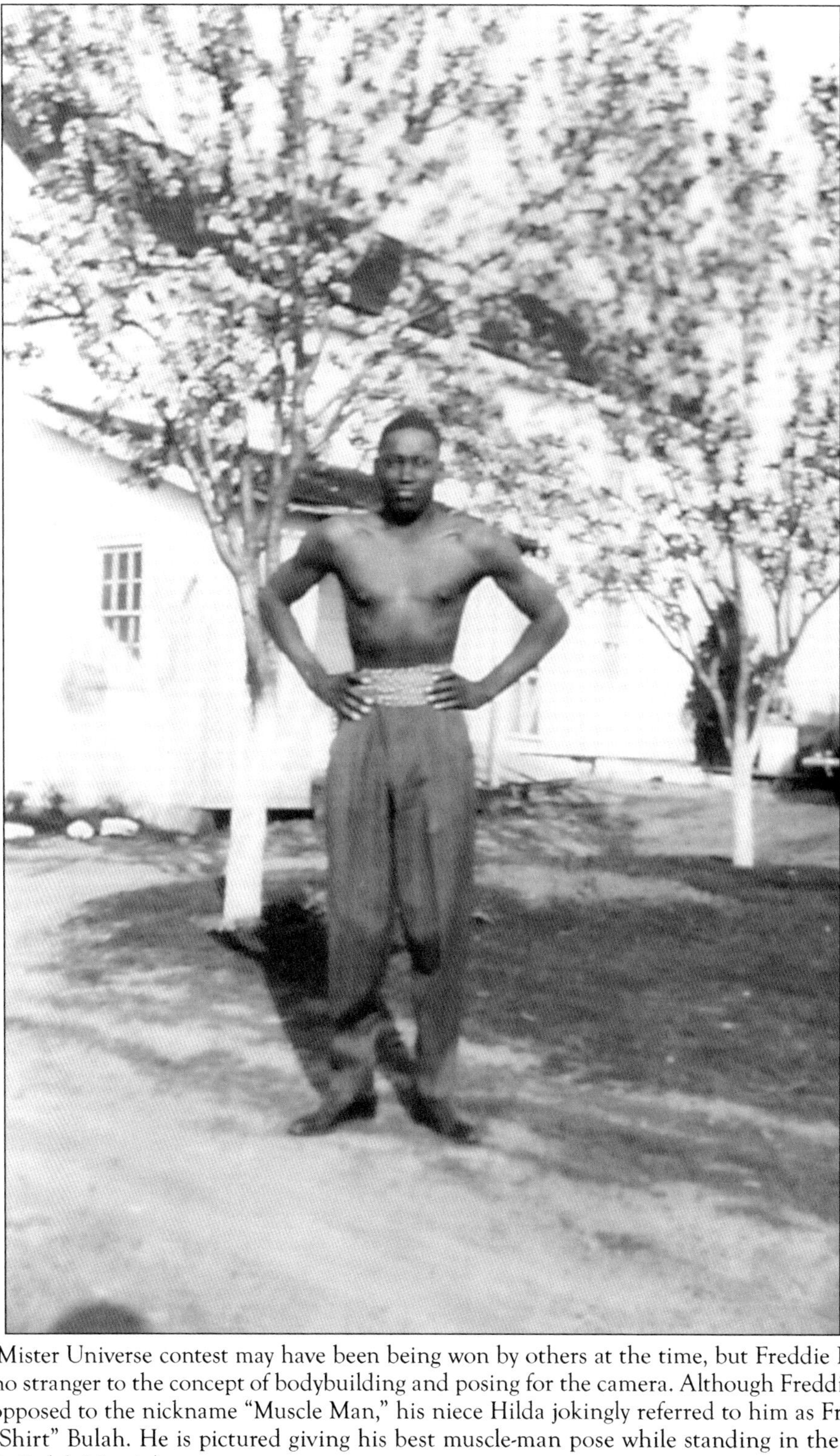

The Mister Universe contest may have been being won by others at the time, but Freddie Bulah was no stranger to the concept of bodybuilding and posing for the camera. Although Freddie was not opposed to the nickname "Muscle Man," his niece Hilda jokingly referred to him as Freddie "No Shirt" Bulah. He is pictured giving his best muscle-man pose while standing in the yard. (Hilda Bulah Morris.)

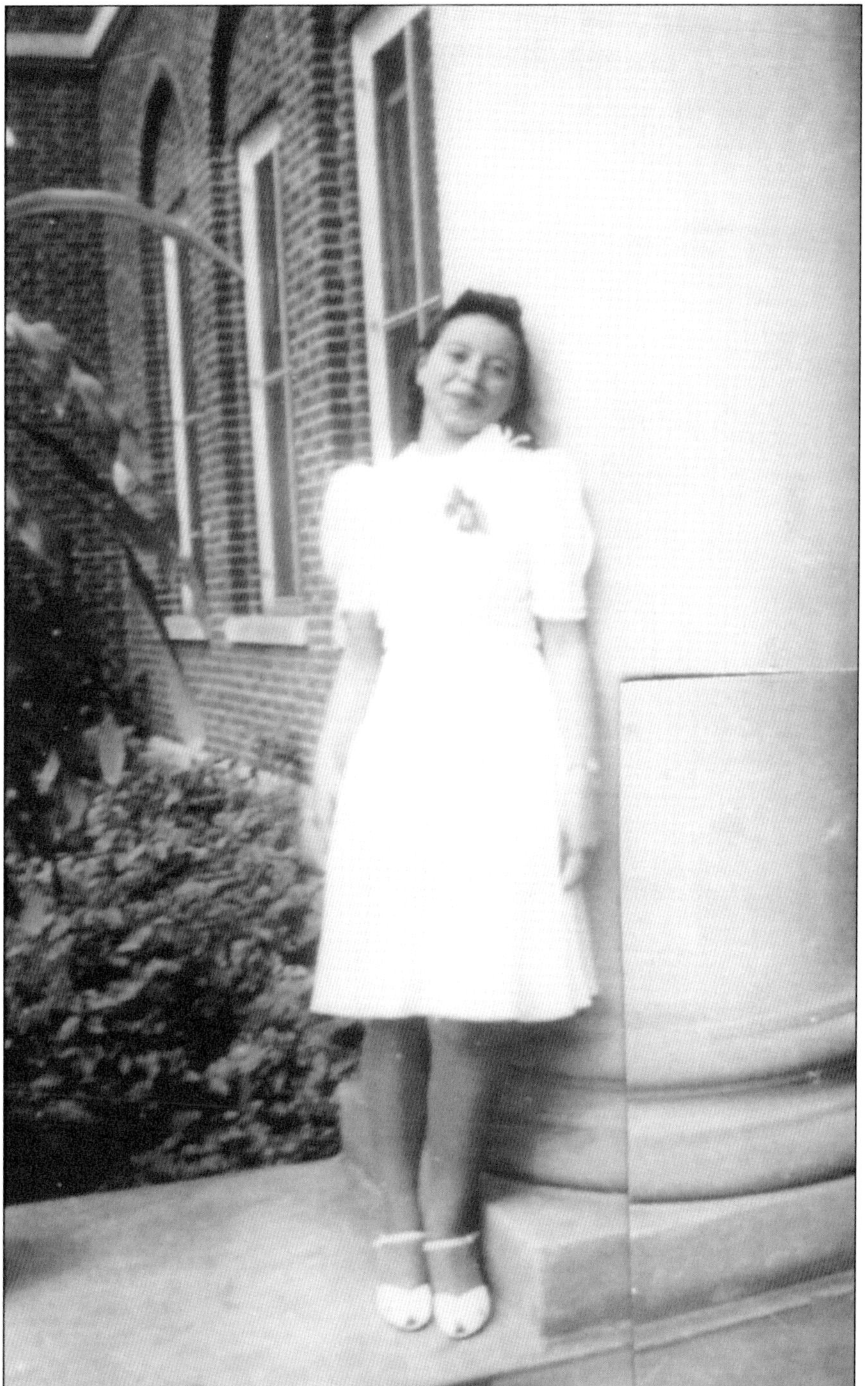

Hilda Octavia Bulah posed as a proud graduate of Howard High School on June 5, 1943, at the height of the United States involvement in World War II. According to local newspapers, the message for the newest graduates included a resounding farewell and well wishes for those charged to move "Forward with Democracy." (Hilda Bulah Morris.)

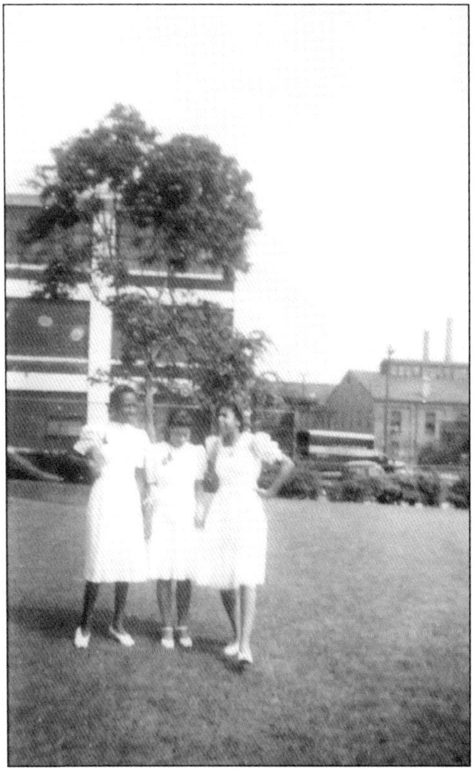

Classmates Dorothy Johnson (left) and Edna Talbot (right) joined Hilda Bulah in a celebratory stroll after their 1943 graduation ceremony on the grounds of Howard High School. (Hilda Bulah Morris.)

Fourteen-year-old Hilda Bulah ascended the ramp outside of Howard High School as she went for a midday stroll while class was in recess. (Hilda Bulah Morris.)

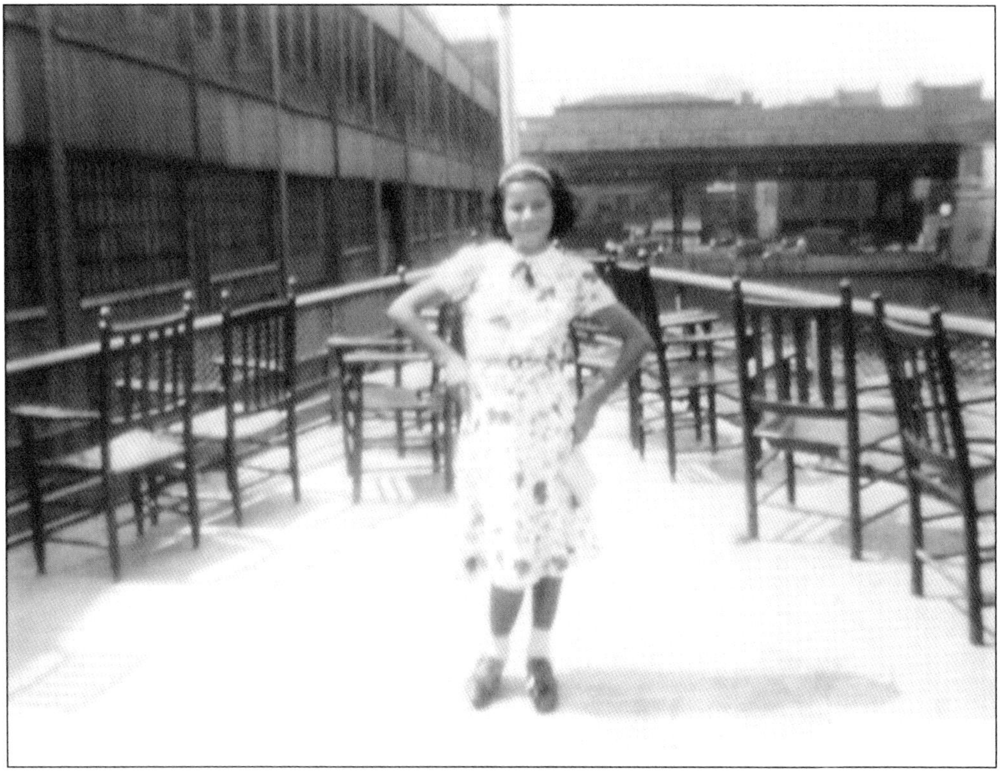

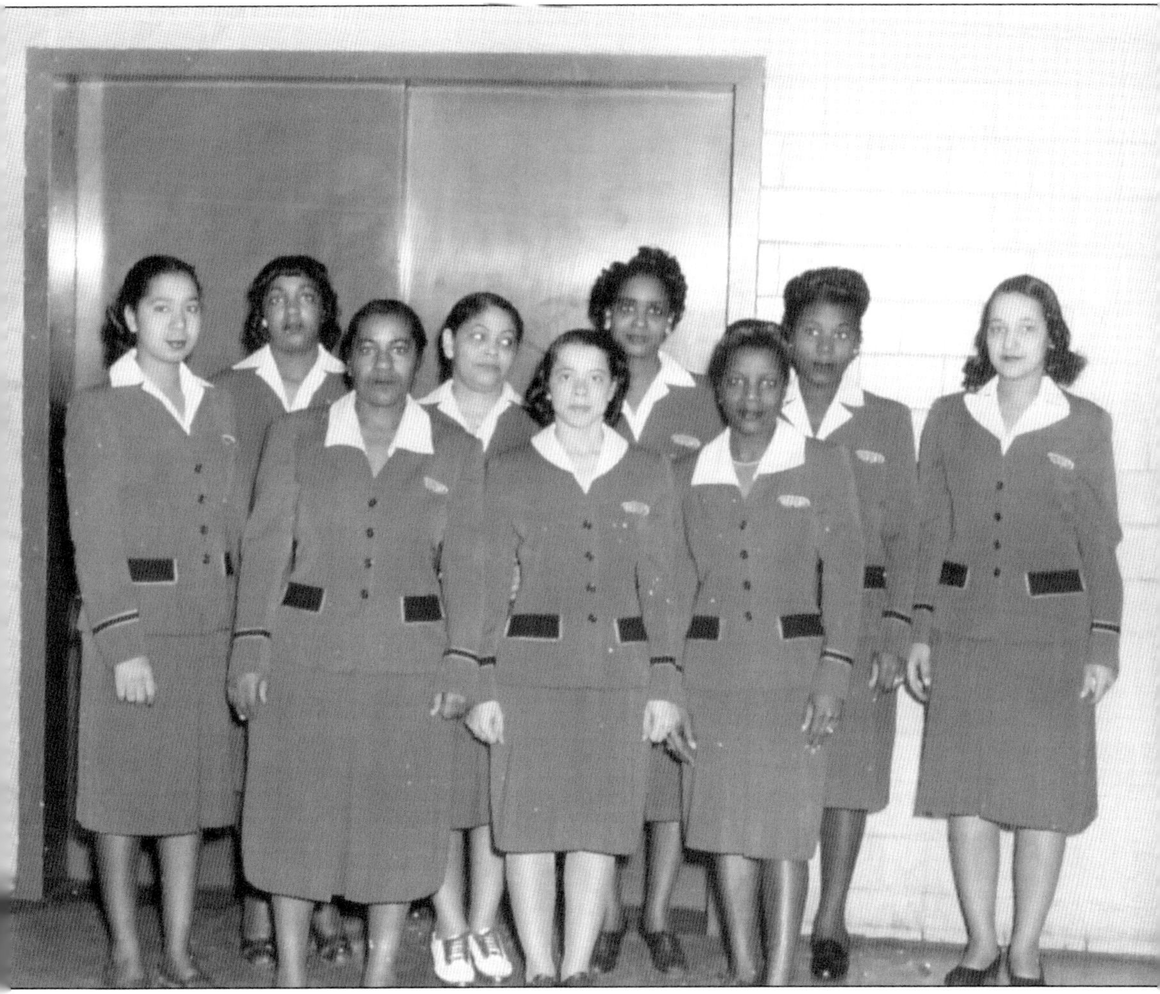

After graduation, Hilda Bulah put her vocational skills to task and secured a job with the DuPont Company. Initially employed with the ammunition corps, Hilda spun silk thread at the silk mill in New Castle. The threads were used to create parachutes for US paratroopers during World War II. After the war, Hilda was hired and selected as the newest member of the exclusive colored elevator operators for the DuPont Company. Pictured here in her uniform (the traditional color of "duPont blue"), Hilda is front and center. This picture was taken in 1947 at DuPont Company headquarters in Rodney Square in Wilmington, Delaware. (Hilda Bulah Morris.)

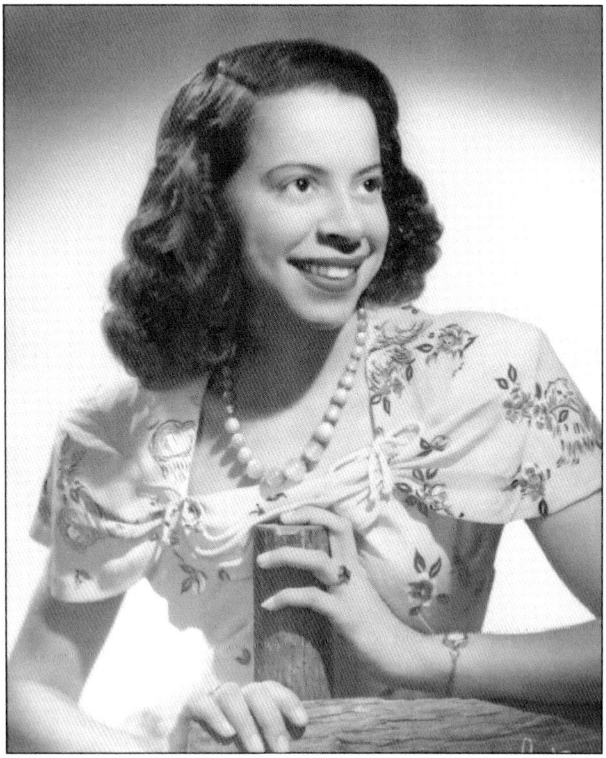

Looking to secure housing closer to her new place of employment, Hilda became a tenant in a flat on Twelfth and Tatnall Streets. She captured the eye of a sailor who had recently returned from the war. Wearing a pink floral dress with her signature ruby birthstone ring, Hilda smiled for the camera in this picture taken in commemoration of her 25th birthday, which she celebrated on July 18, 1948. (Hilda Bulah Morris.)

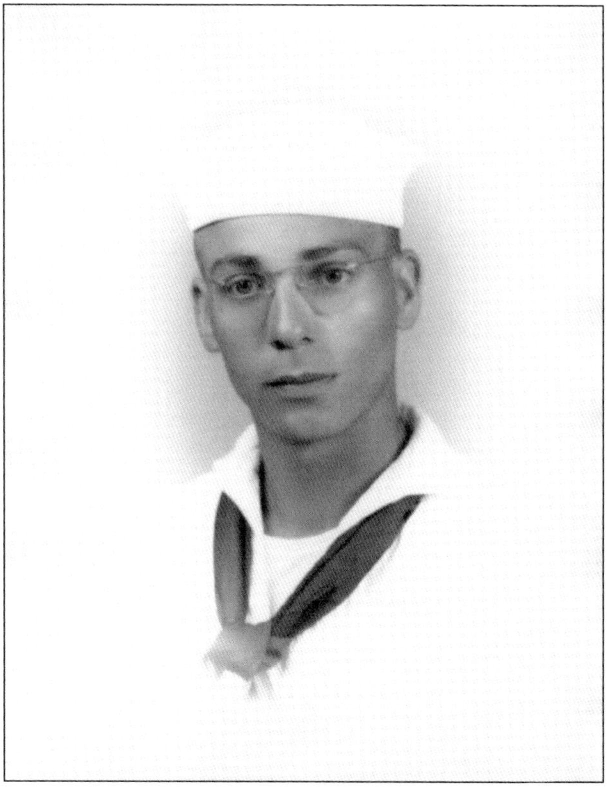

Born in Spottsylvania County, Virginia, Lloyd Morris learned at an early age the meaning of hard labor as he worked in his father's sawmill. He jumped at the chance to leave the mill for an opportunity to live in the big city with his uncle J.B. Stubbs, a physician. Morris worked as a carpenter, building and maintaining homes owned by his uncle. Morris enlisted in the military and became a sailor assigned to the USS *Frontier*. He is pictured in his sailor uniform. After World War II, at age 33, Lloyd married Hilda Bulah on October 9, 1948. (Hilda Bulah Morris.)

Seven

The Case That Shaped the Nation

Bulah Meets Brown

Known as the case that shaped the nation, *Brown v. Board of Education of Topeka, Kansas, et al.*, consisted of multiple cases that were heard by the US Supreme Court concerning the issue of school segregation. Five cases comprised the lawsuit, and two of them were consolidated cases from Delaware: *Belton v. Gebhart*, featuring Claymont High School and Howard High School, and *Bulah v. Gebhart*, featuring Hockessin School #29 and Hockessin Colored School #107C.

Although the facts of each case were different, the constitutionality of state-sponsored segregation in public schools remained the main issue. The Bulah case was the result of a letter-writing campaign in which Fred and Sarah Bulah requested bus transportation to Hockessin Colored School #107C for their adopted daughter Shirley, who was seven years old at the time. After several requests to local and state officials and formal letters of rejection, the Bulahs pursued legal representation. On August 17, 1952, with the assistance of attorney Louis L. Redding, Fred and Sarah Bulah filed a complaint with the State of Delaware Court of Chancery. In the original complaint, the plaintiffs filed against the following defendants: Francis Gebhart, William Horner, Eugene Shallcross, Jesse Ohrum Small, N. Maxon Terry, and James Tunnell (members of the Delaware State Board of Education); George R. Miller Jr., the state superintendent of public instruction; and Gordon Biehn, Frederick Smith, Henry Mitchell, and Ethel McVaugh (representative members of the board of education in Hockessin School District #29).

After the court joined the parties, judge Collins J. Seitz ruled in favor of plaintiffs Bulah of Hockessin and Belton of Claymont. Dissatisfied with the courts' holdings, Delaware attorney general H. Albert Young appealed to the US Supreme Court on behalf of Gov. Elbert N. Carvel. The case went before the US Supreme Court as *Gebhart v. Belton* (1952).

On May 17, 1954, at 12:52 p.m., the Supreme Court issued a unanimous decision (9–0) declaring that segregation in United States public schools was unconstitutional. The court determined that separating children in public schools for no other reason than race violated the 14th Amendment. The cases of *Brown v. Board of Education* and its 200-plus petitioners changed the country. On behalf of the US Supreme Court, Chief Justice Earl Warren declared, "We conclude that in the field of public education, the doctrine of 'separate but equal' has no place. Separate educational facilities are inherently unequal."

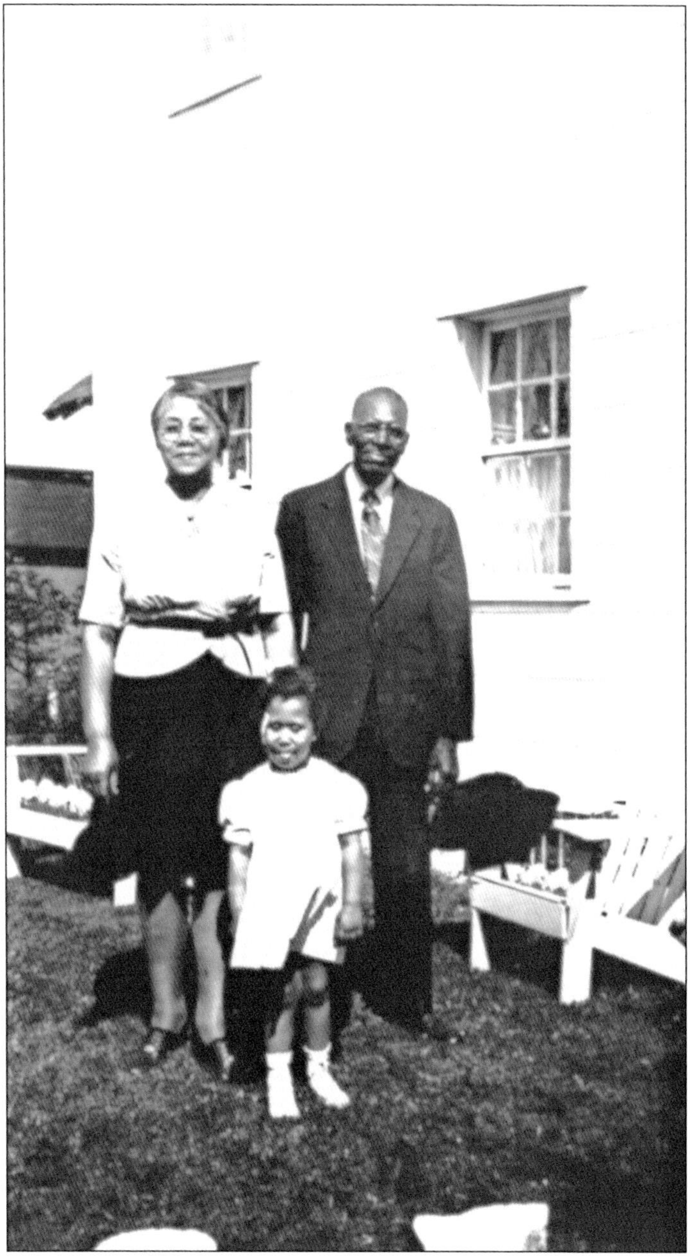

After the death of his wife, Ida, Fred Bulah continued to raise his family. Fred's weekends were filled with activities. One such activity included visiting his brother Rev. Frank Bulah, who worked in Reading and lived in Pottsville, Pennsylvania. During a church social, Frank introduced Fred to a widow named Sarah Corinths. After several months of correspondence and courtship, Fred and Sarah were married on November 14, 1942. Prior to marrying Fred, Sarah gave birth to one son, who died at a very young age. When she met and married Fred, she did not have any children. Upon moving to Hockessin, Sarah became interested in adopting a child. Destiny struck in 1945, when an article in the local newspaper featured an abandoned female toddler found wandering in the corridors of a building across the street from the Wilmington Train Station. Sarah and Fred are pictured here with Shirley around 1948. (Hilda Bulah Morris.)

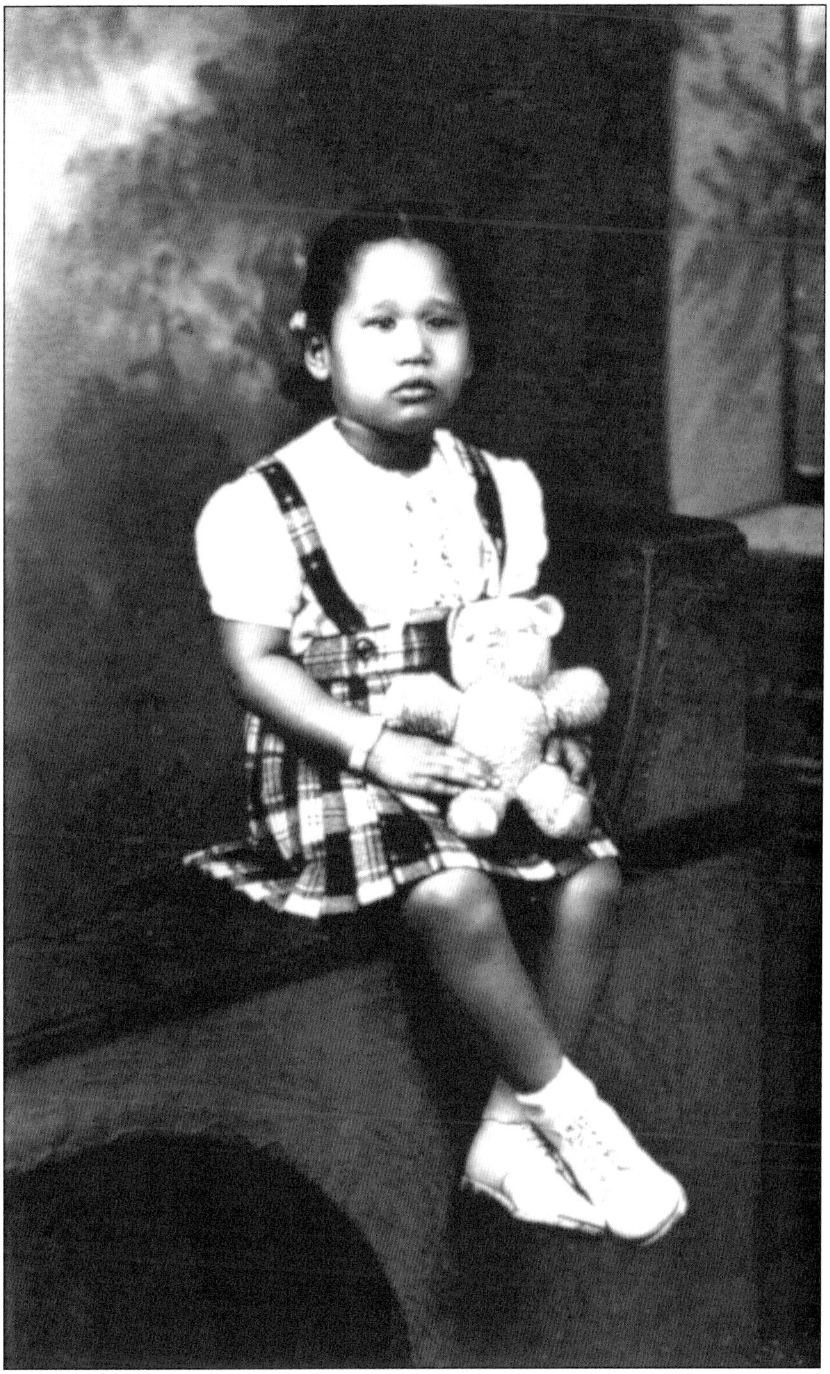

Little is known about the birth of the female baby girl adopted by Fred and Sarah Bulah. Fred and Sarah named their new bundle of joy Shirley Barbara Bulah. Although speculation around her birth and abandonment were well publicized, the Bulahs provided a stable alternative to the labyrinth associated with the toddler. The State of Delaware issued an adoption certificate that established the given name and date of birth for the abandoned child. This is one of the earliest photographs of Shirley Bulah in her formative years. (Hilda Bulah Morris.)

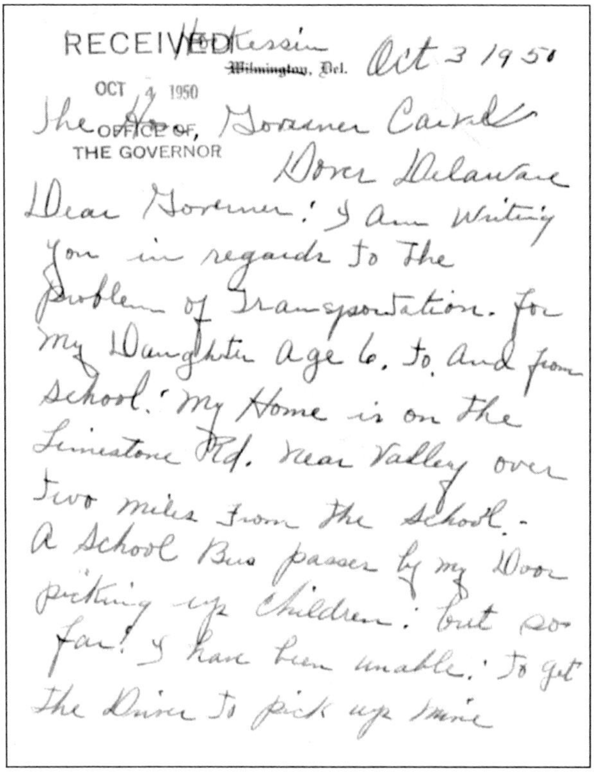

RECEIVED Hockessin
Wilmington, Del. Oct 3 1950
OCT 4 1950
OFFICE OF
THE GOVERNOR

The Hon, Governor Carvel
Dover Delaware

Dear Governor: I am Writing You in regards To The problem of Transportation. for my Daughter age 6. To. And from School: My Home is on The Limestone Rd. near Valley over Two miles from the School. A School Bus passes by my Door picking up Children: but so far! I have been unable: To get the Driver To pick up mine

While the adult sons and daughters of Fred Bulah were well established in their careers, the newest and youngest member of the Bulah family was facing a different set of challenges. Assigned to attend Hockessin Colored School #107C, seven-year-old Shirley was required to embark upon a two-mile walk to and from school. Shirley's mother Sarah was not in favor of Shirley taking the journey alone without the companionship of neighbors and the safety of siblings. For two years, as Sarah was en route to delivering eggs and produce to her customers, she transported Shirley to and from school. Sarah sought bus transportation for Shirley. A bus carrying white children passed the Bulahs' home daily. This letter is a correspondence sent from the Bulahs directly to Gov. Elbert Carvel seeking relief in hopes of granting Shirley permission to ride the school bus.

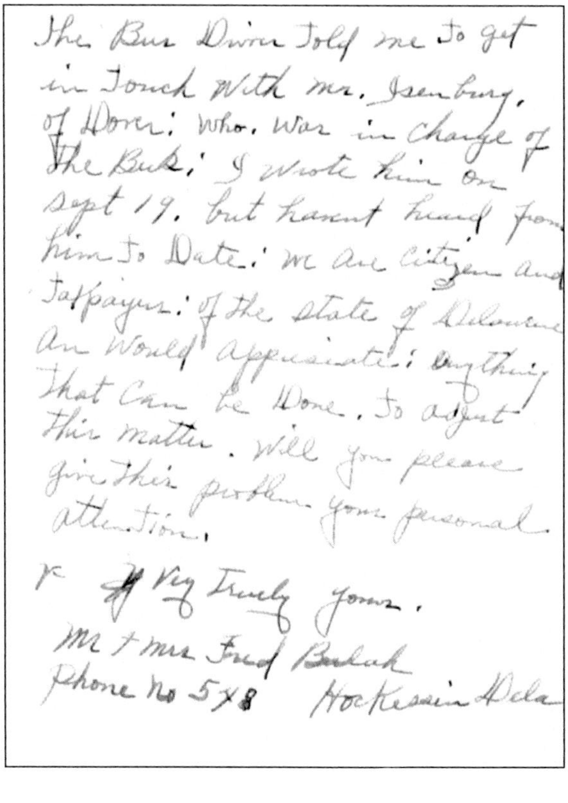

The Bus Driver Told me To get in Touch With Mr. Isenburg, of Dover: who. Was in Charge of The Bus: I wrote him on Sept 19. but hasnt heard from him To Date: We Are Citizens and Taxpayers: of the State of Delaware An Would appreciate: anything That Can be Done. To adjust This matter. Will you please give This problem your personal attention.

Very Truly yours.
Mr + Mrs Fred Bulah
Phone No 5X8 Hockessin Dela

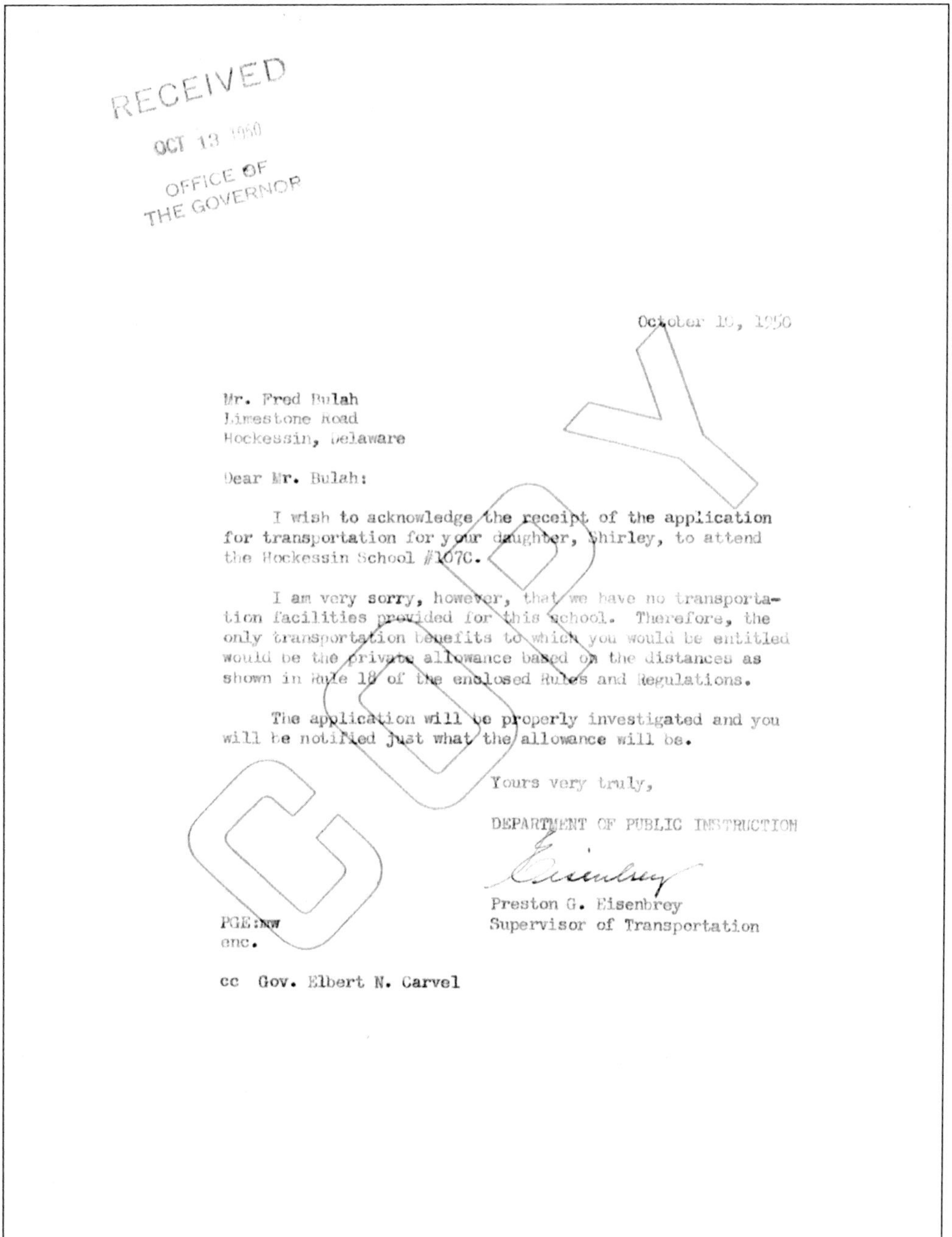

RECEIVED
OCT 13 1950
OFFICE OF
THE GOVERNOR

October 10, 1950

Mr. Fred Bulah
Limestone Road
Hockessin, Delaware

Dear Mr. Bulah:

I wish to acknowledge the receipt of the application for transportation for your daughter, Shirley, to attend the Hockessin School #107C.

I am very sorry, however, that we have no transportation facilities provided for this school. Therefore, the only transportation benefits to which you would be entitled would be the private allowance based on the distances as shown in Rule 18 of the enclosed Rules and Regulations.

The application will be properly investigated and you will be notified just what the allowance will be.

Yours very truly,

DEPARTMENT OF PUBLIC INSTRUCTION

Eisenbrey

Preston G. Eisenbrey
Supervisor of Transportation

PGE:NW
enc.

cc Gov. Elbert N. Carvel

A response to the Bulahs' letter highlighted the state law that governed transportation for children attending public schools. In 1950, according to the law, school bus transportation was provided only for white students. The mandate did not permit colored children to ride school buses. Colored parents paid state taxes, assessments, and fees for public school services that primarily serviced white children.

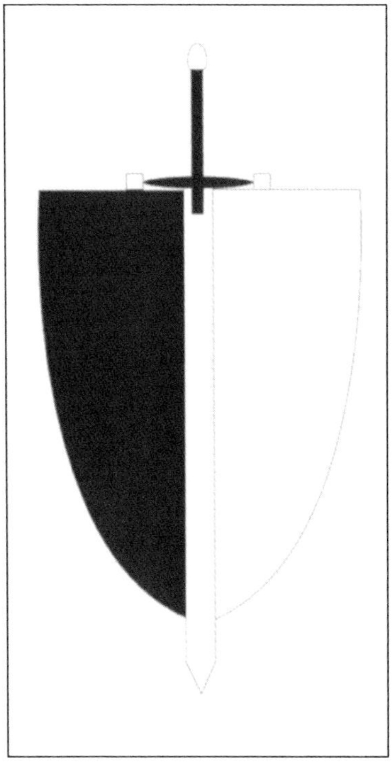

In the spring of 1951, Sarah Bulah contacted attorney Louis Redding to inquire about the rights of colored residents under state law. At that time, Louis Redding was the first and only colored lawyer in the State of Delaware. Attorney Redding suggested suing for the right to receive school transportation for Shirley and for her to attend the whites-only Hockessin School #29. This lawsuit came on the heels of national efforts made by the National Association of the Advancement of Colored People (NAACP) to combat segregated Jim Crow laws that had been enacted at the turn of the 20th century. On August 17, 1951, with the assistance of attorney Jack Greenberg of New York, attorney Louis Redding filed a lawsuit against the defenders of segregation on behalf of Shirley Bulah. Redding specifically charged individual board members. The first name among the members was Francis B. Gebhart. In addition to the Bulah Case, attorney Redding represented another Delaware family seeking admissions to the all-white segregated high school in Claymont. There were 13 named plaintiffs in the case action lawsuit. The lead plaintiff was high school student Ethel Louise Belton, who was represented by her mother, Ethel Lee Belton. The Beltons filed suit against Francis Gebhart and the state board of education on July 13, 1951.

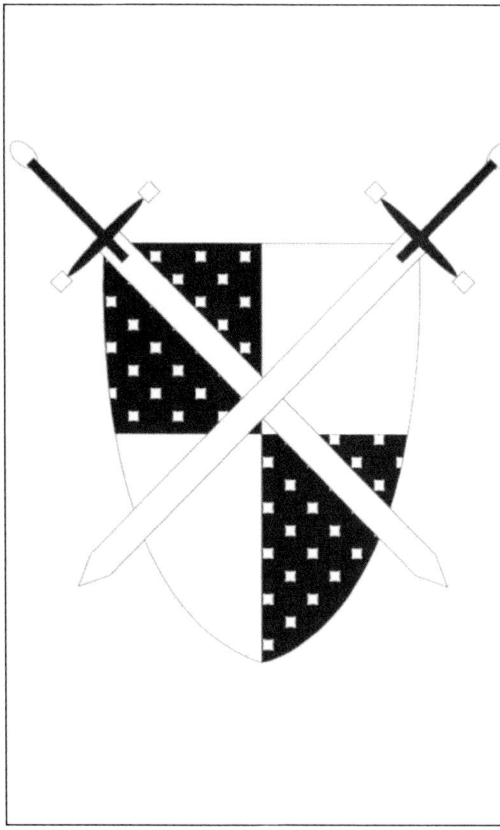

On April 1, 1952, chancellor Collins J. Seitz of Delaware Court of Chancery ordered the immediate admittance of the plaintiffs into the all-white schools of Hockessin #29 and Claymont High School. Judge Seitz ruled that the application of the law of the land established by the 1896 US Supreme Court case of *Plessy v. Ferguson* indicated separate facilities must be equal. Indeed, they were not. August 28, 1952, the Delaware Supreme Court consolidated the Bulah and Belton cases and affirmed the ruling of the lower court. In the fall of 1952, the champions of integration prevailed, and third-grader Shirley Bulah of Hockessin became the first colored student to integrate public grade schools and school buses in the state of Delaware. The ruling only pertained to plaintiffs listed in the original two cases: Hockessin student Shirley Bulah and Claymont students Ethel Louise Belton, Elbert Crumpler, Richard Leon Davis, John Terrell Davis, Spencer Robinson, Styron Sanford, Almena Short, Myrtha Trotter, Carol Anderson, Joan Anderson, Merle Anderson, and Bernice Byrd. Both of the illustrations on this page were created by Trevy Trev Productions.

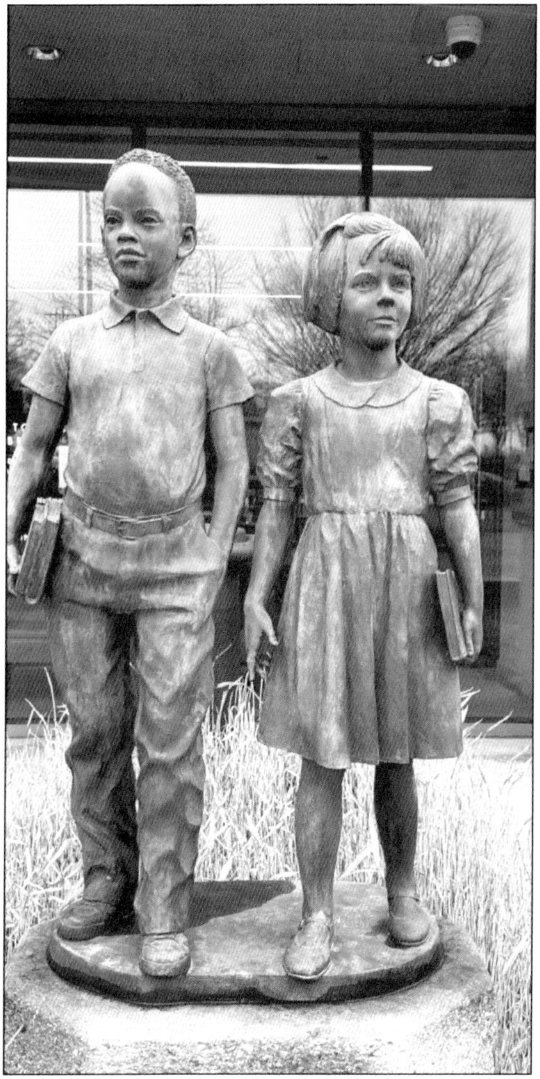

Vehemently opposed to the winds of change, Delaware united with other states to stand firmly in agreement with the Southern Confederate ideology and American Jim Crow society. On behalf of Delaware governor Elbert N. Carvel, Delaware attorney general H. Albert Young appealed to the US Supreme Court to maintain segregated schools in Delaware. *Brown v. Board of Education* consisted of multiple cases from four states and Washington's District of Columbia. The cases were *Gebhart v. Belton (Bulah)*, Delaware; *Bolling v. Sharpe*, District of Columbia; *Briggs v. Elliot*, South Carolina; *Brown v. Board of Education of Topeka*, Kansas; and *Davis v. County Board of Prince Edwards County*, Virginia. The Supreme Court decided to combine the issue into one consolidated case: *Brown v. Board of Education*. Various degrees of explanations have been offered to explain the logic for selecting the Kansas case. One of the popular determinants was Topeka's long history surrounding colored plaintiffs opposing the implementation of segregated schools. The court cases are *Reynolds v. Board of Education of Topeka* (1903), *Woolridge v. Board of Education of Topeka* (1916), *Wright v. Board of Education of Topeka* (1929), *Graham v. Board of Education of Topeka* (1941), and *Brown v. Board of Education of Topeka* (1954). This photograph features *The Classmates*, a sculpture designed by Charles Parks and dedicated in 1999 to commemorate the opening of the new Hockessin Library, where this sculpture stands at the main entrance. (Lanette R. Edwards.)

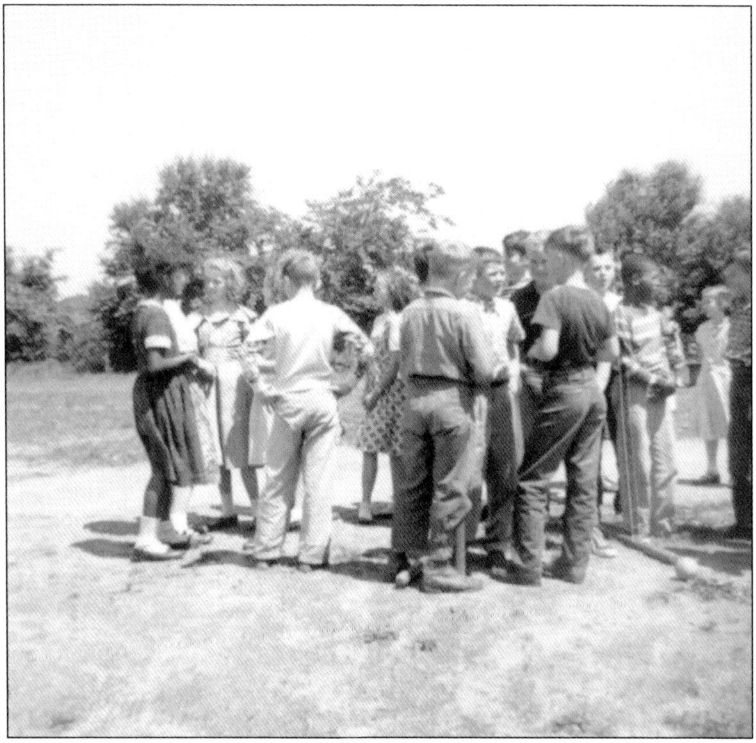

Baseball, a national pastime, became a community balm for the children of Hockessin. As shown in these two pictures, baseball was the backbone to forming the threads of camaraderie among the youth of Hockessin. Pictured here among his classmates is Greg Peterson, who was in the inaugural class of colored male students that integrated Hockessin #29.

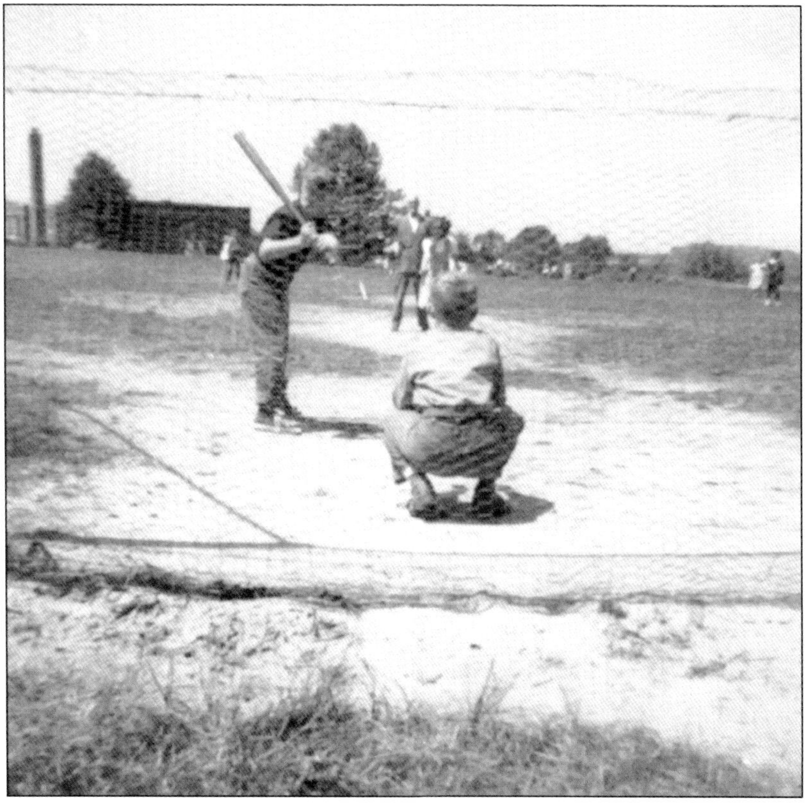

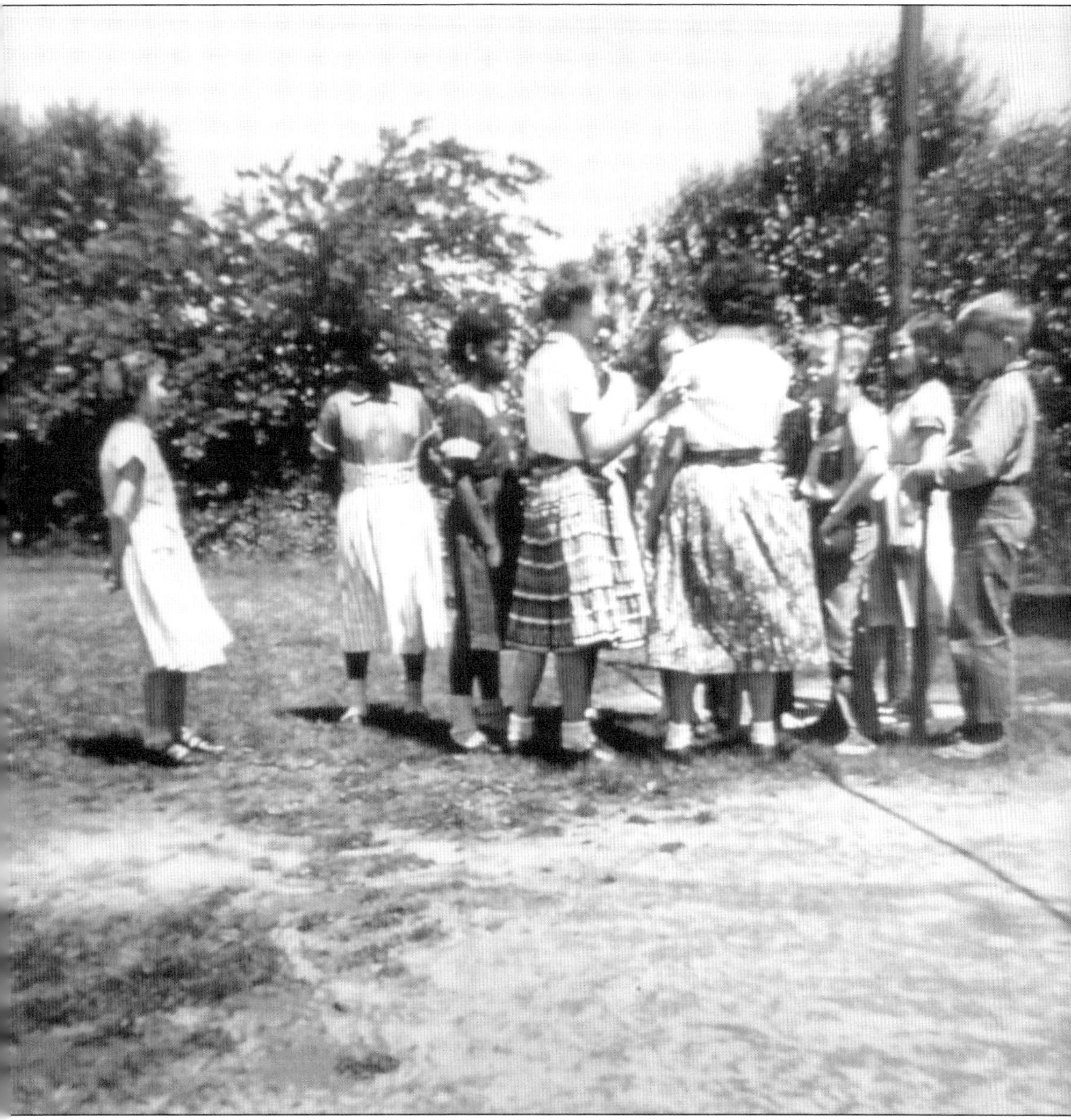

After the decision rendered by chancery court judge Collins Seitz, siblings Lois and Lorraine Williams joined Shirley Bulah in attending Hockessin #29. With great pushback from white teachers, segregated views were at the center of national discussions. Articles were written about the small town of Hockessin fanning the flames of racial unrest. Teachers at Hockessin #29 overtly and venomously refused to teach colored children. They voiced their strong resentment against the mixing of children and races. Among those relentless advocates for isolation and the removal of colored children was Ethel Cheney. Cheney initially introduced Lois Williams to her new classmates through a reading exercise in which she instructed Lois to stand before the class and read to her classmates. The assigned text was *Little Black Sambo*. After the class session, Lois was instructed to read the book in its entirety. Pictured here are Lois and Lorraine Williams on the playground at Hockessin #29 with their classmates.

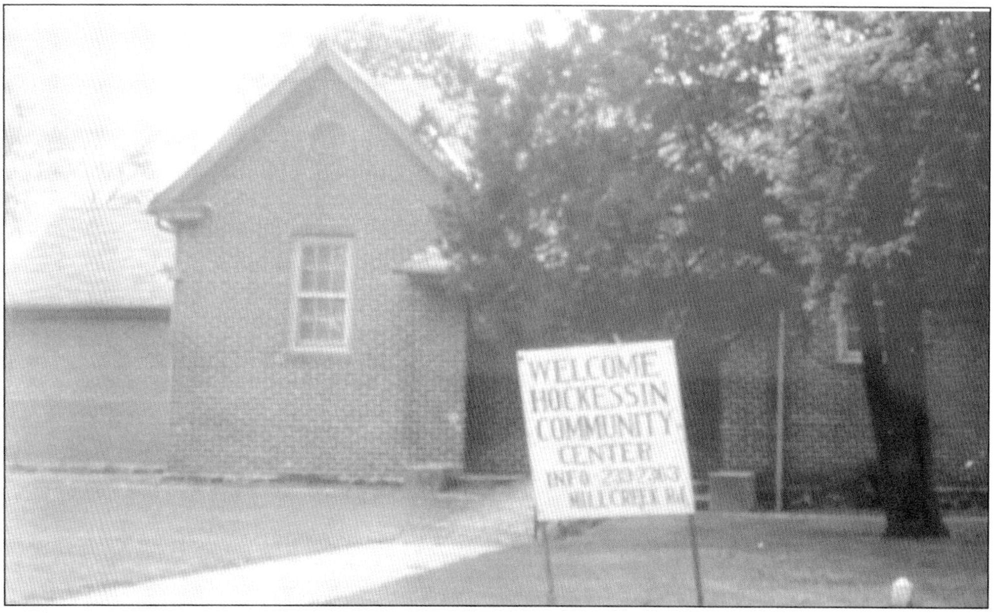

As the 1954 US Supreme Court decision in *Brown v. Board of Education* opened doors to educational progress and charted a trajectory of promise and opportunity, it simultaneously closed the doors of established independent generational educational structures in colored communities across the nation. The Hockessin colored community was no exception. Hockessin Colored School #107C, a stable conduit for 130 consecutive years of learning, closed its doors in May 1959. (Lois Johnson.)

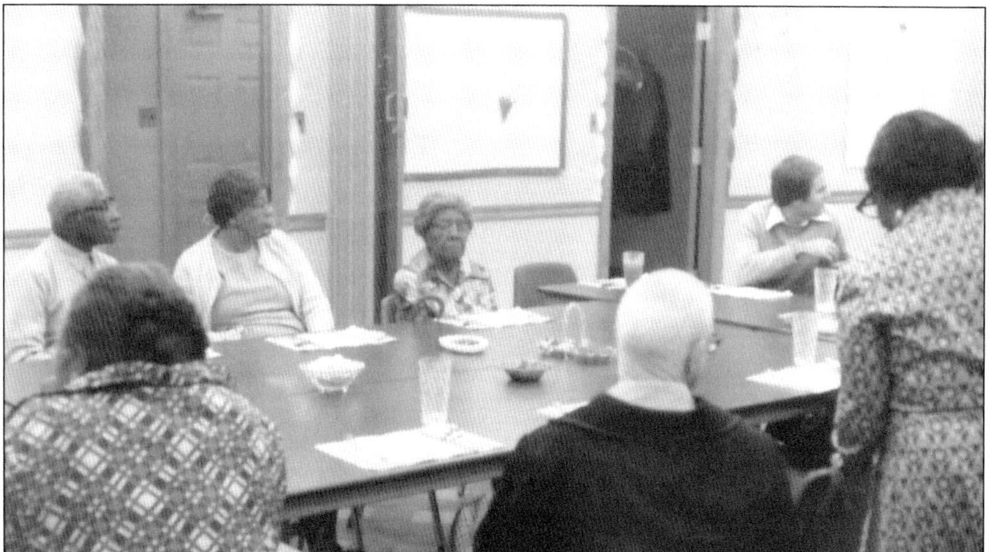

The former Hockessin Colored School #107C became a center for members of the colored community. Serving as a theater, dance hall, and town hall, it became a catalyst for social interaction. Taking on events once held in the aging Grand Hall, the structure was ideally situated adjacent to the school and Chippey AUMP Church. Pictured here are the elders of the community meeting to discuss the state of affairs of the colored community, including programs on education, health, and wellness. Addie Bulah Bostic is second from left seated at the table and facing the camera, and third from left at the table (next to Addie) is Hattie Bulah Murry. (Lois Johnson.)

Among the community's activities were the production of dramas and plays. All were welcome to read for the roles. From talent shows to Broadway musicals, the colored community in Hockessin found ways to enhance their quality of life. Pictured are performers of the Broadway musical *The Wiz*. Although Michael Jackson and Diana Ross were among the stars in the leading roles in the movie, Hockessin featured actors who gave star-quality performances, which were often met with applause and standing ovations. (Lois Johnson.)

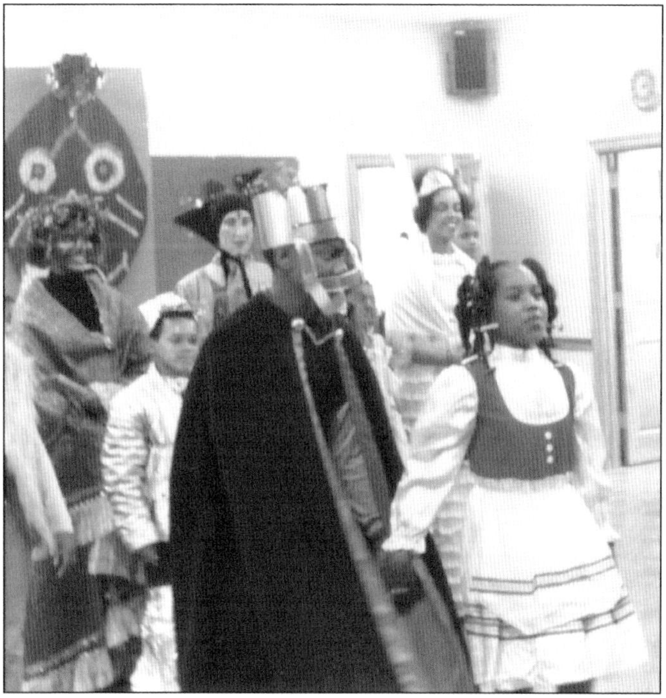

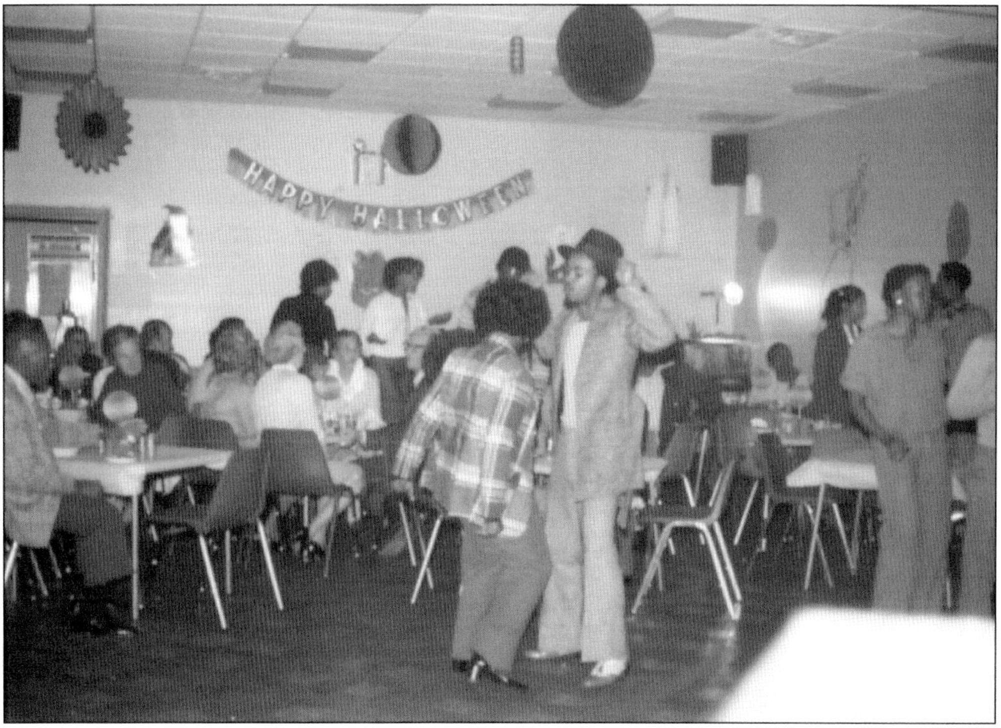

Excitement filled the air when flyers were posted announcing the annual Halloween Dance. Here, members of the colored community are dancing the night away to their favorite tunes. Hockessin residents gathered as entire families—adults and children alike—were encouraged to have a great time socializing with their peers. (Lois Johnson.)

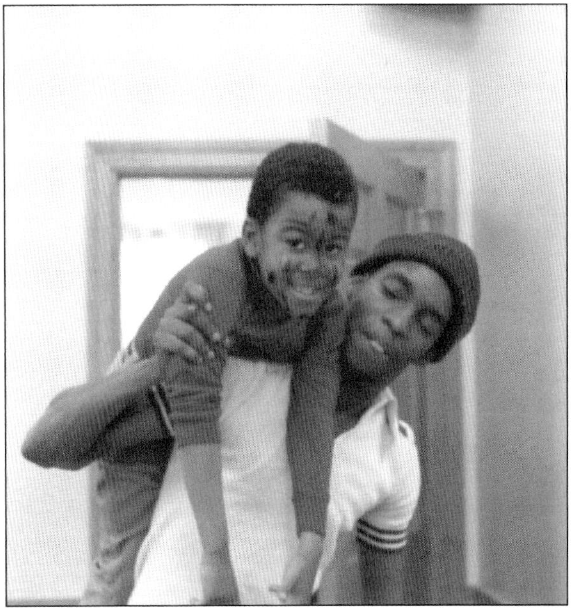

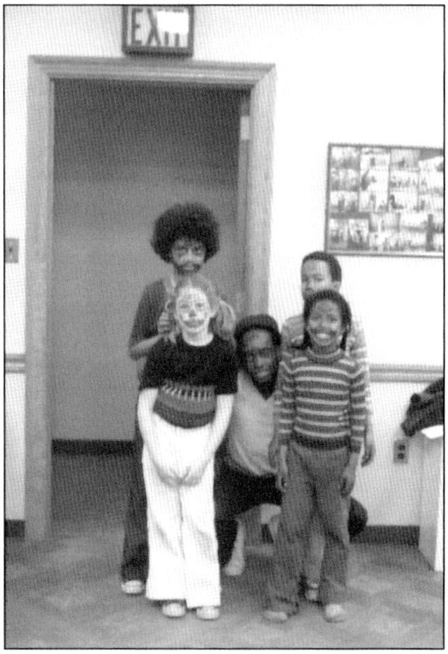

The community center became a great place for fun activities. Students (like the Briscoe brothers, who are pictured above in the image at right) received mentors and tutoring, while other students learned strategic card-playing tips from Byron Harvey (at left in the below image). Face-painting was a favorite among the younger residents. Pictured above left is one of the community center's counselors lifting a young fellow on his shoulders. (All, Lois Johnson.)

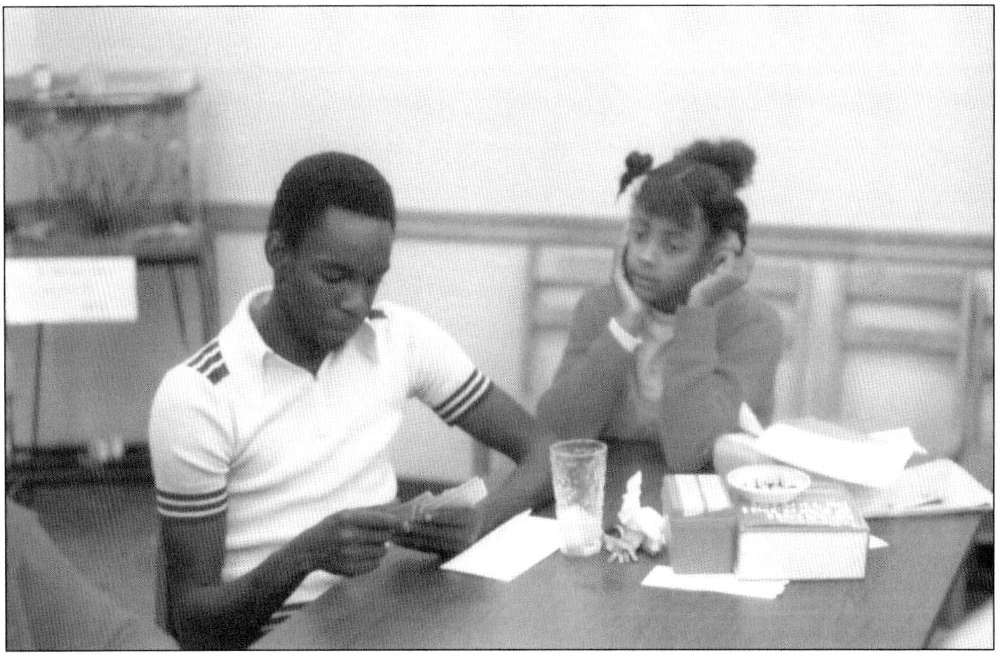

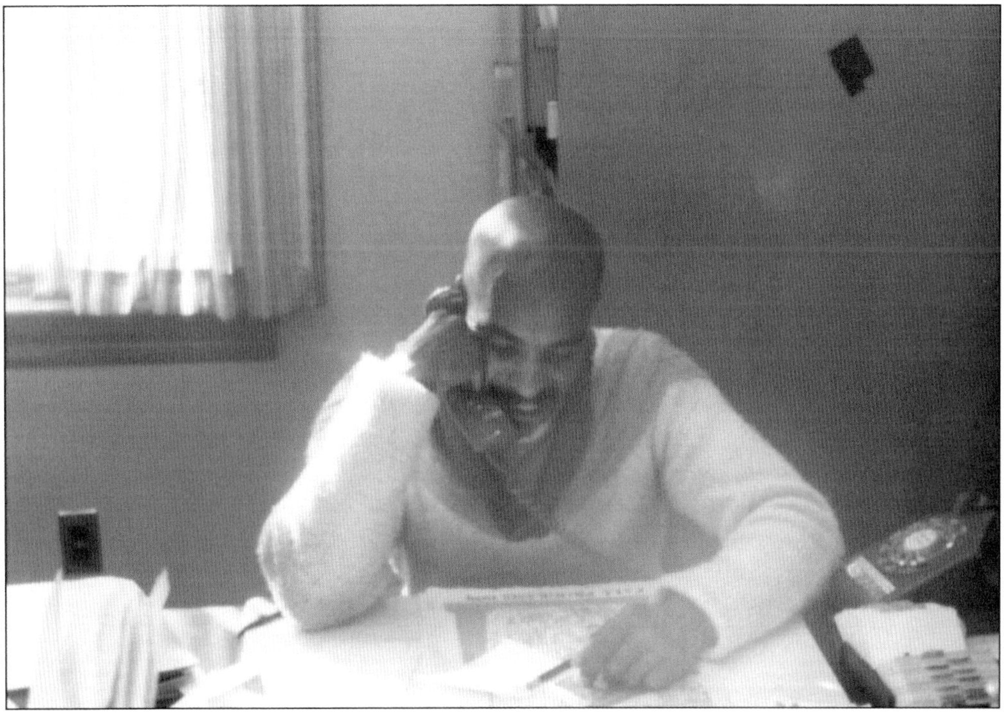

Managers like Jamie Lane were hired to maintain the community center. Shown above sitting at the desk in his office, he was charged with the upkeep of the center. His duties included organizing charitable donations and drives, overseeing operating hours, managing the facility's budget, and programming. Denise Poindexter (pictured below) served as a receptionist at the community center. One of their most popular annual events was the Hockessin Bazaar Community Carnival. (Both, Lois Johnson.)

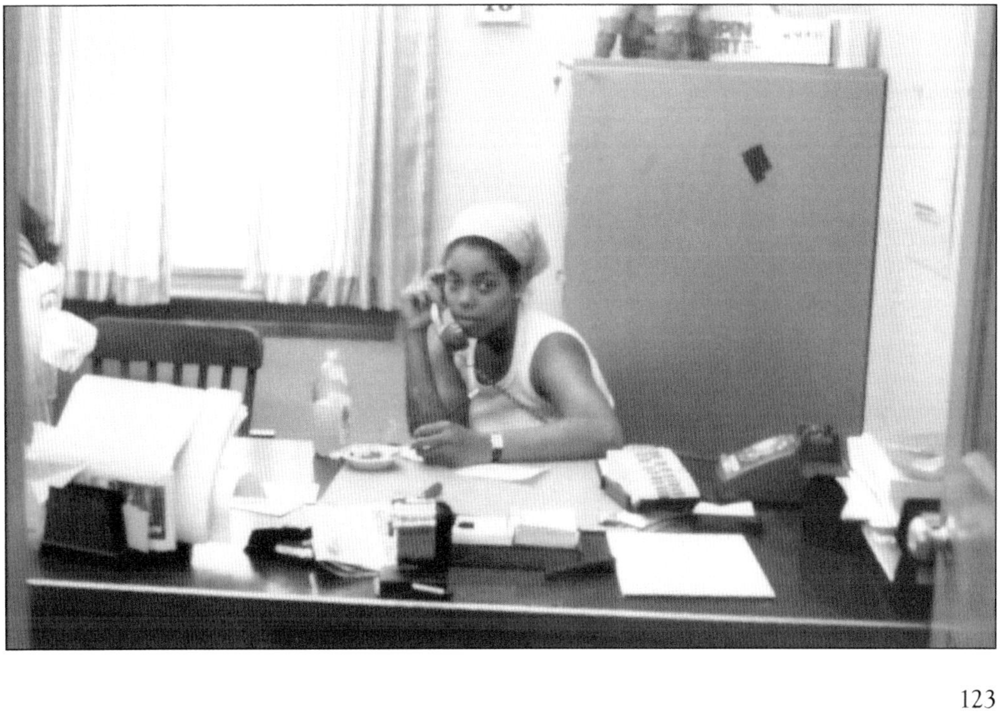

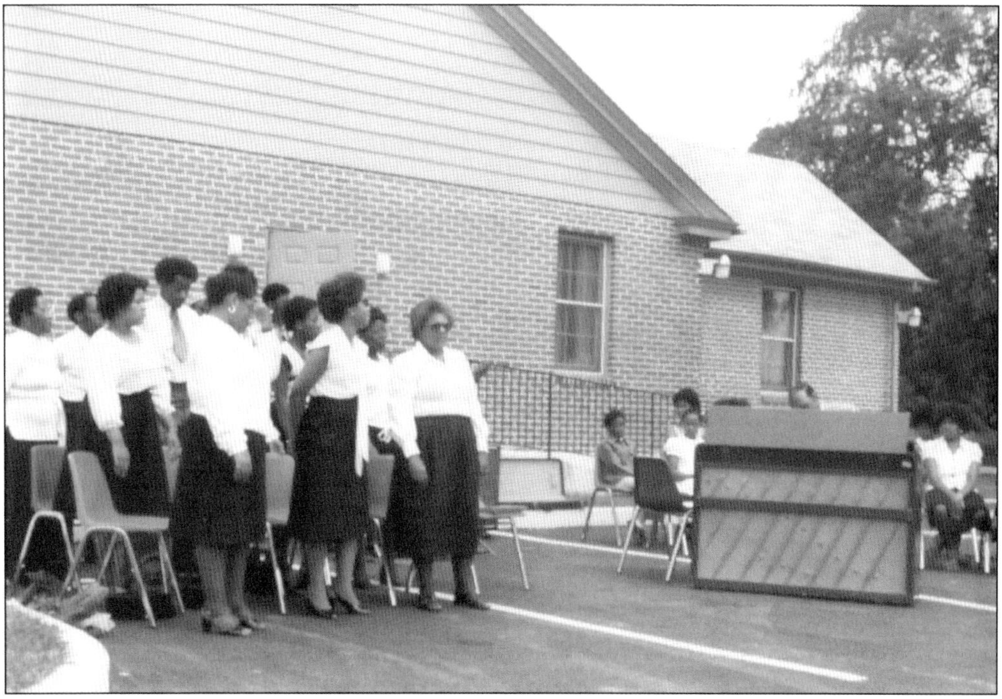

Pictured here are choir and members of Chippey AUMP Church enjoying Sunday worship in the great outdoors. This photograph features Hockessin colored families celebrating the gift of music and worship on the grounds of Hockessin Colored School #107C near playground equipment. All Hockessin Colored School facilities were once properties of Chippey AUMP Church. (Both, Lois Johnson.)

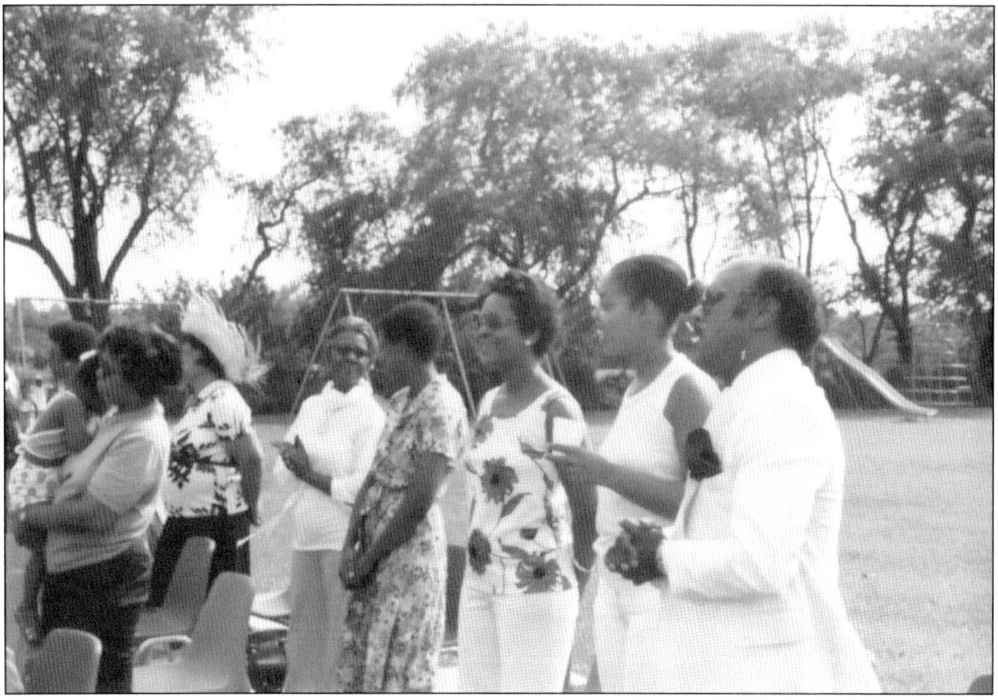

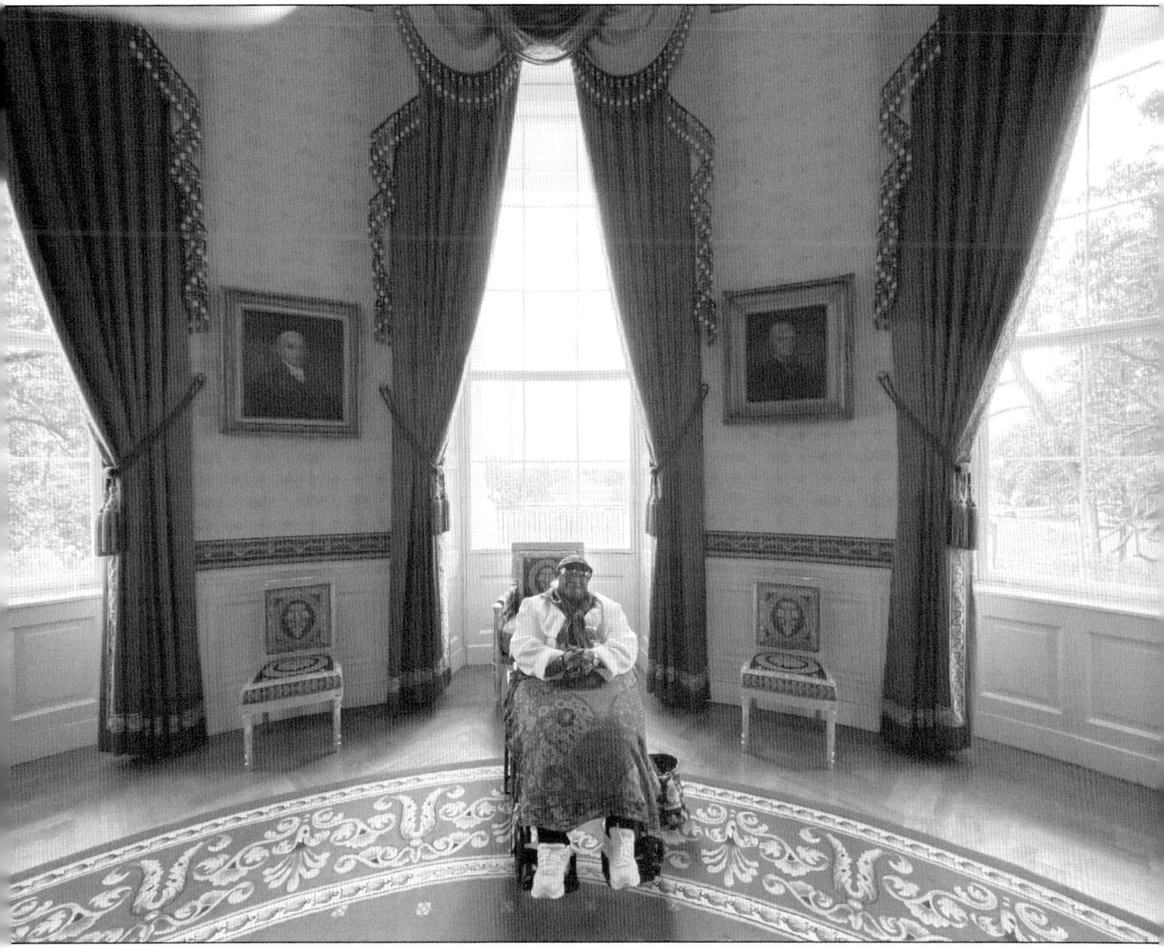

On May 12, 2022, Lois Williams Johnson, the oldest of the few remaining students who attended both Hockessin Colored School #107C and Hockessin #29, joined five of her #107C classmates to witness Pres. Joseph Biden sign into law the affiliate sites of *Brown v. Board of Education*, which included Hockessin Colored School #107C. The bill declared Hockessin Colored School #107C an affiliate site of the *Brown v. Board of Education* National Historical Park Expansion and Re-designation Act. (Lois Johnson.)

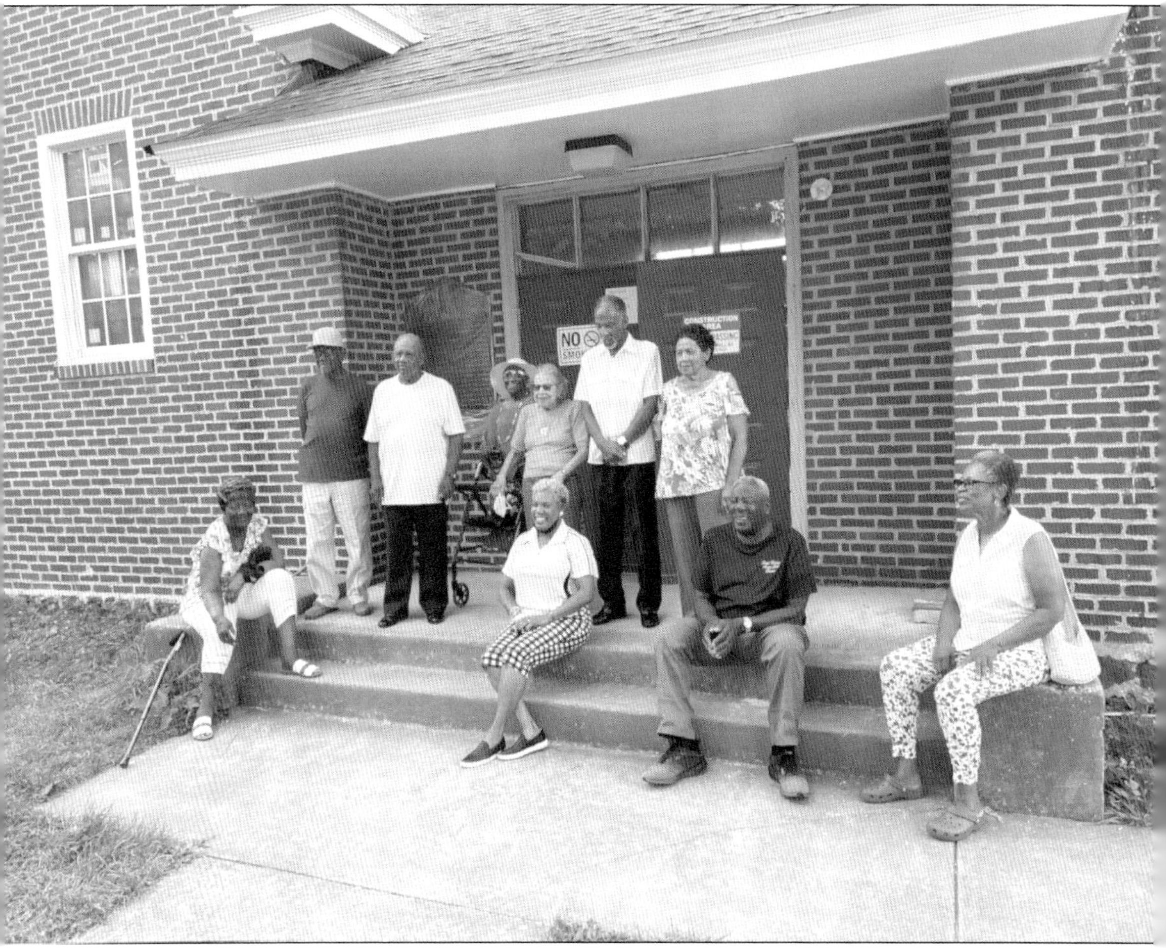

Pictured with the former students of Hockessin Colored School #107C is Dr. Lanette Riddlespriger Edwards, a local historian and the author of this book. Equipped with research spanning a decade, she embarked upon a journey to assist with the renovation of Hockessin Colored School #107C. A former member of the Board of Friends of Hockessin Colored School #107C, she deemed the three-year project a wonderful success. From the #107C schoolhouse in Delaware to the White House in Washington, DC, and many miles thereafter, the former students of Hockessin Colored School #107C and Dr. Edwards formed an everlasting bond. This photograph was taken on July 28, 2022, in front of Hockessin Colored School #107C in celebration of Hilda Bulah Morris's 99th birthday. Dr. Edwards is seated on the steps in the center and is surrounded by the last generation of #107C students—they are, from left to right, Charlotte Knott Emory, Robert Berry, Charles Johnson, Lois Williams Johnson, Hilda Bulah Morris, LeRoy Peterson, Nancy Johnson, James Sonny Knott, and Blanche Knott Tucker. This photograph is dedicated to the memory of Jean Bolden Fleming, Robert Fleming, and S. Constancia Beaujon. (Lanette R. Edwards.)

Bibliography

Adams, Alvin. "What Happened to Negroes Who Won School Suit Ten Years Ago?" *Jet Magazine*, May 21, 1964: p. 16–25.

Brown, Henderson Cheryl. "Recovering Untold Stories: An Enduring Legacy of the *Brown v. Board of Education* Decision." University of Kansas Libraries, 2018. Kuscholarworks.ku.edu.

Chippey AUMP Church. "Welcome New Members Packet," February 13, 2021. chippeyaumchurch.org.

Cole, Kenneth. "*Brown v. Board of Education, Topeka*, research into psychological consequences of racism for black Americans." Washington University in St. Louis, Blackside, Inc., Eyes on the Prize Series, 1985. Repository.wustl.edu.

Delaware Public Archives Hockessin School #107C Files and Photographs.

Gadsden, B. *Between North and South Delaware, Desegregation, and the Myth of American Sectionalism*. Philadelphia: University of Pennsylvania Press, 2013.

Kluger, Richard. *Simple Justice: The History of "Brown v. Board of Education" and Black America's Struggle for Equality*. New York: Vintage Books, 2004.

Lake, Joseph R. *Hockessin: A Pictorial History*. Hockessin, DE: Friends of the Hockessin Library, 1997.

McClave, Marta. "Courage: Woman's Fight Led to 1st State Desegregation Case." *The Morning News* (Wilmington, Delaware, June 16, 1980 – Checkback).

McCullough, C. "*Brown v. Board of Education* (1954): An Analysis of Policy Implementation, Outcomes, and Unintended Consequences." Dissertation for Loyola Marymount University, 2012.

Munroe, John. "History of Delaware." University of Delaware Press, 1979.

Rowan, C. Some "Negro Teachers Favor School Segregation." The *Minneapolis Star Tribune*. December 2, 1953: 1, 10–12.

Sawin, Nancy C. *A Hockessin Diary*. Hockessin, DE: North Light Studio, 1987.

Weekley, Rachel Franklin. *"A Strong Pull, a Long Pull, and a Pull Altogether": Topeka's Contribution to the Campaign for School Desegregation; Historic Resource Study*. Omaha: Midwest Regional Office, National Park Service, US Department of the Interior, 1999.

Weeks, Stephen Beauregard. *History of Public School Education In Delaware*. No. 18. Washington: Department of the Interior Bureau of Education, 1917.

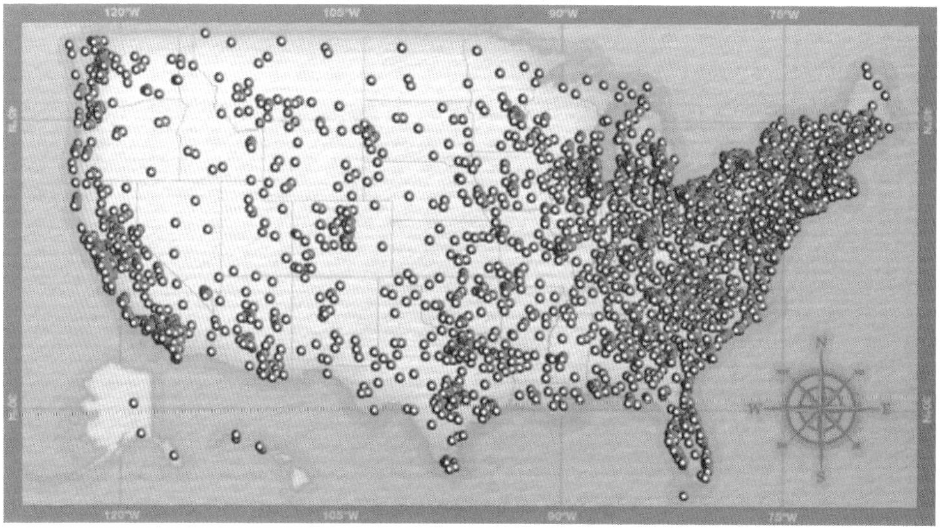